Just Reconci

New International Studies in Applied Ethics

VOLUME 6

EDITED BY

Professor R. John Elford and Professor Simon Robinson,
Leeds Metropolitan University

PETER LANG

Oxford · Bern · Berlin · Bruxelles · Frankfurt am Main · New York · Wien

Just Reconciliation

The Practice and Morality of Making Peace

R. John Elford (ed.)

PETER LANG

Oxford · Bern · Berlin · Bruxelles · Frankfurt am Main · New York · Wien

Bibliographic information published by Die Deutsche Nationalbibliothek.
Die Deutsche Nationalbibliothek lists this publication in the Deutsche
Nationalbibliografie; detailed bibliographic data is available on the Internet
at http://dnb.d-nb.de.

A catalogue record for this book is available from the British Library.

Library of Congress Cataloging-in-Publication Data:

Just reconciliation : the practice and morality of making peace / John
Elford (ed).
      p. cm.
  Includes bibliographical references and index.
  ISBN 978-3-0343-0165-7 (alk. paper)
  1. Peace. 2. Peace--Case studies. 3. Peace-building. 4.
Peace-building--Case studies. I. Elford, R. John.
  JZ5538.J87 2011
  355.02'8--dc22

                        2010051071

ISSN 1663-0033
ISBN 978-3-0343-0165-7

© Peter Lang AG, International Academic Publishers, Bern 2011
Hochfeldstrasse 32, CH-3012 Bern, Switzerland
info@peterlang.com, www.peterlang.com, www.peterlang.net

Printed in Germany

Content

Acknowledgements

The editor thanks the contributors to this volume and others who have co-operated in any way in its preparation. These include General Sir Rupert Smith and the Dean and Chapter of Liverpool Cathedral for hosting his and other lectures which led to some chapters in this book.

Leeds Metropolitan University is also thanked for financial and other support.

JUSTIN WELBY AND R. JOHN ELFORD

Introduction: Modern Reconciliation Activities

On 14 November 1940 a major air raid on the city of Coventry by the Luftwaffe destroyed the beautiful medieval cathedral in the city centre. The cathedral was almost certainly not a target, but from the air must have looked very much like one of the factories producing aero-engines and other munitions of war. The following morning, with the smoke from the bombed city rising around him, in the rubble and ashes of his cathedral, Provost Richard Howard took some burnt wood and wrote behind the high altar 'Father Forgive'. He very carefully did not write 'Father Forgive Them' saying to one of his colleagues '*all* have sinned and fall short of the glory of God'.

On Christmas Day 1940, speaking on the BBC, he called for prayer for reconciliation with Germany. It was not a popular move, and there are still people in Coventry who remember his ministry of reconciliation with bitterness. It appeared to ignore issues of justice, and the need for standing up to evil. Both of these understandings would misinterpret the purpose of Richard Howard. He was fully committed to the necessity of the defeat of the Nazi regime in Germany, but he also looked forward to a post-war world in which Christian values would lead to 'a better more Christ-like world'.

In 1945 a small group went from Coventry to Dresden, in sympathy with the bombing that that city had suffered, and the Dresden–Coventry link has remained ever since. When the Frauenkirche, the main church in Dresden, completed its rebuilding in October 2005 the Dean of Coventry and Bishop of Coventry were invited to be present at the re-consecration, and the cross at the top of the church was a gift from Coventry.

The action taken by Richard Howard, and subsequently by the vast majority of the inhabitants of Coventry, was deeply counter cultural and also against the natural instinctive desire for revenge and retaliation.

Reconciliation work such as this is as relevant to the modern world as it has ever been, as references throughout this book will show. For example, early on the morning of 8 March 2010, the BBC World Service reported riots just south of Jos, in central Nigeria. In a brief but striking interview, a civil rights activist said 'the élite are doing the talking, the grass roots are doing the fighting; all the declarations make no difference without grass roots being involved'.

In the area; small villages, separated by dry fields, dust blows across the low ridges of earth that divide field from field, houses dry and brown in dry weather, drip their walls into the earth when wet. The conflicts vary in their origin, although they are often presented as religious, but they are exacerbated by deep ethnic tensions going back centuries. Competition for farm land between agriculturists and nomadic herdsmen, and extreme poverty and unemployment, all provide fuel for the flames.

Another recent news item was a report from the BBC veteran correspondent John Simpson, this time in Baghdad to cover parliamentary elections. He described the previous day as good, although ninety people had died in bomb attacks, a total that had it happened in the UK would have traumatized Britain for weeks, and be remembered for decades. Conflict (or more properly in Sir Rupert Smith's terms later in this volume, confrontation) is the main staple of daily news, and always has been.

What Is Reconciliation?

Reconciliation has been a word mainly used in Roman Catholic religious discourse where it is used to describe the human sacramental reconciliation with God. For Christians in the Reformed confessions, reconciliation is a word that takes one to St Paul's epistle to the Romans, and especially chapters 5–8. Here the emphasis is on the peace Christians enjoy with God. This has been brought about by the reconciling work of Christ: 'we also rejoice in God through our Lord Jesus Christ, through whom we have now received our reconciliation' (5:11). All this has been wrought by Christ on our behalf. In both of these mainstream Christian traditions the reconciliation referred to is between God and man.

This original sense of the word in Christian discourse is now assuming other meanings. It is a word in transformation, leaking from the religious field into political and social ones. For this reason, politicians find it a useful part of their vocabulary. It is also taught as a subject in war colleges and senior staff training courses within the armed services. Journalists watch a war, report the peace and a week later are asking earnestly 'is there reconciliation yet?' Reconciliation can be a confusing word when it is used as diversely as this.

The reality of reconciliation is both more complex and controversial. It is never a single event and seldom, if ever, quick. Within it are a myriad of competing interests and desires expressed by all the participants in a confrontation. For all these reasons, reconciliation is best understood as the name for a nexus of activities which, when combined correctly, enable a confrontation to be continued without the use or threat of violence. In other words, it permits war to be continued by proverbial other means. These activities will include; confidence building measures, meetings between parties, social developments and economic transformation, grass roots activism and peace-building. It will also include other, even pedestrian, activities which seem but tangentially related. Experience shows that if all this and more is aimed at the same outcome and suitably drawn together by guiding principles and firm leadership, it will sometimes enable violent confrontation to be transformed into peaceful diversity and, hopefully, reconciliation.

If reconciliation is going to be effective it is necessary to understand its complexity and to meet the demands for resourcing its practitioners and the networks and partnerships they work through. Such an approach runs completely contrary to the atomized efforts of nations, NGOs, governments and international organizations as they are set up today. For example, where reconciliation is needed too often international charities set

Work with
Exp'd orders

up reconciliation departments, rather than seeking to partner with others more experienced and effective in the specialism. Governments assume that their armed forces can turn their hands to anything, more or less without warning. In the Iraq coalition headquarters in 2003, in a former palace of Saddam Hussein, there was a room full of desks labelled with such titles as 'Ministry of Justice'. One man sat there seeking to build a national justice system. Even in the days of the British Empire Lord Lugard's concept of indirect rule was understood and applied, and the limits of direct intervention recognized.

Rec'd can be
Transformative
to the way groups
subsequently
think &
behave

Understood in this way, reconciliation is transformative not only of societies, but also of individuals. Its processes can change the way they think and behave. In societies such as tribal ones this can have dramatic effects. The chronicles of reconciliation activity by people like Andrew White repeatedly illustrate this point, often movingly so. None of this ever leads to quick fixes. It often takes years and can seem more punctuated by failure than success. However, when it does succeed the benefits it brings are incalculable. There are notable examples of this. The most easily overlooked and the largest in scale is that of Europe. Between 1914 and 1945 the peoples of Europe conducted the bloodiest, most encompassing, most savage and most destructive wars in human history. The entire continent and large areas elsewhere were reduced to widespread ruin and poverty. The British and Germans alone killed over three million of each other's citizens. Reconciliation efforts after 1918 were faltering and may well have paved the way for the rise of Nazi Germany. After 1945, however, the reconciliation effort co-ordinated every area of society from faith groups through to armies. It involved economic regeneration, school visits, education, and above all the creation of new international links, the European Union and a new currency, the Euro. For two of the nations, France and Germany, the single principal aim of all these efforts was reconciliation, not economic prosperity. Today, war is perhaps not impossible, but is certainly unthinkable, on a continent that is enjoying its longest period of more or less general peace since the fall of the Western Roman Empire. There can be no better or wide-reaching example of the benefits of reconciliation than this.

Long time
many set backs
but
great benefits
Ⓧ *P5*
Ⓧ *P6*

Many other contemporary examples of reconciliation that have to some extent worked remain in progress. In Northern Ireland, more than ten years have passed since the Good Friday Agreement. It is very arguable that while there is cease fire, the conscious process of reconciliation deep in the community needs to continue for the foreseeable future. For all this, however, real progress has been and continues to be made. Whilst the details of the final outcome remain unclear, the hope for its successful achievement grows as time passes. This, in itself, is incrementally confidence-building. What is apparent here is the ongoing need for continued and focused analysis of the roots and origins of the 'troubles' and the creation of the means of their effective resolution. South Africa is similar in these respects. While much has been accomplished there the challenges of persistent poverty and corruption threaten a stable future. Both of these recent examples show that reconciliation may well be a slow and often faltering process, but that it is one can also be punctuated by dramatic success.

While most people agree that reconciliation, understood in this way, matters, there remains the need for proper debate about what it actually is, how it is achieved and made more effective. This book is a contribution to achieving that. Above all, it seeks to understand its place in the wider schema of conflict prevention, resolution and peace-building. In this sense it is far from being an abstract concept. Far from it. It is situation specific, has to do with often not nice individuals, is frequently perilous and its practitioners have to remain ever alert and responsive. The book is prompted in large part by the now perceived growing successes of such reconciliation activities. For this reason alone, they should not be as ignored as they relatively are in the academic study of conflict resolution. Those who do study them are for the most part lone scholars and practitioners devoted to the subject. Their current literature is not great but it is growing. Much of it is referred to herein. The point being made is that this nascent literature must be taken seriously. It must be studied, analysed and developed into the major contribution to peace studies which it should now become.

This literature will not emanate from a single source. Contributions to it will be as diverse in their origins as in their applications. It is important to recognize this for the simple reason that reconciliation often has to be effected between people of different religions and cultures. These will all have their contributions to make often to the surprise of themselves and each other. Any attempt to impose a monochrome understanding of reconciliation would seriously compromise this. It engages people in a common cause and seeks to define ends which they all seek. These ends are the greater part. They are those of peace, social stability, justice and confidence in a better future free from conflict. These so-called 'goods' are the desired ends. Progress to them can only begin when they are recognized by all sides. Bringing this recognition about is, in large part, what reconcilers seek to achieve. They cannot impose it. It has to come from deep within the communities and between the individuals involved. The success of this is neither guaranteed nor assured. The activities often end in failure and have to begin over and over again. Tenacity in the face of failure is, for this reason, one of the hallmarks of the reconciler's art. It is often a long game.

This rich and necessary diversity in the origins of reconciliation and the importance of them in the process of peacemaking must encourage all who seek it to look to their own cultural and religious traditions to see what they can find there of relevance. This is important. If reconciliation is to spring from the wells of the cultures involved they all have to feel valued. This can only be achieved by careful and patient listening which is tempered by an ever ready willingness to accept inspiration from wherever it comes. Much of the writing in this book is by Christians who are involved in the work of reconciliation in various theatres of conflict. Many of them have been for a number of years. In all this the work of Coventry Cathedral has been and remains an inspiration and support.

It is always important to remember that religion is not only the soil from which the concept of reconciliation has sprung. Secular earnestness and good-will has an important part to play. This can noticeably fail, however, if it overlooks the religious dimensions to conflicts as well as the religious resources for resolving them. As we will see in what follows, Andrew White makes this point repeatedly and forcefully. Many efforts at reconciliation fail to deal with the spiritual aspects of conflict. After a cease fire in 2005, militants leaving the swamps of the Niger Delta wanted a church service to confess the sins they had committed in battle and to receive the forgiveness of God. The spirituality of reconciliation is profoundly important, most of all in the church, where its absence is crippling to the church's calling to be a reconciler, with God and amongst peoples. In

Develop this further —

See P7

church disputes the first sign of a breakdown in relationships is the diminution of common prayer. Reconciliation in Christian understanding is a gift of God and thus is rooted in prayer, and above all prayer together.

With very few exceptions purely secular processes of reconciliation will fail. The Oslo Accords of 1993, which so nearly brought about a peace settlement involving Israel and its neighbours, failed to draw in religious leaders. After the Iraq invasion of 2003 there was a period in which religious leadership was ignored. One consequence of this was that that sectarian passions ran out of control and Iraqi society was seriously de-stabilized as a result. This manifest mistake has since been addressed and progress has been made.

The very word reconciliation has useful baggage and reinforcement in the culture of many societies, derived from religion, and linked to love of God and of neighbour. In addition, in many societies in confrontation the only organizations of civil society that continue effectively are the faith groups and especially the traditional denominations of churches whose networks of dioceses and parishes provide a ready-made structure for everything from aid through to the early warning of new conflicts. Ignoring these groups is a frequent mistake.

As we have already begun to see, within the Christian tradition, diversity with love is rooted in the foundations of faith and vision of God in Christ. The doctrine of the Trinity is a central expression of this. It expresses nothing less than reconciled unity of all things in Christ. The Gospel writers and St Paul return to this theme again and again in their writings. He sees the Church as its agency and this is what it has aspired to be ever since. Its central ministry is that of reconciling all things to God in Christ. Such reconciliation is both a present and a future reality: 'Therefore since we are justified by faith we have peace with God through our Lord Jesus Christ' (Romans 5:1); 'We know that the whole creation has been groaning in labour pains' (Romans 8:22). Peace within the church, the body of believers is portrayed by Luke as accomplished at the end of the second and fourth chapters of the Acts of the Apostles. For these reasons, the concept of reconciliation is profoundly rooted in Christian theology and in its understanding of a loving God at its source, who is revealed in the person of Jesus.

This Christian understanding of reconciliation as being of divine origin is why it also emphasizes the importance of the part played by the operative grace of God. This grace, which is the human experience of the love of God in action, is what permits the healing of past hurts and wounds, even of grave crimes against humanity by the leaders of one group against another. Grace in action suffuses secular activity. The hope that exists in South Africa, despite the atrocities of apartheid for generations of South Africans, comes from a gracious giving of absolution by the afflicted and a willingness to receive it by all sides. The Christians who did this there were inspired and supported by the love and the grace of God. Theologically, reconciliation is based on understanding God as one who forgives and is merciful. Within Christian theology it is the dominant theme of human interaction with God, the precedent to a saving knowledge of God. Its manifest result is human flourishing in the image of God. The Truth and Reconciliation Commission offered amnesty, a form of absolution, in return for truth, and that has opened the way to reconciliation in many cases. For reconciliation to be effective there cannot be ulterior or hidden motives, because God's grace is a free gift without condition. The gracious lover loves because she or he has been loved. Such grace is the first casualty of confrontation, and its absence the greatest obstacle to lasting reconciliation.

Why Is Reconciliation So Important?

Politically and economically reconciliation is a tool for achieving what Philip Bobbitt calls the market state.[1] Reconciliation creates sufficient structures of peaceful co-existence to permit the main aims of government to be achieved, principally the creation of a prosperous economy which offers choice to all. This utilitarian or consequentialist view has its obvious attractions. The infrastructure of a market state, however primitive or

1   Philip Bobbitt, *The Shield of Achilles: War, Peace, and the Course of History* (London: Allen Lane, 2002).

sophisticated it might be, is what provides for the commerce which meets daily needs of one kind and another. It creates the confidence for people to invest in businesses and for government to make provision for needs. All this is the infrastructure of civilization. It is one of the first casualties of anarchy. Efforts at reconciliation must be directed to these economic ends where the market has broken down. However, reconciliation has to be more than a means for securing simple economic or material ends, important thought they may be. Its success cannot be judged by them alone.

The provision for basic human dignities is of paramount importance. The cessation of hostilities, provision for shelter, food water and sanitation are chief among these. The urgency of the need for them in disaster zones, sadly and repeatedly, demonstrate this. Evidences for the success of reconciliation are as basic as this. It matters fundamentally because the provision of these necessities is fundamental to human dignity.

Reconciliation is a virtue which shapes the minds of those involved so that they see other human beings in all the dignity of their humanity, and not as objects of hatred, rivalry or menace. It resists demonization, and opens minds and hearts to genuine encounter with other cultures and views, so as to see the richness of the diversity of human talent and expectation. It calls out for mercy and compassion, sends help in disaster and celebrates success. It initially achieves all this, moreover, in the basic ways we have noted. All and even that, however, is only a beginning. Other provisions for establishing the means of human dignity have to follow in the re-construction of civil society.

None of this can be achieved without reconciliation. This is why it is so fundamentally important. We will see in what follows, however, that there are profound issues at stake in all this. Western culture achieves reconciliation principally through the institutions of democracy. These are there taken to be self-evident goods. They identify objectives, seek agreement for them and manage their implementation. That is what democratic governments do. A real question needs to be asked about whether or not this is the only end or objective of reconciliation.

Where Is There a Need for Reconciliation?

The last ten years have seen a growing sense of global confrontation. The attacks of 9/11 appeared to support the theses put forward by those such as Huntington who saw an inevitable series of confrontations, often violent, between different historic blocks, especially a continuation of the 1,500-year-old struggle between Christendom and Islam.[2] Groups within the deeply divided Muslim world accentuate this perception by calling for a global Caliphate. From the Islamic point of view the repeated invasions of Muslim lands by forces from 'Christian' countries is proof of a continued 'crusader spirit', as is the perceived siding of the same co-called Christian countries with Israel (a view that many Israelis dispute) and the failure of Christian Europe to prevent genocidal attacks on Muslims in the Balkans in the 1990s.

Hans Kung argues that religious peace is a pre-condition for international peace, and thus seems to support the view that the clash of civilisations is in certain respects religious.[3] Many people thus argue that reconciliation is needed most amongst and within the great religious traditions. The three Abrahamic faiths do not always live peaceably together. The horrendous and seemingly intractable problem in the Middle East is a daily reminder of this. It is, above all, a historic problem which reaches back to the roots of the three religions. Counter claims about the ownership of Jerusalem more than illustrate this. The need for reconciliation here is poignant to the point of unbearability as the chapter by Marc Ellis illustrates. He is a noted commentator on the Israel/Palestinian problem. The chapter mentions that 700,000 Palestinians were expelled from their land when the state of Israel was formed in 1948. Ellis has a known sympathy with those aggrieved by this. He is also critical of the draconian military measures

2   Samuel Huntington, *The Clash of Civilizations and the Remaking of World Order* (New York: Touchstone, 1996).

3   Hans Kung, *Islam Past Present and Future*, trans. John Bowden (Oxford: Oneworld, 2007).

Israel frequently use to suppress Palestinian revolt. He writes as a 'Jew of Conscience'. This is a group of people who remain faithful to Jewish tradition and use it to criticize the modern state of Israel. He writes: 'Much maligned, even persecuted, and certainly in exile, Jews of Conscience seek a just reconciliation for Jew and Palestinians in the land. Moreover they seek a renewal of the Jewish ethical tradition in a turbulent time.'[4] The chapter concludes with a please for revolutionary forgiveness which seeks justice, the cessation of oppression and equality. Only this, it argues, will lead to a shared life together for the people of Israel and Palestine.

Against this pessimism, however, we need to set other facts. The perception of widespread war is far greater than its reality. Compared to the first half of the twentieth century, in which more than 60 million people died through wars that consumed the world economy and destroyed almost every historic empire, the levels of violence today seem muted. In the period 1945–89 peace was maintained in part not through reconciliation but by mutually assured destruction. The wars of today are better known than their pre-1914 equivalents and this is good, because it prompts international action, but they do not threaten international survival as did the great wars and the cold war. That being said, reconciliation is in some ways more needed. The growing gap between many African countries and the rest of the world economy has been made worse to a large extent by conflict, which is mainly civil. The wars of the world are in many cases small enough to be susceptible to international pressure for reconciliation in a way that would have been inconceivable in 1918 or 1945. We thus have both the possibility and the capability to reduce the volume of extreme violence and that potential is the strongest incentive for reconciliation activity. Reconciliation is needed in all modern conflicts as a tool that both can and will change war to peace. This is not for one moment to suggest that we can achieve the utopia of world peace. It is but to stress that progress in peacemaking can always and must be made by reconciling differences between people whenever and wherever the causes of peace can be progressed by doing so.

4   See p. 108 of this volume.

Who Makes a Good Reconciler?

Many government and other agencies, such as those of the United Nations (UN), exist to bring about reconciliation. These are important and often successful at what they do. Multilateral agencies of the UN have remarkable experience and knowledge in disaster relief work and the management of large numbers of refugees. They are also skilled at from time to time delegating and sub-contracting the field work to smaller groups, and not leading on it themselves, except in the role of kick starting an initiative through their considerable moral authority.

Former national leaders often play significant roles in which they are able to draw on their previous experience and contacts. Tony Blair has taken a leading role in the Middle East; in Africa Kofi Annan and a team of former African Heads of State have been very influential in Angola, Mozambique, Kenya and Zimbabwe. President Obasanjo of Nigeria has made a significant difference in the eastern Democratic Republic of the Congo.

Finally there are the Non-Governmental Organizations (NGOs), of various sizes from the large like the Red Cross to the small like Coventry Cathedral's Community of the Cross of Nails mentioned at the beginning of this chapter. These smaller groups often have a string of successes to their credit. This is invariably based on their local knowledge and the contacts they create.

However, there are two caveats to all this. First, reconciliation may be helped by outsiders but its real work is most effectively done by the actual participants in a conflict themselves. They can be assisted to this end, but they cannot be excluded or excused from taking responsibility for themselves. However skilful the external support may be it is only those directly concerned who can make transformation actually happen. This is why even though larger agencies may be in attendance, genuine and permanent reconciliation is so often the exception rather than the rule. Second, the hard graft of reconciliation is usually done by local NGOs, not by those who pack up, go home and take the credit. The real heroes of reconciliation are, generally speaking, invisible. They are at the grass roots, putting into practice the declarations of the élites.

Many of those most actively engaged in facilitating reconciliation are from religious backgrounds. The St Egiddio community which began in Rome was immensely, even crucially significant, in Mozambique. The churches have played a major role in the Sudan. Religious groups have two principal advantages in reconciliation. They are very often part of international networks and well-established organizations within their own country. This means that they have good access to external advice and support, and are able to work across front lines often almost seamlessly. Thus the Anglican bishop of Freetown in Sierra Leone maintained contact with dioceses in rebel held areas even in the worst of the fighting in the late 1990s. The powerful network of the churches is one that governments and international agencies have been slow to recognize, often at great cost to their own work.

Religious groups will also be able to be realistic about evil. They have the means of confronting and dealing with it. This is no small thing as we shall see in later chapters. Faith in a God of miracles is, to put it ironically, helpful when dealing with wars. A willingness to lose one's life to save others brings credibility to the facilitation of reconciliation. The sense that all need the forgiveness of God enables religious people to reach out to those who have done evil. They can deal with them because they believe they can be redeemed. These are seemingly simple insights, but we will see in much of what follows how powerful they are.

Also, a religious perspective inculcates patience when it is so often needed. Religious people know that ultimate redemption only takes place in the sight of God. They are, therefore, able to live with the imperfection of its manifestation short of that.

Equally importantly, religious people have a passion for peace and an understanding of the means of achieving it. In much of what follows, the Christian reasons for this will be explored.

However, the effectiveness of large organizations is often inhibited by their sheer size. They can only operate when a degree of peace has been established and opportunities for them thereby created. In many war-zones this is far from the case. This is why there is also a need for facilitators of reconciliation who are independent of governments. These are people who can tread where 'angels often fear to go', often at great risk to themselves.

For this reason, great courage is invariably required of them. They find themselves among people who are not nice, who do not, as Andrew White graphically and humorously reminds us, take bagels for tea in London.[5]

Such individuals can only be effective if they are seen to operate without an ulterior personal agenda. These basic requirements rule out many, if not the majority, of candidates for the task. This ironically applies particularly to religious people who are otherwise so suited to the task. Their work is rendered instantly ineffective if they are thought to be covertly evangelizing. Those who are effective, such as those who write for this book, are exceptions who are frequently criticized and even disowned by their co-religionists. The reason for this is because, to go where they have to go to do their work, they have to leave their religious baggage (but emphatically not their faith) behind. They are not explicit evangelists for their religions. They seek only peace. Andrew White, as we shall see, is emphatic and clear in all this. If not, they will often be found working in small groups. They must also be willing to take risks, and be able to listen to all parties without rushing to judgement. Above all, they need patience. Theirs is often a long game, a point we shall return to again and again in what follows.

This book is a contribution to a growing literature in the study of reconciliation. It is edited broadly from within the Christian tradition but many contributions are made by Christians with different viewpoints and by those outside the Christian tradition. It seeks to correlate practical experience and academic analysis. This is facilitated by the fact that many of the contributions are written by those who are actively involved in reconciliation. The number of such writings is steadily increasing. It is important that they do so. Only in this way will a body of practical knowledge and experience emerge which can significantly contribute to the study and development of the work.

John Elford discusses the nature of just war theory. He points out that it is not an exclusively Christian theory. However, Christians who are not pacifists have throughout the centuries turned to it when they have sought to understand the morality, or otherwise, of war. The point is stressed that the theory has always been in a state of development. This

5   Andrew White, *Iraq: Searching for Hope* (London: Continuum, 2005), p. 95.

has been triggered whenever new circumstances and methods of warfare have emerged. He reminds us that hitherto the theory has been in two parts. The *jus ad bellum*, which relates to the conditions which have to be fulfilled before war can be engaged and the *jus in bello*, those which have to be observed once it is. He argues that it is now necessary for the theory to develop again. It should include two more parts. The *jus post bello*, to make provision for arranging the cessation of hostilities and the *jus in pace*, to cover the obligations and responsibilities for the reconstruction of post-conflict civil society.

Justin Welby discusses his experiences of working at reconciliation in Nigeria and elsewhere. He draws attention to our understanding of how conflict occurs within a cycle of developments and to how this helps us to understand how to bring about its cessation. He also shows how the work of the Coventry centre has been seminal in this. An emphasis is placed on the importance of researching thoroughly the background to particular conflicts. Central to this is the need to identify the *dramatis personae*. These are they who will have to be encountered in the reconciliation process. One initial stage in all this is working to relieve immediate need. The need for calculated risk-taking is also shown. Drawing on the parable of the Prodigal Son in the gospel of St Luke, the chapter shows how the work of reconciliation can lead to the healing of individuals and societies.

Elford then writes on the work of Andrew White in Iraq. This is based on Andrew's own writing and on personal discussions between the two of them. He tries to get behind what motivates Andrew and identify the principals which are clearly implicit in all that he does. A number of these are theological. They all focus in some way on how to deal with recurrent manifestations of evil. What emerges is a respect for Andrew's tenacity and vision. The ways in which this is correlated to practical action are also discussed.

Donald Reeves writes on The Soul of Europe and its work in Bosnia and Kosovo. The chapter contains vivid descriptions of encounters with individuals and societies under duress. He recognizes that widespread fear gives rise to a common need for security and for this to be accompanied by the practical relief of necessities. Like Andrew White, Reeves stresses the need to understand and talk to enemies. Out of this emerged a process of peace-building which is ongoing.

Marc Ellis is internationally recognized for his work in the Middle
East and elsewhere. This is centred on his recognition of the need to bring
about what he calls 'revolutionary forgiveness' between warring parties.
He is also recognized for being outspokenly critical of his own Jewish
community. This focuses on his criticism of the state of Israel and support
for many Palestinian causes. He works with a movement called 'Jews of
Conscience'. Through this he shows how deeply his protests against Israel
are rooted in Jewish spirituality.

The Revd Donald Reeves is a similar figure, personally courageous,
and capable of building friendship with the most unlikely people. His work
in the Balkans, done almost alone, like Andrew White in Baghdad, and
in Israel/Palestine demonstrates the role of the religious figure with little
or no organizational baggage.

Ron Roberts, Edina Bećirević and Stephen Paul write on the extent
to which the denial of truth remains an obstacle to reconciliation and
peace-building in Bosnia. This means that the war, they contend, effectively continues. People there have yet to learn again how to live together
in shared public spaces. They comment favourably on the foundation by Fra
Ivo Markovic of an inter-religious choir. This has enabled its participants
and audiences to share different religious traditions and experiences in a
remarkable way. It is an example of just how pragmatic and even simple
effective means of reconciliation can be.

Lakshman Dissanayake argues that attempts at reconciliation in Sri
Lanka must first take into account the nature of the conflict. He shows
that this was an admixture of ethnic, economic and territorial issues. These
affected all levels of society. In general, the majority Sinhalese did not enjoy
the privileges of the Tamil minority. These included attendance at English
language schools and higher education. A consequence of this was that
the Tamils were disproportionately represented in the professions and the
civil service. All this was part of the reason why ethnic riots preceded the
Civil war. However, it is argued that reconciliation will require more than
a focus on this bipolar approach. Local regional and international issues
have also to be considered. A number of reconciliation activities are then
discussed. In this several important points are made. One is that they must
all involve their participants at grass-roots level. Another is that where

aid distribution in involved scrupulous fairness to all must be observed. Another is that the public and private social and economic sectors must work closely, again, with grass-roots social structures. One way they can do this is to respect local custom and precedent.

These contributions demonstrate a range of models and experiences of reconciliation, reinforcing the complexity of the theory and practice and seeking to demonstrate the depth of hatreds that will need to be overcome to find even the barest modicum of capacity to avoid violence. Finally, John Elford draws out some of the themes which have emerged in the discussion. Principal among these is the need for reconciliation activity to be a recognized and programmed part of conflict resolution. He also stresses that it should be properly funded and not left, as it currently is, to self-funding by those who do it. In this concluding chapter attention is drawn to *The Utility of Force: The Art of War in the Modern World* by General Sir Rupert Smith. In this seminal work a distinction is made between the 'industrial wars' of the last century and the 'war amongst the people' which is a feature of the present one. The point made in all this is that the military cannot any longer deliver decisive outright victory to politicians and others who seek peace. What it can do is to work alongside others in seeking peace. In this it has to win battles, but is also has to win the hearts and minds of the people it fights amongst.

Another emphasis is on the subject of the utility of force especially as police action. Necessarily force will have to be calibrated and co-ordinated so that its effect is to create a desire for peace amongst the people, and a sense of the common good that outweighs inherited fears and hatreds or interests and greed. This is a new vision of just war, in that it starts with an outcome of peace and works back to see what may lead to this result. None but the naïve will imagine that in any confrontation all involved seek peace. In most war zones there are vast profits to be made through arms trading, smuggling, protection, mercenary activity and the identification of the market arbitrage opportunities that come when civil society ceases to function effectively.

General Sir Rupert Smith was described recently by another British general as the best thinker of his generation.[6] Elford's references to him are based on a lecture given by Sir Rupert at Liverpool Cathedral in early 2010. It is controversial and provocative, demonstrating the radically different thinking that the General argues is necessary in modern confrontation among the peoples. His immense experience as commander of 1st British Armoured Division in the first Gulf War, commanding UN forces in the Balkans, and finally as Deputy Supreme Allied Commander Europe at NATO during the Kosovo campaign, all give weight to his thinking on the utility of force.

The third aspect is around the issue of principles and relationships and how they interact. Can one be friends with bad people? Is justice something that comes before, as part of, or towards the end of reconciliation? Canon Andrew White was one of a succession of remarkable staff at Coventry Cathedral's Community of the Cross of Nails (also then called the International Centre for Reconciliation). His very individual approach to reconciliation is heavily dependent on personal commitment and a capacity to build deep and genuine friendships with both sides in a confrontation.

The Future

The outlook for reconciliation work is bleak. The major funders are all very short of money. Lack of cross governmental thinking and strategic approaches to foreign policy, security (both political and security of energy and trade) and potential threats, have all led to cut backs in relevant budgets. The most effective reconciliation is in advance of a conflict, and an NGO can work then for several years for a small fraction of the cost than it takes to move a battalion to a conflict in a peacekeeping or peacemaking role.

6   In a private discussion.

There is a lack of understanding of the time frame of reconciliation, of its need to be both political and élite and at the same time communal and grass roots. Special events and initiatives are often used as a substitute for the long graft of the reconciliation process, and expectations are raised that hatred will just go, and bitter loss be forgotten because there is more money and food about. Reconciliation is holistic; to be effective mind, action and spirit must all be committed. The source of its inspiration for Christians is the eternal dignity of the human person made in the image of God. This vision is here shared with all women and men of goodwill who seek peace. For this reason, it is open to the insights they also bring in the hope that the reconciliation of differences between warring people can be achieved and better futures secured for those in need of them.

D.C. WEBB, GAVIN FAIRBAIRN, SEIDU ALIDU AND
AYERAY MEDINA BUSTOS

What Do We Mean by Reconciliation?

Introduction

In this chapter we ask 'What do individuals and societies mean by the term "reconciliation", and how does that affect what they expect from the reconciliation process?' We draw attention to the importance for practice, of the ways in which we conceive of reconciliation and pay particular attention to the question of whether formal apologies should form a part of the reconciliation process.

By way of illustration we will start with a tragic new item. At the beginning of July 2008, Dr Hayford De-Graft Yankah, a fifty-five-year-old Ghanaian urologist, who had worked in the United States for thirty years, hanged himself in his home near Accra. He and his wife were no longer living together. Shortly before hanging himself, Dr Yankah had telephoned a friend and asked him to come to his house. The friend set off, but when he was about thirty minutes away Dr Yankah, telephoned again asking how far away he was. The friend arrived at the house at about 10am, to be met by Dr Yankah's house boy, who had been asked to wait at the gate to let him in. When Dr Yankah responded neither to knocking at his door, nor to telephone calls, his friend forced open the door and found him hanging by a computer cable. Dr Yankah had left a hand-written will and a note saying that he had failed to 'reconcile with life'.

This story, reported in the Ghanaian press[1] raises questions about what was going through Dr Yankah's mind as he took the steps that ended his life. Suicide is a complex phenomenon that can have many meanings and be underpinned by many intentions.[2] Though self killing is not the focus of our chapter, the story of Dr Yankah's death introduces the notion of reconciliation, which we want to examine in some detail. Dr Yankah's note said that he had failed to 'reconcile with life'. What could that mean? What is it to reconcile oneself with something, whether it is life as a whole, or some aspect of life, some experience, some disappointment, some tragedy or some trauma? In Dr Yankah's case it might be that what he really could not reconcile himself to was the fact that he was no longer living with his wife. We will never know.

For some people reconciliation involves the attempt to come to terms with and make sense of events and their repercussions, as part of the process of coming to terms with oneself, and attempting to create a comfortable sense of identity. Others, on the other hand view reconciliation, whether as a process or as an outcome, as a way of dealing with history and their role in it. Alternatively it may be conceived as the task of individuals and groups, in coming to terms with events and their results, or of 'making things right' between the parties in a dispute.

Although the idea of reconciliation is used in relation to human conflict of many different kinds, our main concern here will be in the context of peace building after violent conflict during which there were periods of government characterized by human rights abuse. In particular we will use take examples of two such conflicts with which we are familiar

---

1   General News, 'Suicide doctor invited colleague shortly before hanging' Tuesday, July 8, 2008, accessed at: http://www.ghanaweb.com/GhanaHomePage/NewsArchive/artikel.php?ID=146510 on 10/07/08.

2   Gavin Fairbairn, 'Suicide, euthanasia and assisted suicide: does it matter what we call it when people choose to die?' *Annals of Psychology*, 2009 and Gavin Fairbairn, *Contemplating Suicide: The Language and Ethics of Self Harm* (London: Routledge, 1995).

– Ghana[3] and Argentina[4]. In this context reconciliation is generally viewed as a necessary step toward individual and/or societal healing. However, reconciliation can mean different things to different people, depending upon their experiences, understandings and beliefs and this can create difficulties. Susan Dwyer notes that:

> The notable lack of any clear account of what reconciliation is, and what it requires, justifiably alerts the cynics among us. Reconciliation is being urged upon people who have been bitter and murderous enemies, upon victims and perpetrators of human rights abuses, upon groups and individuals whose very self-conceptions have been structured in terms of historical and often state-sanctioned relations of dominance and submission.[5]

Responding to Dwyer, David Bloomfield picks up on the 'deep confusion that still surrounds the term 'reconciliation', and its practice in post-violence peacebuilding', and draws attention to the fact that

> there remains great disagreement over what reconciliation actually means and, in particular, how it relates to other concepts and processes, such as justice, peacebuilding, democratisation and political development.[6]

Bloomfield then also considers the question of what we might believe the purpose of reconciliation to be:

> Is reconciliation a national, societal, even political process? Is it an individual, psychological, even 'theological', process? Is it a process at all, or does it describe a state of relationships at the end of a process?

3   Seidu Alidu, 'Achieving Reconciliation in Ghana: The Role of the National Reconciliation Commission', PhD thesis, School of Applied Global Ethics, Leeds Metropolitan University, 2010.
4   Ayeray Medina Bustos, 'Constructing Peace through Justice, Memory and Reconciliation in Argentina', PhD thesis, School of Applied Global Ethics, Leeds Metropolitan University, 2010.
5   Susan Dwyer, 'Reconciliation for Realists', *Ethics and International Affairs* 13/1 (1999), pp. 81–98.
6   David Bloomfield, 'On Good Terms: Clarifying Reconciliation', Berlin: The Berghof Research Center for Constructive Conflict Management, Report No. 14, 2006, p. 3.

Bloomfield's questions are rhetorical and he goes on to share his answers to them, and to comment on the answers that have been given by many others. What is clear is that 'reconciliation' is neither a simple term, nor a simple phenomenon. A number of authors, including Bloomfield, write about it as both a process and an outcome. It has both political and interpersonal (sometimes even intrapersonal) manifestations. Viewed like this it involves the building of a relationship between conflicting groups or individuals that can lead to an end state where both parties can co-exist peacefully. In addition, situations occurring after violent conflict or abuse that have left behind extremely deep psychological scars, self reconciliation will usually involve those who have suffered admitting and coming to terms with what s/he has gone through. Something similar is true, also, for those who have perpetrated violence and been responsible for the suffering of others. They may have even more difficulty in reconciling their views of themselves with the truth about what they have done.

Johan Galtung, founder of the International Peace Research Institute, has identified twelve approaches to reconciliation after violence, pointing out that none of them are able to deal with the complexities of the situation on their own. Galtung suggests that, as there is no panacea, perhaps they will all have something to offer. The possible approaches to be explored include attempts to change the perception of victim and perpetrator by identifying the true causes of the conflict; the possibility of reparation or restitution; the administering of a theological penitence and/or secular justice; the relating of individual's stories; and the use of rituals and practices that are important and relevant to the specific culture(s) involved.[7] We will address these particular approaches by examining the mechanisms and processes that are often employed and the concepts which they attempt to address.

---

7   Johan Galtung, 'Twelve Creative Ways to Foster Reconciliation After Violence', *Intervention* 3/3 (2005), pp. 222–34.

Truth Commissions

In a post violent conflict situation, the reconciliation process is often provided by a body such as a Truth, or Truth and Reconciliation, Commission. According to Mark Freeman, a lawyer and independent consultant on human rights issues:

> A truth commission is an *ad hoc*, autonomous, and victim-centred commission of inquiry set up in and authorized by a state for the primary purposes of (1) investigating and reporting on the principal causes and consequences of broad and relatively recent patterns of severe violence or repression that occurred in the state during determinate periods of abusive rule or conflict, and (2) making recommendations for their redress and future prosecutions.[8]

The Truth and Reconciliation Commissions that have been set up over recent years have adopted differing approaches in the attempt to achieve reconciliation, depending on whether they look at things as restorative or retributive justice, as a way of uncovering truths; or as a mixture of all three. Although such a Commission may have clearly stated aims and objectives in relation to process, there may not be an ostensive definition of what is generally understood by the term reconciliation. Perhaps the best that can be expected is to examine the ways that the term is used and to try to note the relationships between those uses, in an effort to understand what kind of work is being undertaken. It is obvious that there is a need to be clear about what 'reconciliation' initiatives are aimed at achieving from the outset. Unless all parties to the process understand what they are committing themselves to, there will always be a danger that some people will not be satisfied with the outcomes and then, even if they seem publicly to accept them, they may nurture continuing ill feeling and hurt in private and this may in turn fuel further conflict. A third party can often help to ensure that all sides understand the aims and objectives of such a reconciliation process.

---

8   Mark Freeman, *Truth Commissions and Procedural Fairness* (Cambridge: Cambridge University Press, 2006), p. 18.

The problems that may follow from a failure to agree on exactly what is expected of reconciliation processes, and about what is needed in order to reach a successful conclusion with such a process, may be seen if we consider the different expectations that the various interest groups in such processes may have. In Ghana, for example, Robert Ameh draws attention to three different identifiable groups with different views of what the reconciliation process should involve.[9] The first group acknowledges Ghana's bitter past, but believes that investigating it may not necessarily lead to reconciliation but merely re-open old wounds. Ameh refers to them as the 'Amnesia Group'. Typical members are alleged perpetrators of human rights violations during violent conflict, who advocate amnesty as an important component of the reconciliation process. The second group think differently, arguing that any reconciliation process should result in punishment of the perpetrators. Ameh refers to them as the 'Retribution/Vengeance Group'. In Ghana some actually threatened to perform their own acts of vengeance if the reconciliation process did not deliver a satisfactory result. Finally, Ameh refers to a 'Reconciliation Group', who believe that any attempt to re-visit the past should lead to a rebuilding of relationships between former feuding parties. In the case of Ghana this group consists mainly of faith based victims of abuse.

These examples demonstrate how differently people can think about what reconciliation should mean. Failing to take account of the different expectations of these and other groups in designing a process aimed at achieving reconciliation may create problems for the future. Groups similar to those outlined by Ameh as being present in Ghana, are also evident in other post conflict situations. For example, following the so-called 'Dirty War' in Argentina, the former military leaders called for amnesty (cf. Ameh's 'Amnesia Group') whereas almost all the victims believe that reconciliation and justice can only be achieved through punishment of the perpetrators (cf. Ameh's 'Retribution/Vengeance' Group). However, in this case there

9   Robert Ameh, 'Doing Justice after Conflict: The Case for Ghana's National Reconciliation Commission', *Canadian Journal of Law and Society* 21/1 (2006), pp. 85–109.

is little evidence for a 'Reconciliation Group', probably because there was no public acknowledgement of human rights abuse, perpetrators often either denying their part in such activities or showing no regret and even saying that they would do it again.

Traditional Community Practices

Among Galtung's approaches to reconciliation mentioned earlier is one that employs the use of traditional cultural methods to resolve disputes and conflicts. Galtung refers to this as the ho'o pono pono approach – named after the Hawaiian traditional method of reconciliation and healing through community and neighbourhood gatherings. A moderator (healing priest or family elder) oversees the process that requires harmony to be restored by confession and forgiveness.

Similar reconciliation processes in Africa involve tribal, ethic or kingship rituals specific to a particular culture. They are seen as ways of re-establishing relations between the people and their ancestors. The processes involve the participation of the whole community and are usually held as a kind of festival in which the Elders act as mediators and ensure that the process is culturally embedded. One such indigenous traditional process has been the subject of international examination recently. The challenge of administering justice in post-genocide Rwanda that is acceptable to the international community has proven to be an expensive and time consuming process. On the cessation of violence over 120,000 people were arrested and imprisoned following the 1994 genocide. The Rwandan government agreed to the International Criminal Tribunal for Rwanda (ICTR) established by the UN in 1994 to prosecute persons responsible for genocide and other serious violations of international humanitarian law. However, only thirty-four cases have been completed so far with a further

twenty-four in progress.[10] National courts were also used to try around
10,000 suspects up to 2007. Roxanne Lawson, Associate Coordinator of
the Africa Peacebuilding Program at the American Friends Service Com-
mittee noted that:

> It has been evident since early in the reconciliation process that the western justice
> system, embodied in these two courts, would need a hundred years to be able to
> handle all the case.[11]

In order to expedite the process the traditional communal justice system
of Gacaca courts has been revived and modified. The objectives of the over
8,000 Gacaca courts established include revealing the truth about what has
happened, eradicating the culture of impunity, reconciling Rwandans and
reinforcing their unity.[12] Lyn Graybill and Kimberley Lanegran describe
the process:

> *Gacaca* encompasses three important features of relevance to broader experiments
> of reconciliatory justice. First, *gacaca* rewards those who confess their crimes with
> the halving of prison sentences [...] Second, *gacaca* law highlights apologies. Part of
> the procedure of the traditional *gacaca* system, apology has been maintained in the
> new variant as an important ingredients to promote reconciliation. Third, repara-
> tions to victims are a cornerstone of *gacaca*. Those found guilty must contribute to
> a compensation fund and/or perform community service.[13]

The term 'Gacaca' refers to the village area where people meet. Judges are
elected from the elders of the community and although the system has

---

10   *International Criminal Tribunal for Rwanda*, United Nations – http://69.94.11.53/
     ENGLISH/cases/status.htm, accessed April 2010.
11   Roxanne Lawson, 'With Gacaca, Rwanda Combines Traditional and Modern Justice
     Systems', *Peacework*, American Friends Service Committee, November 2005 – avail-
     able at http://www.peaceworkmagazine.org/pwork/0511/051110.htm – accessed
     April 2010.
12   Initial Service of Gacaca Jurisdictions, http://www.inkiko-gacaca.gov.rw/En/
     EnObjectives.htm, accessed April 2010.
13   Lyn Graybill and Kimberly Lanegran, 'Truth, Justice, and Reconciliation in Africa:
     Issues and Cases', *African Studies Quarterly*, Vol.8, Issue 1, 2004, pp. 1–18.

been much criticized by Amnesty International,[14] for example, it is a system created by people disillusioned by the international community.

A further illustration of the traditional practices and social norms that exist in Africa is provided by the concept of 'mato oput' in Uganda. Here, a trusted independent third party plays shuttle diplomacy between the two conflicting parties and they decide when it is possible to talk without bad temper. At the right time the case is taken to the chief and a neutral venue is fixed at which the offended side is invited to present their case and their demands. The family or clan of the offending side must then work to raise the agreed compensation.

As the former Permanent Secretary of the Ministry of Foreign Affairs of Kenya, Bethuel Kiplagat, points out 'the spirit of mediation is very much part of the African heritage' and the act of reconciliation is not so much a bargaining session but one of healing:

> a re-establishment of relationship between people and also with their God. There is a holistic approach to the process, working with the community as a whole, invoking spiritual forces to be present and accompany the community towards peace.[15]

Truth, Consensus and Trust: Apology, Forgiveness and Blame

We want now to focus on some thoughts about the part that truth; consensus and trust; apology, forgiveness and blame, play in the reconciliation process.

14 Amnesty International Report AFR 47/007/02, *Rwanda: Gacaca; A Question of Justice*, 17 December 2002, available at http://www.amnesty.org/en/library/asset/AFR47/007/2002/en/b65d04e4-d769-11dd-b024-21932cd2170d/afr470072002en.pdf, accessed April 2010.

15 Bethuel Kiplagat, 'Is mediation alien to Africa?', The Ploughshares Monitor, Volume 19, No. 4, December, 1998.

Many and perhaps most people believe that truth must play an important role in any attempt to achieve reconciliation and truth might indeed be considered by many as a necessary condition for reconciliation. In other words, in order to come to terms with the past, it is sometimes assumed that those who have lived through and experienced conflict may need to know the truth about the fate of their loved ones and/or about what went on during periods of abuse/oppression/conflict (especially if they, or their loved ones, were victims) and/or they may need others to know the truth about what happened to them, and for their own personal account to be verified.

These assumptions make psychological sense. Many of us will have had the experience of listening to the stories of people who have been upset or bereaved, who frequently tell and retell their stories as they begin to absorb the truth about what has happened to them. Such storytelling is therapeutic, in the sense that it is only when we have accepted what has happened, or have been able to construct some kind of understanding and explanation of events, that we are enabled to move forward.

Mark Freeman and Priscilla Hayner (from the International Center for Transitional Justice) argue for the importance of truth as one of many possible elements in the pursuit of reconciliation:

> true reconciliation might depend on a clear end to the threat of further violence; acknowledgement by the state or by perpetrators of the injuries suffered; a reparation programme for the injured; attention to structural inequalities and the basic material needs of the victimized community; the existence of natural linkages in society that bring formerly opposing parties together; or, most simply, the passage of time.[16]

It is important to determine what we expect of the concept of truth and how we think we will recognize truth when we come across it. How are we to distinguish truth from untruth? How are we to recognize lying when we meet it?

---

16   Mark Freeman and Priscilla Hayner, 'Truth-Telling', in *Reconciliation after Violent Conflict: A Handbook*, edited by David Bloomfield, Stockholm: Institute for Democracy and Electoral Assistance, 2003, p 112.

Truth is not a simple matter, especially when we are dealing not just with physical facts, but with social and moral ones. John might say something that is untrue, believing it to be true; and Jane may say something that is true, believing it to be untrue. Which is telling a lie – and which the truth? If we allow that lying is always about the intention to deceive, then it is clear that John is no liar, while Jane, in this instance is. Add to this the possibility that a person might have problems with memory and they may 'fill in' their recall of events, by picking up details from others, whose version fits with, and perhaps reinforces, their own interpretation. There is also the possibility that what we recall will be influenced by the way that we experienced an event, rather than simply by the event itself, and it becomes clear that 'truth' cannot be taken as a simple matter.

Michael Ignatieff poses a series of questions about national reconciliation, including 'can a nation be reconciled to its past as an individual can, by replacing myth with fact and lies with truth?' He distinguishes between truths told for the purpose of reconciliation, and truth told for its own sake and notes that:

> One should distinguish between factual truth and moral truth, between narratives that tell what happened and narratives that attempt to explain why things happened and who is responsible...Truth commissions were more successful in promoting the first than the second.[17]

The events surrounding incidents of violent conflict are often confusing and are obviously subject to strong emotions. It is not always clear at the time what is happening, why it is happening, or sometimes, even, who is involved and to what extent. Different people, including bystanders, will often have quite different perspectives and/or points of view. A variety of accounts and interpretations of the same event are nearly always presented during attempts at reconciliation. Perpetrators will usually construct their version of what occurred in an attempt to minimize their guilt. Victims, on the other hand, will often want to emphasize the hurt and pain they have

17   Michael Ignatieff, 'Articles of Faith', *Index on Censorship*, 5, September/October, 1996, p. 113.

suffered, and the extent to which those with whom they are or have been in conflict were responsible for that hurt and pain. Both will also attempt to construct a story that makes some sense to them and to others, in order that it becomes understandable and believable for them. At times it may be necessary to take account of both an individual's version of events, what we might refer to as their 'individual truth' and a common or 'communal truth' – the generally accepted story constructed by bringing together individual stories, official histories, documentation etc.

Individuals need their individual truth to be validated and accepted as a description of the past and of their experiences in order to help them to come to terms with what has happened to them, to their community and to their friends and loved ones. Society needs to establish an official and validated version of the truth in order to identify the guilty; to support victims, and to understand causes and the circumstances that allowed them to come about in order that they can attempt to prevent recurrences.

In thinking about the importance of truth, of course, we need also to consider its converse, *deceit*, and not just deceit in the sense of lying to others, but also the possibility of self-deceit. As we have already hinted, lying involves deliberately telling untruths, or deliberately withholding the truth as we understand it and believe it; self deceit is more complex, and involves fooling oneself about things – 'pulling the wool over one's eyes'. Though it is easy to believe that perpetrators of dreadful acts may at times enter into self-deceit in order to avoid facing up to the facts of what they have done, it is less easy to think of victims as doing so. However, it is possible, for example, for a victim to forget selectively the acts of aggression that they or their group have been responsible for in earlier times, and they may view these acts as justifiable even when the same acts on the part of the 'other' are viewed as heinous.

Truth and Narrative

The assumption that people need or want to know the truth (or to construct a 'true' story) about the past has led most Truth Commissions to conduct their hearings in a narrative form, where both offenders and victims are expected to talk respectfully to each other about their part in the events under consideration. Based on his studies of language development in British children Gordon Wells notes that:

> When storying [referring to narratives] becomes overt and is given expression in word, the resulting stories are one of the most effective ways of making one's own interpretation of events and ideas available to others. [18]

Putting personal stories into the public arena as a way of building a shared narrative, is arguably one of the central points of Truth Commissions. Janice McDrury and Maxine Alterio's work on storytelling as a learning tool has led them to believe that acknowledging and sharing experiences about the past provides 'an opportunity for reflective learning and the development of deeper relationships with others'.[19] However, the assumption that disclosure of what actually happened during past abuses could, by itself, bring about reconciliation, is questionable. In fact, in their study of South Africa, Rwanda and Sierra Leone, Lyn Graybill and Kimberly Lanegran have identified a number of problematic issues concerning transitional and restorative justice and they suggest that there is no substantive evidence to back the claim that merely telling the truth about what has happened in the past leads to reconciliation.[20] Drawing on experiences obtained through trauma counselling and anthropological fieldwork, Brandon Hamber and

---

18   Gordon Wells, *The Meaning Makers: Children Learning Language and Using Language to Learn* (Portsmouth, NH: Heinemann, 1986).

19   Janice McDrury, and Maxine Alterio, *Learning through Storytelling in Higher Education: Using Reflection and Experience to Improve Learning* (London, Kogan Page Limited, 2002), p. 34.

20   Lyn Graybill and Kimberly Lanegran, 'Truth, Justice, and Reconciliation in Africa: Issues and Cases', *African Studies Quarterly*, Vol.8, Issue 1, 2004, pp. 1–18.

Richard Wilson go further and doubt that there could be such a thing as national reconciliation purely as a result of truth revealed before Truth Commissions.[21]

In our view, truth is most likely to be helpful in achieving the goal of reconciliation when, as well as meeting the needs for truth that we have already pointed out, it assists in some other way as well. For example, finding out the truth about the causes of abuse may lead to steps being taken to address them and identifying the victims of abuse can help them achieve compensation for their suffering. In addition, the identification of perpetrators of abuse can, where this is possible and appropriate, result in their being punished and in justice being seen to be done. It is therefore important that, for the purposes of reconciliation, the search for truth is carried out for positive reasons. Following the establishment of a democracy in Argentina in 1983, President Alfonsin created CONADEP, the National Commission on the Disappeared, at the same time as he repealed the amnesty declared by the previous military regime. The people of Argentina were then able to see the Truth Commission as a way of uncovering truths that had not previously been recognized

However, the search for truth does not always have positive results. In Ghana for example, the ex-president Jerry Rawlings successfully masterminded two military coups, each of which witnessed extensive human rights abuses. Although he apologized for some of the crimes committed during his term he refused to participate in the Truth Commission set up by his successors, believing it to be nothing more than a witch hunt. In addition, the transitional provision in the Ghanaian constitution makes prosecution impossible. Rawlings appears to have retained a number of sympathizers within the military and so prosecutions for war crimes and human rights abuses in Ghana may not only be inappropriate, but actually impossible.

21　Brandon Hamber and Richard Wilson, 'Symbolic Closure through Memory, Reparation, and Revenge in Post-Conflict Societies', *Journal of Human Rights*, 1, 2002, pp. 35–53.

Consensus and Trust

Reconciliation is often assumed to be possible when two conditions are met – the development of consensus and the development of trust. One rationale for this belief would be the idea that groups can only live together in peace and mutual respect if they agree to do so, either implicitly or explicitly, because each trusts that the other will be true to their word. Where written or unwritten pacts such as these exist, people can more readily trust and relate to each other. It is neighbours that form our immediate world and environment, but where consensus is lacking and neighbours become suspicious of each other, harmony is gradually lost. This is usually the first early warning of enemy construction which can eventually lead to conflict.

Building consensus between neighbours requires trust and in their work on trust and negotiation in intergroup contexts,[22] Roderick Kramer and Peter Carnevale argue that there seems to be a close relationship between cooperation and trust. They note both that trust can lead to cooperation, and that cooperation can reinforce trust. In this process, a mutual relationship is created. Looking at reconciliation between nations, Arie Nadler and Tamar Saguy contend that where the parties in conflict harbour distrust, they are less likely to cooperate, because each is likely to misinterpret the intentions of its rival.[23] For example, mistrust is a major problem that has made the peace process between Palestinians and Israelis so difficult. Although a number of peace treaties have been signed between the two parties, there is still a high level of distrust between them. They may share an uneasy coexistence, but it seems highly unlikely that they can be reconciled, while the current level of suspicion and mistrust persists.

22   Roderick M. Kramer and Peter J. Carnevale, 'Trust and Intergroup Negotiations', in R. Brown and S. Gaertner (eds), *Intergroup Processes* (Oxford: Blackwell, 2001), pp. 431–50.

23   Arie Nadler and Tamar Saguy, *Reconciliation Between Nations: Overcoming Emotional Deterrents to Ending Conflicts Between Groups*, in Harvey Langholtz and Chris E. Stout (eds), *The Psychology of Diplomacy* (New York: Praeger, 2004).

Therefore, if part of the role of reconciliation after conflict is to establish harmony between formerly antagonistic neighbours, or at least a consensual agreement to coexist peacefully, then it is essential that mutual trust and understanding be established between them so that long lasting and meaningful agreements can be achieved.

Harmony/Peaceful Coexistence

It is not only property and human lives that are lost during violent conflict; at such times, any sense of common security that may have been previously enjoyed by the community is likely to be severely damaged. In addition, during an internal or civil war the concept of communal living and togetherness is often replaced with mistrust and suspicion. After the violence has ended, although the dead will not return and injuries sustained by some might ensure that they will never be the same again, property that is lost can be restored with time and some wounds will heal. How, though, can trust and togetherness be rebuilt to unite the community? This is one of the roles of peace building, but successful conflict reconciliation processes can help ensure success. Reconciliation is thus a bridge to attaining trust in those who may have lost hope.

As an illustration of the differing ways in which people from diverse cultures might attempt to establish harmony between former antagonists, we might consider some traditional practices and social norms that exist in Africa. In Ghana for example, wisdom about living an ethical life and relating well to one's neighbours is passed on by way of proverbs. The struggles of life are illustrated in a Dagbani saying *'zinli min nyena gba zab'ra'* which means that even the tongue and the teeth which live together in the mouth often fight each other. This underscores the fact that disagreements and conflicts are an unavoidable part of human life. However, when they do occur, if we are motivated by a wish for harmony and peaceful coexistence, dialogue needs to take precedence over violence as illustrated by a saying from the Akan language '*o bi nka obi*', meaning 'let's not bite one another.' This proverb emphasizes belief in the idea that dialogue and compromise should be used to handle grievances and we should not resort to violence when we are offended. This approach to achieving harmony with one's neighbours is aptly captured by the concept of *ubuntu*. Encompassing the western notions of 'humaneness' and reciprocity, *ubuntu* is often expressed by the Xhosa saying '*umuntu ngumuntu ngbabanye bantu*' which translates as 'people are people through other people.' The Christian religious philosopher John Mbiti explains this in terms of a relationship between people in which whatever happens to the individual happens to the whole group and whatever happens to the whole group happens to the individual. Therefore the individual can only say; 'I am, because we are; and since we are, therefore I am.' [24]

On a more personal level, reconciliation can also be thought of as re-establishing balance or equilibrium between an individual's past and present. For some people this will involve telling and retelling their story, the idea being that by reconstructing and relaying the events that they lived through and the experiences that they had, a person can come to absorb them, to accept that they happened. This emphasizes the potential healing power of narrative. However, it is important to recognize that in some cases it may be initially beneficial for the victim to blot out some of the events of the past in order to survive psychologically. Dwelling too much on what has happened can be debilitating. In some cases, the experiences of the victim may have been so horrific that recalling them would involve reliving their pain and anguish almost to the same extent that they were felt at the time. If too much time is spent on recalling and on thinking about what happened, it can interfere with every day life to the extent where day to day conversations and interactions with others (especially family and friends) may be affected. In this way the victim may be prevented from rebuilding their lives. In extreme cases they may even be unable to come to terms with the present at all, which could lead to attempts to end the

24   John S. Mbiti, *African Religions and Philosophy* (London: Heinemann, 1969), pp. 108–9.

suffering by taking their own life. Therefore, when the event is too close it may be too painful to dwell on it. Something similar may be true for a perpetrator who feels guilt over his actions – especially if they were carried out in the heat of conflict or under orders which he did not feel able to refuse. In the same way that a victim may need to leave the horrors of the past to one side for a while and concentrate on rebuilding something like a normal life, perpetrators may need a breathing space – a chance to put aside difficult thoughts about what they have done until they have re-established themselves and their lives after the conflict has ended, and they are then able to cope with the possible consequences of dealing with what they have done.

Although it might seem that these two approaches are contradictory, in fact they are not and it may be purely a matter of 'horses for courses'. Some people will find it helpful immediately, to talk through their experience, to tell their story and to go over it again and again, while others will be more comfortable keeping it in until the time is right. For some people telling their story will ultimately be unhelpful, because it will not assist them to move on. On the other hand, some people who sublimate the horrors that have happened to them and refuse ever to talk about them may suffer psychologically as a result, as they cut off part of themselves forever. It may therefore just be a matter of timing. Those who find it too hard to address what has gone on may need to wait until they are ready and when, in order to re-establish harmony, their past and present need to be reconciled. The amount of time that is needs to elapse before this can successfully take place will depend upon a number of factors including the physical and mental state of the individual; recognition of the importance of forgiveness and/or admission of guilt; the extent to which support is available within an accepting society or group and the possibility of arrest (for the perpetrator) or recompense (for the victim).

Forgiveness and Apology

Apology and forgiveness are often considered to be prerequisites for reconciliation. This is probably because conflict in one-to-one interpersonal relationships can frequently be 'healed' if the transgressor apologizes and the person who has been offended accepts the apology and offers forgiveness. However, apology is not a simple thing, and in drawing to a conclusion we will pay some attention to the complexity of apology, as a feature of the process of reconciliation.

It is sometimes assumed that victims who have suffered the actions or inactions of perpetrators possess the power to forgive those who have harmed them. Even when they do have the human and moral resources to do so, victims will often expect those who have harmed them, not only to apologize, but to show remorse for their acts and perhaps, to make a commitment to refrain from acting in similar ways in the future. The question therefore arises as to whether perpetrators mean it when they say they are sorry. Though some will do so, as part of a genuine expression of remorse and in order to demonstrate to their victim or victims that they have changed, the fact that a person, a group or a nation says 'sorry' does not in itself mean anything. 'Apologies' can be little more than words. Unless they are accompanied by the right intentions and feelings, they mean little. Some would also go so far as to say that unless an apology is accompanied by appropriate actions, it means nothing. In Ghana, for instance, some people believe that the behaviour of former President Jerry John Rawlings does not live up to and hence confirm the apology he made to the nation for the atrocities committed during his eleven years or more of military rule in the country.

Consider the difference between an offender who 'apologizes', means it and 'lives' it and one who apologizes but neither means it, nor lives in ways that suggest it is meant. Interestingly there could also be situations which, for personal or cultural reasons, an offender doesn't (can't) apologize, but means to (and lives as if they are sorry). In such a case, the fact that an 'apology' is withheld may be of less importance that the fact that remorse is shown in behaviour. We can perhaps appreciate the complexity of the situation by considering all the possible positions taken up by victim and perpetrator. For example, those who have offended may or may not wish to apologize. In each case, they may also then have the ability to apologize or they may not. Then, in each case, they may or may not actually express their sorrow and even then they may or may not be genuine in their expression of remorse. Finally, they may openly demonstrate the authenticity of their regret and/or apology (or lack of it) by the way they behave.

The situation for those who are offended against is similarly complex. In this case they may or may not be willing to receive an apology and then they may or may not feel able to offer forgiveness for any apology offered. Once more the authenticity of their acceptance of an apology and/or offer of forgiveness will be revealed by their future behaviour and the way they live their lives.

Taken together, these possibilities show at least some of the difficulties both perpetrators and victims may feel about the need to apologize or to accept apologies. In cases where perpetrators are able and willing to render an apology, there is still a possibility that the victims may be unwilling or unable actually to forgive, even though they may want to. Feelings of resentment and bitterness after being harmed, persecuted or attacked may run too deep to allow them simply to forgive. At one level they may be so filled with the desire to seek regress or even for revenge that they find they cannot forgive, even though at another level they may wish to do so. In some instances, pressure from others in the group may inhibit those who would be willing to forgive from actually saying that they do. In addition, some victims who choose not to forgive the people who have offended them may nonetheless be able to believe and accept an apology that is offered sincerely. In this case they may attempt to live with their inability to forgive and try to reconcile their past with the present.

Concluding Remarks

Peace does not follow automatically when violent conflict ends. The attempt to reconstruct post conflict societies, heal wounds and rebuild trust and confidence takes a great deal of effort. This is the work of peace building, in which it is now recognized that reconciliation plays a major part, alongside considerations of justice. Even in situations in which the pain experienced by victims of war and oppression may not be forgotten (or even forgiven) it is possible for individuals and communities to reconcile themselves with past actions and experiences, so that they can eventually coexist peacefully with former adversaries or oppressors. In this way the cycle of violence that results from the neglect of painstaking peace building and reconciliation, may be broken.

At national level, the attempt to achieve reconciliation requires difficult political decisions as governments initiate and then work to sustain processes aimed at acknowledging and remedying the wrongs of the past. It also requires difficult decisions at an individual level, because activities that attempt to bring reconciliation can be painful and humiliating as people have to relive dreadful experiences and come face to face with truths about their lives that they might have preferred to have been left untold. However, it is by confronting those difficult issues and dealing with them that healing can occur. That is why reconciliation processes must hold a realistic hope of benefit for individuals and groups, and why every effort must be made to fulfil those hopes. Individual members of governments can hamper such activities and processes for their own personal or political reasons, especially when their own role during the period in question was less than innocent. In addition, governments may initiate investigations simply in the attempt to establish some legitimacy in the international arena. At best such apparent reconciliation initiatives, instigated and/or carried out for ulterior motives, will only patch over deep seated problems; at worst they will generate frustration, anger and general dissatisfaction, leading to further violence.

People don't always have shared views of the nature of reconciliation, with the result that they can develop differing expectations of it. That is why the nature of reconciliation, what it might involve and what its outcomes might be, deserve and require careful consideration. In this chapter we have tried to begin to explore some of the ways in which reconciliation may be conceptualized (including the ways in which it can be considered as both a process and an outcome) and some of the work is expected of it in relation to peace building. In doing so we have drawn attention to its relationship to other concepts, including 'apology' and 'forgiveness', and to a number of important practices, including the attempt to develop shared narratives, that play a central role in much peace building. *En route*, we gestured at the importance of truth in all its forms. This is an area in which we think there is much work still to be done.

R. JOHN ELFORD

Just War Theory: Reconciliation and Reconstruction in the Christian Tradition

Introduction

In this chapter we will look at why peacemaking is so important in the Christian tradition. In so doing we will see why some Christians are pacifists and others not. It will be shown that there is, effectively, only one tradition in which Christians, with others, have subjected war fighting to moral criteria: the Just War tradition. This will be explained and the need for its development in the modern circumstances of war fighting will be discussed. In brief, it will be argued that the classic two parts of the tradition needs to be expanded to include two more which embrace arrangements for hostility cessation and the reconstruction of post-conflict civil society. In conclusion, those developments will be specified and some of the means of their implementation explored.

Peacemaking in the Christian Tradition

Christians carry a particular responsibility for peacemaking for the simple reason that they are charged by Jesus to be peacemakers (Matthew 5:09, Mark 9:50, Luke 1:79). It is not possible to be a Christian and ignore this injunction, simple as that. The reason for this is because Jesus was identified as the Messiah, the Prince of Peace, prophesied in Isaiah (9:06). In his person the Messianic age became a present reality. In him the visions and expectations of the old order were fulfilled. Peace was no longer to be longed for in the Messianic future. His person actualized that future. In him the Messianic peace had arrived. No understanding of peace in the Christian tradition is adequate unless it is rooted in these fundamentals about Jesus as the Messiah. This is nothing less than staggering. To be a Christian is to live in the Messianic present and to carry dominical responsibility for peacemaking. This is the major difference in the understanding of peace between the Old and New Testaments.

In all probability, Jesus was a pacifist. Those who wish to argue that he was not have precious little evidence to cite for their opinion. That most commonly referred to is his turning the money changers out of the Temple (Matthew 21:12). But this stretches credulity. To infer from this incident that Jesus would, therefore, approve the use of force in other situations is simply reading into the text something which is evidently not there. Jesus was a (very) strange Messianic figure who proclaimed the Kingdom of God (Mark 1:15) and enjoined his hearers to prepare themselves for its imminent arrival, the *parousia*. He believed that he lived in the last moment of time before all earthly rule would be overturned and the Kingdom of God would arrive on earth. When this did not happen and his ministry finished in the ignominy of the Crucifixion, his followers had to include in their recol-lections of his teaching the story of his life, as well as to adapt his radical preaching to ever changing circumstances. The New Testament is the record of how, initially, they achieved this. They all make the crucifixion central to their understanding of his person. They do this, however, in different ways. The most different is Luke who, as we will see below, took a different view of history from Mark and Matthew. For Luke the crucifixion narra-tive is neither so central or climactic. It points, rather, to the ascension of Jesus into heaven. This event is pivotal to the ending of the gospel and the beginning of the Acts of the Apostles (the only sequel to any of the gospels by the presumed same author). The gospel writers all approached the prob-lem of the delay of the parousia in different ways. The earliest gospel, by St Mark, takes Jesus at his word and expects the arrival of the Kingdom to be imminent. The slightly later Matthew's gospel acknowledges the delay (it had no choice) but believes that the arrival remains imminent. The later, possibly much later, Luke's gospel is radically different in this respect. It accepts the permanence of history and constructs a schema which explains the place of the risen and ascended Christ at God's right hand in glory. This is a vision which is more or less what Christians still believe. That Jesus was the Messiah, that he inaugurated the Messianic age, but that the full realization of that age was yet to be fulfilled on earth when he returned in glory. In all this, the foundations were laid for a partially mistaken first-century Palestinian Messianic movement to become a major world religion. The writings of St Paul were also, of course, crucial in this respect. This was a religion in which peacemaking, for the reasons we have briefly considered, became and remains an imperative for its adherents.

Seen in this light, Jesus' pacifism was of his particular life and times. Changing circumstances were soon to require otherwise of his followers. This is the view we will here take. However, it is contested with force and integrity by many Christians who believe that changing circumstances should not alter this fundamental truth about the person and work of Jesus. He was a pacifist and for that reason alone they claim, his followers should never be any other. This is the bedrock of the pacifist traditions in the Christian churches. Some, such as the Quakers and the Mennonites, have made it the central reason for their existing as they do. Other Christian churches have many pacifists in their ranks. In all, they have produced many fine examples of people who have and still do witness to and argue for this, to them, fundamental truth. Pacifism of this kind is sometimes called 'pacifism of principle'. For the purposes of analysis it is important to distinguish it from other types of pacifism. One such is 'pragmatic pacifism'. This is not based on principles, but simply on the claim at in the end it is the only thing that will work. Those who, as here, disagree with them, do well to respect their integrity and keep their witness always in mind. To believe other than pacifists do is no small matter and to be held constantly to account for so disagreeing is important. This is why, at their best, these two Christian traditions the pacifist and non-pacifist have existed side by side. As times and circumstances have changed the one tradition and then the other has come to the fore. This is a strength of Christianity and not a weakness. It requires that its adherents be peacemakers and that they think things out for themselves in ever changing circumstances, throwing themselves on the mercy of God when they decide to act as they do.[1]

---

1   See my *The Ethics of Uncertainty* (Oxford: Oneworld, 2000), Chapter 5.

These necessarily brief remarks on pacifism barely do it justice. They do, however, enable us to recognize the reasons for its central importance in Christian tradition: an importance that all should recognize, including those of us who disagree with it. Pacifism, it may be generally observed, is no longer the dominant approach to war in the Christian tradition. For reasons we will now briefly consider, that approach has been to understand and support the notion of limited warfare. The origins of this are, again, to be located deep in the history of the Christian church and even before that.

The Just War Tradition

The early Christians were ambivalent in their attitude to the state, which was of course the Roman Empire. It is differently depicted in the New Testament. On the one hand it is seen as the agent of righteousness (Romans 13:1–7, 1 Peter 2:13–17) and on the other as the Great Beast (Revelation 13). Jesus was specifically confronted by a question about to whom loyalty is deserved and famously answered that it was necessary to render unto Caesar 'the things that are Caesar's and God the things that are God's' (Matthew 12:17). Notwithstanding their horrendous persecution by the Roman authorities, Christians for the most part existed peacefully within the confines of Roman society. With the expansion of Christianity, however, all this was to change in a historically short time-span. The persecution of Christians by the Roman authorities came to a formal end in March 313 CE with the Edict of Milan. From then on Christianity could be practised without let or hindrance. The consequences of this were almost immediate. Christianity grew phenomenally in strength within the structures of Roman society. The main outcome of this was the election of the first Christian Roman Emperor, Constantine, only ninety-seven years later in 410 CE. Christians were now enfranchised citizens of the Roman state who had to share in and take responsibility for its well-being. This is commonly referred to as Constantinian Christianity.

One of the fundamental responsibilities of the state is, of course, the responsibility to defend its citizens. For this reason, Christians had to come to terms with the responsibilities of civic power. Little wonder that this exercised some of its best minds. They were principally Ambrose of Milan and St Augustine. They both reconciled Old Testament notions of war as an instrument of God's righteousness and the Roman understanding of *justum bellum*. This is, in fact, a central example of the way that Christian thinking became a part of Western culture. It no longer existed in isolation. It was part of a wider picture of wisdom and tradition. This drew deeply on Classical, Greek and Roman sources and brought them into dialogue with its own biblical traditions.[2] More widely, of course, this included the synthesis of Christian thought and Greek philosophy, again principally, but not exclusively at the hand of St Augustine. All this marked the initial engagement of Christianity with thinking about the justice, or otherwise, of war in Western culture. This has continued ever since. The resultant *just war tradition* is not for these reasons exclusively Christian. It has always been and remains a forum for open debate. Throughout the centuries there have been notable Christian contributions to its development by Gratian, St Thomas Aquinas and others. In fact, it has received the attention of most mainstream Christian thinkers throughout the ages and it still does. All this is proper and to be expected, given the deep origins of the peacemaking obligations in Christian tradition.

One marked feature of the just war tradition has been its evolving nature. It has been re-formulated whenever changing circumstances have required it to be so. The history of this is well documented and need not detain us here. All we need to draw from the forgoing is: the importance of peacemaking in Christian tradition, the reasons why the majority of Christians eschew pacifism, the engagement with the wider discussion about the justice of war and the willingness to remain open to the development of that discussion whenever changing circumstances require it. In what follows we will look both at reasons why the tradition now needs to develop again and at the form those developments might now take.

2   Cf. my 'Christianity and War', pp. 171–82, in *The Cambridge Companion to Christian Ethics*, ed. Robin Gill (Cambridge: Cambridge University Press, 2001).

The Present Need for the Development of the Tradition

First we need to be clear about what the tradition already says. Only then will we be able to understand why it needs to be developed. One of its marked features is the simplicity of its formulation. As it stands, it is in two parts. The first, the *jus ad bellum*, is about the conditions which have to be fulfilled before a war can be considered to be just and the second, the *jus in bello*, is about the criteria which have to me met for the conduct of the war also to be so. Chief among these, as we shall see, is the requirement to *discriminate* between military and civilian targets and to use only force which is *proportionate* to the end required. Before we consider these further some comment is necessary on the use of the word 'just' in this context.

All war is a human tragedy. It involves death and suffering including that of the innocent who get caught up in it. We are probably now more aware of these ugly facts than we have ever been because of the speed at which we receive images of and information about war through the media, particularly television. Some of these are harrowing simply to look at, let alone experience. The pacifist claim that none of this can ever be justified is immensely strong at this point. It is from here that not being a pacifist is poignantly difficult. The first thing we have to do is to stand back and try to see the wider picture. This can be considered a dispassionate thing to do, but it is necessary if we are even to begin to consider the tragedy of it all in a wider perspective. When we do this, it immediately become obvious that there are some states of affairs that at least compare with and invariably eclipse war in their horror. Systematic genocide is an obvious case in point. Similarly harrowing pictures of this are sadly commonplace. For whatever reason (and Christianity has, of course, particularly relevant views on this) people are capable of inflicting incredible acts of cruelty, suffering and death on other people. The capacity for this, moreover, is seemingly unlimited. Tribal warfare in areas where state control is weak or non-existent is a now common example. Inter-religious warfare is another. The havoc and suffering these cause is ceaseless. At its worst it creates situations which are more horrendous in the scale and depth of the suffering they cause, than would be the limited and controlled suffering which would be entailed in preventing them in the first place or stopping them once they have broken out. To acknowledge this is to recognize the fact that there are some states of human suffering that are worse than war. It is only in this dire and limited sense that military actions to prevent such suffering can be thought to be 'just'. This is only contextual justice. It is not absolute. Resort to it has to be, as we shall see, last resort and, again as we shall see, it has to be strictly limited. Given all this, the use of the word 'just' is highly conditional. It is important to remember that at all times. This is not simply a passing caveat. It is a fundamental reminder to all who even begin to contemplate the justice, or otherwise, of wars.

Briefly, for a war to be even contemplated as just in this sense, it must be: of last resort, and fought by a legitimate authority after a formal declaration. It must also have a reasonable chance of success. Once engaged the means used should discriminate between military and civilian targets. The means should also be proportionate to the end they seek. These conditions look simple enough, but they are invariably complex and controversial in their application. For example, they do not state that civilian casualties invalidate the 'justice' of such a war, proving that they are not an intended consequence of any particular action. This has been and remains a point of delicate discussion. The question is this. Can we, or can we not, be held morally responsible for foreseen but unintended consequences of our actions? To claim that we cannot is not an easy thing to do with a clear conscience. This is not an arena for the pursuit of easy conscience, anything but. This is one of the hardest things that supporters of the theory have to face. They can only do it by keeping in mind the wider justices they earnestly seek. Any who claim that this is straightforward are of easy conscience. The way ahead is harder than they even imagine.

For our purpose, it is important to notice as we have done that traditional just war thinking falls, broadly into two categories. First, the conditions that have to be met *before* a war and be considered just in the sense we have been describing. Second, those that have to be adhered to once it *is engaged*. It is equally important for our purpose to notice what these conditions presume about warfare. Namely, this is that wars come to end in victory or failure at some given point. Also, that they end naturally

when victors vanquish foes. It was, of course, once true that major wars
ended in this way, in final victory and defeat. The two great World Wars
ended in this way. We know exactly when they finished and accounts and
images of their doing so are etched in our memories. All this dates from
a time when war was a mighty and industrial conflict between clearly
identified opposing sides. Nothing less, in fact, than a shoot-out-to-the-
finish which both parties and their allies earnestly desired. The fact that
all this has now changed radically is the main reason why just war theory
needs re-visiting. (There are others which we will consider below.) It has
to adapt itself to a world in which, for the most part at least, war fighting
is of a very different kind.

This difference has recently been powerfully described by a distinguished General whose conclusions are wrought from his own war-fighting
experiences.[3] Sir Rupert Smith describes foregoing 'industrial war' and sets
out the reason for its demise. This was caused by the use of the atom bombs
in August 1945, which he describes as the last act of industrial warfare.
Fire power had now become so massive that, short of being deployed as a
means of unimaginable mass suicide, it could not be an effective instrument of war fighting. As has often been ironically remarked, it made the
world safe for war fighting. This is, precisely, what it did. It opened the way
for smaller limited wars. But these were not only different in scale, they
changed their nature. Rupert Smith analyses this change and describes
modern war generically as 'war amongst the people'. This occurs in a world
which is very different from pre 1945.[4] The sequence of war to that date
was, invariably, peace–conflict–resolution–peace. Since then 'there is no
pre-defined sequence, but rather a continuous criss-crossing between confrontation and conflict, whilst peace is necessarily either the starting or
the end point; and whereas conflicts are ultimately resolved, this is not
necessarily the case with confrontations'.[5] He illustrates this by saying that
the Cold War was resolved, but the Palestinian/Israeli conflict is not. In

3   Rupert Smith, *The Utility of Force: The Art of War in the Modern World* (London:
     Allen Lane, 2005).
4   Ibid., p. 183.
5   Ibid., p. 181.

modern war fighting, force has it utility, not it providing dramatic solutions, but as part of a wider political processes. Politicians and the military work together, albeit with defined roles. In all this, the use of force has to be carefully managed to meet agreed political objectives. What these actually are in any given circumstance might well not be clear and subject to constant revision. Hence, the provisionality of it all.

This view of the changed nature of war fighting in the modern world requires extensive new thinking about the just war tradition. In this chapter we are drawing attention to just one aspect of that. Recall, again, that the tradition focussed on *ad bellum* and *in bello*. The marked presupposition here were that you could (a) contemplate a war before you commenced it and (b) that you could control its conduct once it was engaged and (c) that it would end decisively in its own time and circumstance. This latter, for reasons we have briefly considered, is now far from the case. Uneasy truces have to be worked at politically and economically by all sides. They are invariably punctuated by fragile cease-fires, complex negotiations between multiple parties and the attendant plethora of media attention and analysis. In all this it is hoped that confidences can be restored and the conditions of civil society re-established. The military may or may not come in and out of any of these processes and if they do it may well be as peacekeepers than as offensive military campaigners. They are on-hand, integrated and strictly limited in their objectives. Their primary function is to fight. The just war tradition has to accommodate all this if it is to provide warfighting (in the new sense) with the means of controlling its morality. This will not be an easy thing to achieve. The conditions of military engagement of this kind can be immensely complex. They can change, in a given situation, from street to street and by the hour. Recognition of this has been generally dubbed as 'law fighting'. This illustrates the pressure put on operative troops as they deal with complex and ever changing ground circumstances. One moment they might be fighting with fire, then next peacekeeping, the next nursing and the next civil engineering and so on. For all this they will subsequently and rightly, held accountable. The suggestion here being made is that some light can be thrown onto all this if the desired objectives of a military intervention are defined as specifically as possible before it is engaged.

Modern military interventions can be necessary for whatever reasons and, goodness knows, there are enough of them. They will all entail collateral damages. By far the paramount among these, of course, are deaths, both military and civilian. Modern methods of controlled war-fighting can limit these, but they are unavoidable. Even one is a tragedy. Traditional just war thinking has been preoccupied with this inevitability of conflict and it will, rightly, continue to be so. What we need to go on to think about are other damages. Military interventions are so drastic that the situations they bring about are often worse than those previously prevailing. This need not invalidate them but it does mean that they require special attention prior to intervention. These are all those damages which are done to the infrastructures on which civil society depends. The most obvious are; the provision of food, shelter, medicine and security. Providing all these, and more, requires sophisticated collaborations between occupying and indigenous populations, the international order and professionals of all kinds. Where these do not come into play effectively when conditions require them, confrontations can soon degenerate into chaos and be tragically counter-productive of their initial aims, however lofty they might once have been.

The experience in Iraq has shown an un-preparedness for all this by the occupying powers. They had no plans for how the country was to be governed after the invasion. Things were made worse than they might have been by the fact that in May 2003 the American Pro-consul, Paul Bremer, dissolved the Iraqi army. The Coalition force was then too small to impose order. This was a possibility that had been foreseen and warned of by some military commanders, but was ignored by the US Defence Secretary Donald Rumsfeld. Terrorist attacks increased with resultant deaths on all sides. Bremer also removed Baathist public officials from office because of their alleged sympathy with the overthrown regime. More incredibly still, he removed from office many University and School Teachers, Nurses and Doctors for the same reason. By these actions the Americans and their allies could scarcely have made things worse for themselves, not to mention the decent Iraqi people in whose best interest they were ostensibly acting. All this is sensitively summed up by Andrew White who was and remains an observer and participant in Iraqi affairs.

The Coalition Provisional Authority was a well-meaning shambles. There were so many hundreds of experts – but they were experts at setting up systems that work in America. And not everyone was even that: the man who was given the job of reviving the Baghdad stock exchange was a junior soldier who had never worked in finance! Paul Bremer, who took over the reins from ex-general Jay Garner and his very short lived Office of Reconstruction and Humanitarian Aid, was a splendid man but he knew nothing about the Arab world. His previous experience, as ambassador to the Netherlands and 'ambassador-at-large for counterterrorism' under Ronald Reagan, did not qualify him for overseeing one of the most complex societies in the world. It was reportedly his unilateral decision to dismiss every last man in the Iraqi army and police. Clearly, some people had to go, but the result of sacking everyone was the anger and anarchy that engulfed the whole country. Suddenly hundreds of thousands of men trained to fight (and still in possession of their weapons) had no job, no income, no status and every reason to revolt.[6]

All this clearly added to the problems of social reconstruction and probably did so largely unnecessarily. Clearly, any good intentions which lay behind these actions had not been subjected to critical analysis. In fact, those very good intentions were probably a part of the problem. Americans and others did not question the moral virtue of what they were doing. Even more, they relied on that virtue alone to sort out the subsequent problems of civil disorder. Less virtuous aspiration and more attention paid to the political realties would have at least created the possibility of foreseeing some of the difficulties. Only then could those political realities have been anticipated, understood and dealt with.

In the absence of all this, the situation was chaotic. It created a milieu in which tribal warlords could flourish as they preyed on the vulnerabilities of ordinary people who were in fear of their lives and desperate to secure the day-to-day means of survival. Desperate men were available for cheap hire. In these ways, the war was won in a military sense, but the peace was then lost, even squandered, by the very powers who did the winning. If their initial aim was to restore the basic humanitarian conditions of civil society it was corrupted by their own incompetence, or perhaps as we have suggested by their moral blindness. This is not because they were

6   Andrew White, *The Vicar of Baghdad* (Oxford: Monarch Books, 2009), p. 76.

bad people. It was because they were too convinced of their own virtuosity and, as a result, totally unprepared for the harsh realities which stood in the way of creating a sustainable and just peace. Of all this it has been well observed that: 'The post-conflict situation in Iraq should help to convince us that the path of moral responsibility and the path of prudent realism converge in the pursuit of limited and specific objectives in the post-war world.'[7] For all these reasons and more there are clearly profound lessons to be learned from the post-conflict mismanagement of Iraq. If they can be put to good effect they will help to avoid untold and unnecessary misery in the future.

Things in Iraq, are getting better as some conditions of normality return. Even this, of course, is occasionally punctuated by horrendous killings. Iraqi people are, however, now taking more and more responsibility for their own welfare and an envisaged security without foreign troops. British troops have moved out well in advance of their 31 May 2009 deadline. US troops will be following later in 2010, save for those remaining to support Iraqi normalization. People in Basra are no longer primarily concerned with security as normality returns. Their preoccupation is now with securing electricity, sewage and jobs. The question here is, could the path to the re-construction of civil society been made been smoother and quicker? It, surely, could have been if before the conflict began (a) the difficulties had been more precisely envisaged and (b) strategies for coping with them put in place as a matter of moral requirement. This requirement, moreover, should be made a matter of moral obligation *from the outset*. A part, that is of Just War thinking.

In other words, just war provision now needs to be not just *jus ad bellum* and *jus in bello*, but also *jus post bello* and *jus in pace*. The terminology here is important and there are evident equivocations in the literature of its emerging use. Here we will use the phrase *jus post bello*, to refer to the creation of means for ending wars. This has to be done simply because, as we have observed, wars no longer end naturally and conclusively in final

7   Charles Reed and David Ryall (eds), *The Price of Peace: Just War in the Twenty-First Century* (Cambridge: Cambridge University Press, 2007), p. 234.

outcomes. Those ends have to be created wilfully, politically and militarily. They are the more difficult to achieve because they have to be created while conflicts are still raging and antagonists are still hoping and fighting for elusive 'final' victories. This is an area of study which is in urgent need of attention. The late Sydney D. Bailey recognized this when he published his magisterial two volume work on the subject.[8] He was a distinguished Quaker pacifist of principle but he was also of pragmatic outlook. Clearly, he believed that we would be better placed to stop wars if we knew more about how this had already been achieved. He studied eighty-nine conflicts in the period 1945–54. In each instance he summarizes the background to the conflict, identifies the main actors, and evaluates the effectiveness of cease-fires truces and armistices. No overall conclusions are drawn from this magisterial study, but it contains a wealth of insight. It detailed methods are also exemplary.

All this what we are calling the *jus post bello*. This is necessary because in the absence of the 'natural' cessation of conflict in conclusive military victory, ways have to be found to end hostilities. Without them conflict can be interminable, inconclusive, tragic for all concerned and counterproductive of the achievement of ends it was initially engaged to secure. The conflict in the Middle East is more than illustrative of this need. It is all the things we have just identified. As we know all too well from that conflict moving from cease-fires to negotiation and from there to peace is seemingly impossible. This is reason enough to include in the considerations of the morality, or otherwise, of future contemplated conflicts, binding obligations about how and when the cessation of hostilities will be secured. People who will be involved in achieving this need, as far as is possible, to be identified beforehand. These will include both local leaders and those who will negotiate with them in attempts to reconcile their differences. None of this should be treated casually. Detailed plans need to be drawn up. These should include cost analyses and budgets for the work to be carried out. In addition to this there also needs to be detailed consideration about

---

8   Sydney D. Bailey, *How Wars End: The United Nations and the Termination of Armed Conflict, 1946–64*, 2 vols (Oxford: Clarendon Press, 1982).

the nature of desired objectives which might well have to be scaled-down if they were too ambitious and unrealistic in the first place. All this is now beginning to receive proper attention and discussion.

This chapter is suggesting that even this important development of Just War theory is not enough. That development also needs to include consideration of ways to establish *jus in pace*, justice in peace. Only when this is achieved as fully as possible can military interventions be said to be completed. For this reason, the theory of the just war needs not only its now emerging third part, but also its final and fourth part.

Only with this development will the tradition be able to adjust to the changed circumstances of conflict which we have observed. Only in this way, will it be able to envisage, from the outset, the awesome range of moral obligations which are encountered in the path to peace. None of this will be achieved overnight. Its difficulties are too complex for that to be a realistic expectation. All that can be expected is that we make some reasonable progress with developing a theory (the only one) which has enabled us to subject war to moral scrutiny. The precise details of that development will have to be wrought from previous and ongoing experiences. Only in action and in retrospect will they be seen to be desirable or not. In the extremes of moral exposure which war entails, it is the only theory we have to help us. Nigel Biggar recently says of it: 'On the one hand, it demands of those who would use lethal violence that they have the patience to meet the demands of a system of elaborate moral criteria. But on the other hand, it requires of those who rightly fear the awful horrors of war, the courage to admit that sometimes, tragically, just peace can be bought at no lesser price.'[9]

The emerging analysis of the invasion of Iraq provides a good illustration of all this. At the moment it focuses on the *jus ad bellum*, the justice or otherwise that is of the invasion in the first place. Three reasons have been given for it at various times:

9   Reed and Ryall (eds), *The Price of Peace*, p. 75.

(a) That it was to pre-empt the development and use of stockpiles of weapons of mass destruction.

(b) That is was justified by the need for regime change in the name of humanitarian relief.

(c) That it was a necessary part of a wider war on terror.

Whichever of these is given priority, their subsequent evaluation will depend greatly on what happens to Iraq and its people in the longer term. If Iraq descends into irretrievable chaos then none of these will seem to be justified. If, however, the lives of Iraqi people improve for the better and seemingly permanently, then one or the other, particularly (b) will look plausible. It is still too early to say with confidence, but the signs are that things are now getting better in Iraq much more quickly than could have been expected in the recent past. Whether or not and if so to what extent this will have been the result of the General Petraeus-inspired military surge, only the analysis of time will show. What all this illustrates is that analysis of the *jus ad bellum* is now contingent not only on the *jus in bello*, and the *jus post bello*, it is also crucially dependent on the *jus in pace* which we are discussing. In other words, a complete doctrine of the Just War now needs to include not the two parts as has been traditional, or even the third the *jus post bello* which is now being recognized, but also the fourth the *jus in pace*. Unless this last is seen to be and actually is effective, then the preceding three parts cannot, on their own, provide a rationale for the justice of war.[10]

The *jus in pace*

An important caveat needs to be made at this point. It concerns the nature, aims and objectives of the involvement of those who were responsible for the intervention in the first place. Where these are of American, British

---

10   Cain O'Driscoll, *The Renegotiation of the Just War Tradition and the Right to War in the Twenty-First Century* (New York: Palgrave Macmillan, 2008), p. 163.

and European origin there is usually some presupposition that social reconstruction in peace will lead to some form of social democracy. Indeed, this
presupposition has recently been identified as something of an ideological
crusade based on utopian ideals.[11] John Gray forcefully argues that this is
not only mistaken, it is also dangerous. Western liberal democracy is not,
as many of its proponents believe, destined to conquer the world. Other
forms of government will always exist and for complex reasons to do with
cultural history, tribalism, and diverse ethnicities they will invariably do
so with more effect than Western democratic methods could ever achieve.
This is because these indigenous social arrangements are part of the history of their cultures. They are owned and understood by those who live
with them. For this reason, they are more likely to establish workable solutions which will be embraced by peoples for whom liberal democracy is an
alien concept. In the future just as in the past the world will be governed
by many different kinds of regime.[12] The point that Gray makes is that it
is facile and dangerously utopian not to accept this. Recognition of this
evident truth places particular obligations on invading ideologues. Given
that the world is as it is, they will have to learn to put their own political
ideologies aside whenever they are inappropriate to the task in hand. This
will require a humble respect for different cultures and the patience to
understand how to enable them to work effectively in the best interests
of their populations. Achieving anything of this will require nothing less
than the curbing and perhaps even in many instances the end of political
and economic ideological imperialism. The prospect of this is awesome.
It will require revisionary thinking with little precedent to go on. Only in
this way will different countries and cultures and religions be able to live
together in their own ways side-by-side to the greater good.

The views expressed in this volume all claim that one of the first tasks
which has to be achieved in post-conflict social reconstruction is the establishment of reconciliation between previously, or even still, warring parties. Without this they will be unable to communicate with each other let
alone work collaboratively for effectively social re-construction. This, of

11   Cf. John Gray, *Black Mass* (New York: Penguin, 2008).
12   Ibid., p. 241.

course, particularly applies to those who will be required to play whatever key roles in the process. Activities to bring this about are, for obvious reasons, carried out at the cutting-edge of sensitivities. For that reason they are vulnerable in the extreme. They also require immense courage of those involved. Territories have to be crossed, misunderstandings clarified and trusts between suspicious parties created often in the most difficult of circumstances. Much of this work needs to be carried out well in advance of more established political processes. For that reason, alone, it will often be confidential and even under-cover. From the little we still know, there are indications that this was the case in Northern Ireland and in other theatres where reconciliation activities have been effective. Still warring parties often meet in deepest secrecy to explore the means of peace.

Arrangements for such reconciliation activities clearly not only need to be put in place at the earliest possible opportunity, their existence should also be a pre-requirement in the *Jus in pace* criteria. (When we have recognized other such requirements in what follows we will conclude with some considerations about where that should happen and who should be responsible for it.) This will, as we have seen, first require the identification of the individuals, parties and factions to be included. The obvious key issue here is the willingness, or otherwise, to talk to enemies, even those described as terrorists. There can be no baulking at this. No self-righteous, stand-off, indignation. Only the earnest desire to make progress whatever that might require. For this reason it is clearly arguable that there cannot be any room in this process for not talking to whomever, even the most despised of enemies. More and more evidence of these processes indicates that there cannot be room for such refusals to talk and stand-offs. Successful political outcomes to conflict can only be established if all the key players are given a hearing. More than that, even, given also roles in the sought for process of reconstruction. In Northern Ireland for example, again, the fact that alleged former terrorists are now respected, if cautiously, politicians is more than evidence of the fact that these endeavours can be made to work. The many, though not enough, such instances of this happening are proof enough if its possibility. Of course, it will not always work. That is not the point. Nothing works all the time. All that has to be recognized from the outset is that everything has to be done to make it work in the growing knowledge that it so often does.

None of this can be achieved without the good-will and co-operation of the warring parties. It cannot be imposed. This is why, in the very first instance, they have to learn to talk to each other. This does not happen spontaneously. It needs catalysing by third parties. The newly emerging reconciliation agencies and their activities are a real sign of progress and hope in this crucial area. They go where others usually fear to tread. The justice they seek is importantly not retributive. This point is crucial to their work. They do not seek to apportion blame. Their noble aim is restorative. They envisage a better future and seek ways of enabling warring parties to discover precisely what contribution they can make to that end. The first stage in all this is to find ways of establishing a social order which respects and provides for the fundamentals of human rights, common decency, and self-respect. This is a profoundly human enterprise. It cannot be passed over or ignored. It is the foundation of all that can follow. Pre-empting this with civil engineering projects, important thought they subsequently become, can be counterproductive. Unless these are owned and indigenous responsibility for them taken from the outset they will not play their part in the wider scheme of things. There are simple reasons for this. The grand projects have to be grounded in actual needs which are defined by those who experience them. This is the very reverse of vague persons from somewhere else deciding what is best. Only local communities can understand local needs and this means that they have to be given the authority and the means to secure them. Indigenous social reconstruction does not come more profoundly than this. As far as is possible, their views and needs should be taken into account, or at least envisaged, before conflict is engaged. In what follows we will conclude with some reflections on how this might be achieved.

The sheer logistics of achieving anything like this are, of course, formidable, expensive and labour intensive. For this reason alone, they should become part of the initial budgets, strategic thinking and contingency planning. Not all of this thinking, of course, will be new. Much of it will already be established best practice. This needs to be researched and built upon. The management of the sheer logistics of achieving anything of this kind is probably best managed, initially at least, by the military. They will also know how best to operate under extreme conditions which invariably prevail. This is a good illustration of the point mentioned earlier based on the observations of Rupert Smith about military involvements now being an integral part of wider peace-building processes.

We have already alluded to the impracticality of thinking that Western style democratic structures will always be the best form of government when regimes are removed. However, the first task is to envisage what sort of at least interim government can be created. Obviously this will require the identification of the key indigenous personnel. Initial, at least, contact with them will have to be during conflict. This makes it all the more difficult for obvious reasons. Pre-intervention military intelligence should be directed to this end. The next thing to establish is the nature of the relationship between such identified persons and the invading forces. Whatever this might be, it should be collaborative and only dictated by imposition under dire and strictly identified circumstances. Such a relationship will also change as the tasks in hand proceed and this, also, should be planned for. Appropriate language speakers will be central to all this. As such personnel become active the needs for the involvement of people in the reconciliation movements will become a priority. Many of those involved will be former enemies and suspicions will, therefore, abound. All this is awesome enough, but it is only the beginning. The point here being stressed is that the reconciliation activities should be (a) initially planned for, (b) sensitive to the cultural specifics of any conflict and (c) financially provided for.

Once achieved, however, tentatively, the first task of such interim measures is to provide for humanitarian relief. Medical care is the most important. Much of this already happens as we see increasing use being made of military hospitals for the treatment of civilians, even enemies. This then needs to be followed by provisions for security, food and the myriad of daily common decencies and requirements.

These two first steps, the identification of personnel and enabling their effective operation, should be seamless with the cessation of hostilities. So much so, in fact, that at its earliest it should pre-date them. Only in this way will opportunities be closed off to the unscrupulous who will seek to exploit peoples' basic needs for their own manipulative ends. Stories of Warlords employing impoverished Iraqis desperate to earn money for food and seeing nowhere else to turn, more than illustrate the need for this.

In all this, peacekeeping forces will have to emerge to keep the necessary levels of order which alone make doing anything possible. How will they be constituted? How will they include the indigenous populations? What role will the UN play? How will their work be scaled-down as civilian order becomes established? The questions are endless. But and this is the point, they are not unknown. Even brief reflections such as these can identify at least some of them. All of them become readily apparent when previous best practice is analysed. Not all of this is unknown territory. We have been here before more times than enough. One of the central lessons of Iraq, as we have stressed, is that we did not pay enough attention to enough of these obvious questions before, by our own actions, we (in the West) made the tasks in hand much more difficult than they ever should have been. What is now so patently obvious was unbelievably not only five or so years ago.

The point of my argument is, to repeat, simply that *Jus in pace* thinking of this kind needs to be formalized and given its proper place within the established and wider framework of Just War thinking. Only in this way will it ever become a clarified matter of moral obligation. This is precisely what the tradition is for and what it delivers at its best. It will be for others to suggest how the agencies to affect it should be mobilized. They are, even on brief reflection, too numerous to list even provisionally. An obvious first question will be to ask whether or not the existing structures of the UN and other international agencies are suitable for the purpose, or whether new ones will have to be created. The nature of the obligations towards these by national governments will also have to be examined. The challenge is awesome. Given that the world is at it is and that some of our recent experiences in these areas have been so woeful, it cannot be ignored.

The suggestion being made here, that all this should become a fourth part of formal Just War thinking. More than that, it also makes it a part of international moral obligation. This means that it will have to become articulate in its intentions, explicit in its methods of achieving them and accountable for its conduct. All this is what the Just War tradition has proven itself able to deliver over the centuries. This does not mean that it solves all the problems or settles all disagreements. No way of proceeding will ever do that. What it does is the more subtle and effective. It provides a framework in which those who are morally earnest can go about their business. That is more than enough to be going on with. These reflections have set out to do no more than suggest one way in which the much needed urgent progress can be made with that.

It is no longer enough for war to be entered into for just reasons and for it to be conducted justly. The nature of the outcome of these actions must now be studied as an intrinsic element in the assessment of their virtue or otherwise. This calls for nothing less than a new realism, a new pragmatism in fact and a new admission that unless peace is secured after conflict wars are ultimately lost. Worse than that, they are at least futile and, at worst, immoral.

What we have been suggesting here is one practical way of addressing this now urgent problem. This will be achieved not by abandoning the criteria which have served us well over the centuries, but by extending them in some such ways as we have tentatively suggested. Given that the world is, sadly, as it is, military interventions will continue to be justified for humanitarian reasons. Their necessity is now a fact of life and a permanent feature of the international order. They will cease to be morally justified, however, unless we pay as much, and perhaps even more, attention what they leave behind them and to ensuring that justice is as evident there as it is in any other part of the complex moral apparatus with which we contemplate war. Only in this way will the now evident weakness of the Just War tradition in dealing with post-conflict realities be redressed. Unless this is achieved, world peace will remain as elusive as ever. In conclusion, I shall let a telling reflection on twentieth-century history unequivocally make the point. Johan Verstraeten writes:

> From European history we have learnt [...] that the total neglect of future-oriented peace building after the First World War, and particularly the merciless revenge against Germany, paved the way for the success of the Nazis and the Second World War. On the other hand, peace-building in Europe after the Second World War, via the Marshall Plan, European integration and different attempts to generate a spirit of reconciliation, has built sustainable foundations for a lasting peace between former enemies whose borders have become insignificant for EU members and who have accepted a common currency.[13]

---

13   From Just War to the Ethics of Conflict Resolution', *Ethical Perspectives: Journal of the European Ethics Network* II/2–3 (2004), p. 107. This article makes many of the points mentioned in this chapter. It also refers to similar discussions elsewhere.

JUSTIN WELBY

Reconciliation in Nigeria

Introduction

In November 2002, serious rioting broke out in Kaduna in the middle belt of Nigeria. Two advisers from what was then called the Coventry International Centre for Reconciliation (ICR) went at the end of the rioting, which killed several thousand people in three days and left more than 25,000 homeless. Though apparently a religious conflict, as will be described later, the reality was far more complex. A return visit in January by the Coventry team involved a conference for Anglican clergy in the Diocese of Kaduna on the subject of reconciliation. It was bitter and difficult, with many of the clergy very hurt by the events in which they had seen. Churches had been burnt, parishioners killed and injured, they were seeking revenge not reconciliation.

The work of the conference centred around the book of Jonah. Key to the book is Jonah's anger with God in Chapter 4, because of God's forgiveness of the people of Nineveh. Essentially Jonah is saying to God 'I did not refuse to go to Nineveh in the first place because I was afraid, but because I knew you were the kind of God that would forgive and I wanted them to suffer'. Exploring this theme with the clergy, one of whom was encouraging parishioners to arm themselves and be ready to strike back, brought out many deeply painful feelings. At the end of the conference it was unclear to what extent emotions and desires for revenge had, in fact, changed. However, returning a few months later, the Coventry team found that a number of reconciliation initiatives had by then been started. The Bishop of Kaduna (the Right Reverend Josiah Fearon) had continued his work of reconciliation and dialogue with Islamic leaders. At parish level there was also action. One involved a parish which made contact with local Muslims through the church members deciding to buy bread from the local Muslim baker. Contact created by this step enabled the Muslims and the Christians mutually to protect each others' places of worship during services (both the mosque and the church had been burned or severely damaged during the rioting). These steps led eventually to mutual co-operation in areas of health and social need in a very impoverished part of the city.

I have begun this chapter with this story to provide an illustrative context for the definitions and theory, which will follow.

What Is Reconciliation?

In this chapter I am defining it as 'a framework for processes which, when combined correctly, enable a confrontation to be continued without the use or threat of violence'. This distinguishes it from arbitration, which is usually a settlement arrange by a third party, very often on a middle ground. It is also distinct from mediation, a facilitated process by which parties in a dispute reach agreement. Essentially, reconciliation is proposed as a framework within which other forms of conflict resolution and mitigation can take place. Reconciliation does not end disagreement, but is used to enable parties to continue to disagree without violence or mutual destruction. In many ways, democracy and general elections are simply reconciled forms of civil war. The struggle remains in place, feelings may run very high, but the means by which the dispute is then carried on does not normally lead to death and violence (Romans 3:16).

For Christians, reconciliation is at the very heart and basis of faith. The foundation of that faith is the work of Christ in bringing reconciliation, or at least the possibility of it, between human beings and God, 'all this is from God who reconciled us to himself through Christ and gave us the ministry of reconciliation' (II Corinthians 5:18). In the Sermon on the Mount Jesus himself set a broader context of God's will for reconciliation, and commitment to the principle of peacemaking: 'Blessed are the peacemakers, for they shall be called children of God' (Matthew 5:9). Of course, the reconciliation that God brings goes much further than the definition given above, it involves the inner transformation of the human person, but that is beyond the scope of this chapter.

In modern times, and especially within the Christian evangelical tradition, this process of reconciliation has often been seen as entirely vertical, that is to say essentially between the individual and God. It results in the assurance of a relationship with God as Father, of sins forgiven, and the beginning of the individual's Christian journey. That view is obviously essential, but also, when taken too simplistically, limits the power of the Christian doctrine and experience of reconciliation. Professor David Ford develops the theme of the overflow of God's goodness as one of the sources of human flourishing.[1] Reconciliation is far too great to be contained by one person, or even within the Church. Jesus' words in the Sermon on the Mount speak to the transforming impact of genuine reconciliation, which should overflow from the individual and the Church into the world around. Christians should not just be recipients of reconciliation they should also be the source of rivers of reconciliation flowing to the places of conflict and trauma around them in their own families, in their workplaces and communities and across the entire experience of human kind. One model among many for doing this is the subject of the rest of this chapter.

The Nature of Conflict

The nature and pattern of conflict and confrontation is extremely complex and the application of force, of policing, of peacemaking and reconciliation, is an interactive process on which there is much writing. It is important to understand this nature if we are to make any progress with bringing reconciliation to bear on its resolution.

---

1   David F. Ford, *Self and Salvation* (Cambridge: Cambridge University Press, 1999).

The recognized pattern is essentially a bell-curve. The first phase, the long introductory period, which may last many years, is one in which the structures of society fail to enable normal tensions within communities and wider society to be articulated and resolved. As time goes on, and factions form, it becomes increasingly evident that they are inevitably preparing for more violent approaches to settling their disagreements. Rumours of this will emerge, and carefully targeted words will be used to demonize opponents. In public debate language will itself become more violent, using the vocabulary of war rather than of peace and resolution. Arms will begin to be traded, hidden and prepared for use. This phase may, again, last for several years. In the second phase, there is usually a very rapid escalation of confrontation, which will often last as little as a few weeks. Sporadic killing and raiding will occur within the area concerned, there will be demonstrations often leading to violence, riots and arrests, usually without the due process of law. Ordinary crime will increase very significantly and human rights violations will become widespread.

This second phase will normally lead to outright fighting within an area or across an entire country. At this point, all normal forms of civilian and civil society life will come to a halt. There may be emergency relief, but distribution of food and the necessities of life, the provision of education and health and any form of law and order will disappear. The length of the crisis will vary according to the resources of the parties. In a full blown civil war or international conflict, this may last some years. However, in recent years crises of this kind have tended to be relatively short. The 2007 war in the Lebanon is a very good example. Long periods of preparation, and rising tension, were brought to a head by border incidents involving the kidnapping of Israeli soldiers. The crisis involved invasion and heavy fighting, with sustained aerial rocket and ground based bombardments. After a relatively short period there was a very rapid deceleration of violence under the impact of international pressure and the achievements of certain objectives by one side. During the deceleration there is likely to be mediation, some agreement at least on ceasefire and the re-opening of the most basic forms of civil society and economic activity. One of the most surprising aspects of conflict is that within days of a conflict ending, schools will start to re-open in one form or another. At the time of the disturbances in

Kenya following the 2007 elections, I was in Eldoret, and found schools opening in refugee camps with classes of two to three hundred children, only a couple of days after the Kofi Annan brokered agreement.

It is at this point that, often, reconciliation talk and even action may begin. It is not the ideal moment. Pre-emptive reconciliation is even more effective than pre-emptive violence. A famous manager of Liverpool Football Club, Bill Shankly, once said: 'I teach my boys to get their retaliation in first.' In conflict management and mitigation one might say: 'I teach the parties to get their reconciliation in first.' Following the outcome phase in post crisis life, there is then a form of peace with diminishing levels of violence and a tail. If reconciliation is happening, as in Europe after World War II, this tail will eventually lead to deeply established peace and the prospect of renewed war being unimaginable. Without reconciliation, the situation is more likely to be as that between 1918 and 1939, where there are openings for those who will wish to renew violence. In this worst of all situations such as this, the bell curve repeats itself. The repeated wave like patterns will then continue until there is a change of influence and a transformation of society through a reconciliation process. A UN study in 2002 suggested that since 1945 only just under half of all serious civil conflicts had failed to re-start in five years after a brokered outcome. Even in circumstances where peace has been established through the outright victory of one side, for the seeds of future conflict not to be sown, albeit perhaps a generation away, it will be necessary for there to be reconciliation, at least in progress.

The next thing to understand is the levels at which reconciliation can be expected to work. Like a bonfire, conflict operates at three levels. First, the roots of the conflict, the fuel, which may go back generations, and be made up of ethnic, economic, religious or historic causes. Second, the triggers of a conflict, the petrol that is put on the fuel to start a good blaze. These will be shorter term in focus, such as perceived impunities before the law, biased policing, unfair distribution of revenues or advantages in society and similar features that make the roots apparent to those affected. Third, the top layer is the manifestations of conflict, the match, which is what is seen in the media. It may be rioting or all out war, but it is the area which is least important for the pursuit of reconciliation, but often the one that gets all the attention. The roots are the proper object of its affection.

For Summy see my Diag (B) P 222

The 1960s in Northern Ireland is a good example. The roots of the troubles were buried deep in its history. Among the many triggers was the perceived discrimination against the Roman Catholic and Nationalist minority by the Protestant and Unionist majority, and in particular the overwhelming proportion of Protestants in the police force. Triggers do not of themselves constitute conflict, but added to the roots they provide a highly dangerous situation.

The methodology that will be set out below seeks to engage with the roots, discovering them, enabling people to recognize them, and then developing the structures which permit them to be addressed. If the roots are removed, the triggers become powerless and the manifestations of violence do not occur. If only the manifestations are dealt with, perhaps by police or armed force, all the ingredients remain for new violence to occur. Out of such reconciliation activity the capacity might emerge for building civil society. A good example would be a project in which the Coventry team was involved in Nigeria, where training of law enforcement agencies meant that a road traffic accident involving different communities, which previously would have lead to violence, was dealt with through negotiation. No progress can be made without reconciliation at the deepest level of the society involved.

A Model for Reconciliation

The rest of this chapter is an exploration of the model developed at Coventry Cathedral, which permits a systematic approach to the work of reconciliation to begin in the ways described above. In order to earth it in Christian spirituality, the model will be applied to a reading of the story of the Prodigal Son (Luke 15: 11–32). In summary, the story of the Prodigal Son is interpreted here as a journey by both sons towards the grace of the father. At their best, churches are the channels of this grace.

The Coventry model is based on six words beginning with R, Researching, Relating, Relieving, Risking, Reconciling and Resourcing. It is not a linear model, but one that seeks to hold together a complex matrix of actions and reactions by the reconciler. Some of the Rs will start later in a process, but once started none ceases as far as the reconciler is involved. They will all remain in focus. A Christian reconciler will bring all these resources to bear. In the context of all this, the empirical facts of the given situation need to be kept in mind. We will now discuss the relevance of the six Rs in turn.

Researching

As described above, in November 2002 severe riots broke out in the Nigerian city of Kaduna. It came at a similar time to the Miss World competition being held in Abuja and other parts of Nigeria. In the UK the press portrayed them as the Miss World riots, with a caricature of supposedly ignorant religious fundamentalists (by which was meant Muslims, using a popular and absurd stereotype) attacking Christians in a perverse effort to resist an inane but harmless event. This 'analysis' was, in some parts of the reporting, refined into a discussion of a clash of civilizations. On one side was portrayed the more Westernized 'Christian' approach and on the other a more fundamentalist 'Muslim' approach. The inspiration for this farrago was Samuel P. Huntington's book *The Clash of Civilizations and the Re-Making of World Order*.[2]

In his highly influential (and very sophisticated) book, Huntingdon points to the inevitable clash between what he defines as a number of different civilizations. From the point of view of American foreign policy, and much media analysis the most significant of these two civilizations were the Christian and the Muslim. This chapter is not the place to discuss the book, but suffice to say that its theories were strongly supported by some

2   Samuel P. Huntington, *The Clash of Civilizations and the Remaking of World Order* (New York: Simon and Schuster, 1997).

and also widely challenged for a lack of understanding of the internal work-
ings of the different blocs, which he identifies, and especially a tendency
towards treating Islam as monolithic, rather in the way that Christendom
was presented in the Middle Ages.

On arriving in Kaduna the signs of violence were everywhere. Travelling around, we were taken to a church, which had been burned; on one
whitewashed wall were the words 'The Christians will seen the DEATH
[*sic*]'. Outside on the road were burn marks where the minister of the church
had been necklaced (killed by having a tyre full of petrol put round his
neck which was then lit). Two hundred metres away were the ruins of a
mosque, with holes in the walls from the effects of explosive. A Christian
former army officer commented: 'The Muslims attacked us first but we
killed more of them than they did of us.' Severe atrocities had taken place
across significant portions of the city.

However, it quickly became apparent that the initial impression of
a purely religious conflict was inadequate. More persistent questioning
revealed that the rioting had been started by a competitor in the forthcoming elections for governor of the State of Kaduna, who, seeking to portray
the existing Muslim governor as too soft, had paid unemployed youth to
begin riots. This was not a religious conflict. It was political chicanery.
Such a simple example illustrates the importance of researching conflicts
carefully. There are some clear principles to remember when doing this.
It is essential to begin by putting aside judgement. Apparent causes and
rights and wrongs may very often, with further examination, prove to be
too simple. It is essential to include both sides in the research, even if the
initial impression is that one side is more to blame. In order to be able to
hear what people are saying truly, the researcher must empathize with the
suffering of the people to whom he is talking, and try to see what they were
seeing through their eyes. Research must be repeated again and again: the
principle of iteration is essential. Above all, anyone involved in reconciliation who is an outsider, must assume persistent ignorance and inability
fully to comprehend what they are seeing and hearing.

In the story of the Prodigal Son, the father was looking, searching,
listening, waiting. There was no rush to judgement, but rather a willingness
to receive, to be vulnerable. The results of research should be a continually

deepening perception of the elements and realities of a conflict, with an openness to correction and vulnerability to being shown to be wrong. Key players will be identified, relief needs will be measured, and the potential for success can be established.

There are two particular outcomes from researching which may seem surprising. First, potential spoilers will be identified. A spoiler is someone who has a vested interest in the continuation of the conflict, rather than in its resolution. They may be arms traders, or other criminal or semi criminal organizations, whose requirement is to inhabit an environment of force and violence to their own profit or benefit. In certain circumstances even the legitimate armed forces of the State may choose to be spoilers, seeing an end to flows of resources and hopes of popular support if there is no fighting. An example of this which should be remembered is that in the eighteenth century a standard toast in the officers' mess of British regiments was 'to a sickly season and a bloody war', in order to ensure promotion. Spoilers are very important because in most circumstances its will be improbable that they will participate in reconciliation. Their identification and the establishment of a plan for dealing with them is an absolute pre-requirement of any reconciliation activity.

This links into the second key result, the role of policing and enforcing peace or security in the context of reconciliation. Very often reconciliation is presented as an alternative to the use of force, but any effective reconciliation will frequently require policing action (including armed force) in order to create a context going beyond the crisis point of the bell shaped curve referred to above.

Sir Rupert Smith, looks at this issue from the other side, that of the professional soldier. The military need those who will be doing the 'touchy feely' work because, as Sir Rupert argues so cogently, the army's principle role is to win conflicts, not to settle confrontations. It is no more realistic to believe one can have reconciliation without enforcement, where there has been already significant civil disturbance and violence, than it is rational to imagine a society with no police force.

Check out Archieve of lecture Smith gave at Liverpool Cathedral - on their web site?

Relating — INTENTIONAL; INDESCRIMINATE; genuine Rel^s; Be Vulnerable;
LIKE GOD
Be Personable, NOT OFFICIAL; WARM; EMOTIONALLY OPEN; Sympathetic

All effective reconciliation depends on facing the truth. Both sides have
to face the truth about themselves, to look in the mirror and see who they
are and what they have done. They have to re-imagine a new face, not aris-
ing from victory, but from a transformation of conflict. They also have to
face those whom they have demonized, opposed and sought to kill. They
still, in many conflicts, may have to face those who have sought to do those
things to them, but against whom they have retaliated only in self-defence.
The early stages of reconciliation are too soon to bring in considerations
of concepts of justice and retributive action.

Relating begins by the reconciler setting a pattern and a model for
it. Once again, it has some very important principles. Relating should be
indiscriminate (almost), that is to say one does not relate to people because
they are good but because they are there. In the same way God reaches out
to human beings not for their merit but out of His love. The limits to indiscriminate relating are very difficult to establish, but they do exist. Where
an individual or an organization will only use meetings to manipulate, or
to establish a position, or where there is no interest in meeting, or if they
are highly likely to kill anyone who comes to see them, a line has to be
drawn. There is a need for fine judgement here.

Subject to these limits, the relationships must be genuine. It is essential
that those involved in reconciliation have a genuine commitment, which
makes them personally vulnerable in the relationships they establish. They
have to relate to a person, not an office. One cannot see a 'militia leader'.
One has to see a named individual with feelings, emotions in whom the
blood flows and who has worries and loves like everyone else. Relationships
must be affective. They need to show signs of personal engagement, to
affirm, to encourage and to be warm in their expression. Such relationships
will necessarily be emotional. Conflicts are emotional places to be in. Very
often a leader or significant figure in a conflict, as well as those involved as
foot soldiers, will need someone to whom he or she can speak who is not
a potential rival for power within their organization. They need someone
with whom there can be honesty. They may seem very busy, but a visit
from an outsider provides an opportunity for a change of pace and gear,
and where the outsider is sympathetic in their nature, such an opportunity
may provide an element of healing merely by its happening.

My former colleague Canon Andrew White is especially skilled in this area. His deep commitment to those with whom he works, from either side of a conflict, is so obviously apparent to them and those observing, that it is a major force in breaking down barriers and enabling the beginnings of reconciliation. The foundation of relating is that the very existence of a relationship is more important than the process of reconciliation. In the story of the Prodigal Son, the elder brother seeks process. He refuses to come in until it is clear that his father promises to exert the necessary family discipline and ensure that the younger brother is suitably admonished and even punished. The younger brother is drawn back to the family through relationship, because the father seeks the fullness of life.

In Iraq, a number of religious leaders, whom I met after the invasion of 2003, sought immediately to build contacts with their potential enemies from other religious communities. In one case, this was despite more than forty members of the individual's family having died under the regime of Saddam Hussein. Relationship here was much more important than process. Once again, this raises issues of justice. Before relationship can be established, one might argue that it is essential that there is a foundation of justice. This may seem apparent, but is in fact false. Justice cannot be established in depth and with confidence in the absence of profound relationships, in which trust has begun to emerge. In this way, comes before justice.

Underlying this fact is the importance of recognizing that reconciliation is enormously demanding, and its relatively frequent failure is very unsurprising. For people who have been involved in violent conflict to be expected to put aside their hatreds and their desire for 'justice' in the sense of retribution, is a very tall order indeed and goes against many of the instincts of human nature.

Relieving — Life Preservation: meeting needs & intro justice as appropriate.

Genuine relationships encompass the whole person, and their social and economic context. 'If a brother or sister is naked and lacks daily food and one of you says to them, "go in peace, keep warm and eat your fill", and yet you do not supply their bodily needs, what is the good of that?' (James 2:15–16). Understanding the levels of a conflict illustrates the need for this clearly. Relief aims to alleviate the socio economic roots of conflict, as well as validating the commitment of relationship. In 2004 I visited a town in the Niger Delta, more than two hours journey into the swamps by small speed boat from Port Harcourt. It was a place of profound deprivation, fought over by different groups seeking to extract significant economic value from control of the area. No roads reached it, clean drinking water was in very short supply, and electricity was only through local generators. Within sight of the edge of the town, the lights of an oil company flow-station lit up the night. It generated enough electricity not only for itself but for the town, should it have chosen to share it. The company was also well supplied with water, excellent food and first class medical treatment. The flow station sat over an exceptionally productive oil field, and payments to local communities to keep them quiet were one of the major sources of conflict. The contrast was almost overwhelming. A visit to that town involved meeting militias who were at various times threatening and dangerous. However, for me it was hard to imagine that I would have been any different if I had grown up in such a place. Relieving looks to the issues of life preservation. In the parable of the Prodigal Son, the father meets the immediate needs of the returning son in every possible way. He clothes him, gives him shoes, gives him a ring to symbolize the return of his authority as a son of the house, and thus security, and feeds him and welcomes him, meeting both physiological and psychological needs. The elder brother would have had him punished, and he even seeks through the accusation of wasting money on prostitutes, to worsen the division with the father.

Relief or relieving is a slightly dangerous word, not least because relief itself is often misused. Relief as mere donation very often goes astray in areas of civil conflict, and can be put to the purchase of weaponry or to the maintenance of lifestyles for militia leaders or warlords. It is often a major source of corruption. In that town in the Niger Delta the kind of relief required was in the form of basic infrastructure provision as well as forr opportunities for business development, especially through microfinance. It is not being argued here that relief is not important. It is, but has to be intelligent relief.

An obvious consequence of the requirement for relief is that reconciliation will involve numerous agencies and significant partnership working. It will be very rare that one organization has all the resources, including people with the right attitudes, and the ability to deliver the different requirements needed. Relief itself is an extremely complicated activity, with many sub-specialities ranging from crisis relief to long term sustainable development. Sustainable development can go a long way to prevent the early stages of conflict we referred to earlier from gaining hold. The Niger Delta, again, demonstrates the importance of sustainable development, whether through external relief or, better still, from home-grown projects. In 2004 there was a significant cease-fire brokered with the militia. It resulted in more than a thousand fighters leaving the swamps and returning to Port Harcourt under an amnesty. A similar programme is presently happening at the beginning of 2010. However, the 2004 project failed for a significant number of reasons. First, corruption and poor governance meant that the promises made were not delivered by State agencies. Second, there were no clear economic programmes into which returning militia could go and where they could find training and sufficient means of earning a living, starting a family and having hope for a future. Third, militia activity for the sake of justice easily slips into criminality under the influence of money coming from politicians seeking office.

At the same time that I was observing and being involved with the problems in the Niger Delta, where one of my colleagues led the effort, I was also researching and then following up building relationships with radical Muslim groups in Northern Nigeria. In the course of this project, I found that the state government in Kano had developed a programme which gave a clear, short term alternative to the temptation offered by violent groups, for unemployed youth. The programme involved paying them to train, with the clear possibility of remunerative work at the end of their training.

It is important not to be naïve about all this. The dangers of relief have recently been set out clearly and radically by Dambisa Moyo.[3] However, not all aid has been wasted and examples of small scale local projects, run by local people, often produce more positive results than the large scale work done by foreign governments.

---

3   Dambisa Moyo, *Dead Aid* (London: Allen Lane, 2009).

So far, I have sought to play down the role of justice. It cannot be deployed easily at the early stages of a reconciliation programme. However it is in relieving that for the first time justice moves towards the centre of the stage. Life preservation is a core concept within ideas of justice, and a major force in enabling justice to be done for both perpetrators and victims following civic disturbances.

Conflict involve Risk - Personal, Kidnapping etc.

Risking

Risk Analysis - Be Aware ; of Failure ; of Making conflict worse &/or Sooner ; Be Wise / Constantly Review

Any involvement in areas of conflict necessarily brings risk. The obvious personal risks need to be taken seriously as the kidnapping, wounding or killing of an outsider is extremely damaging to any reconciliation process. Careful risk analysis, and the use of local intelligence and well informed advice is essential for the participant, and risk should be something that is never forgotten, from the moment that research starts. However, there are far more significant risks involved in reconciliation, which have nothing to do with the 'heroics' of going to areas of conflict. The staff and supporters from the local area will almost invariably take far more risk than the outsider.

Two particular areas of risk arise from reconciliation work. The principles set out earlier of *almost* indiscriminate relating mean that the reconciler will be speaking to and developing relationships with those who are seen as evil and who may well have been involved in terrible crimes against others in the conflict. The status of the reconciler is very important in handling this risk. Reconciliation work done by governments will always be more difficult, as government officials meeting 'terrorist' groups always gives them validity and authority which they would not possess otherwise. By contrast, reconciliation, whether through faith based groups or individuals from them carries with it less baggage. A good example would be dealings with Hamas in the Middle East. Any contact between Hamas and for example, officials of the British Foreign and Commonwealth Office quickly leads to reports that Britain is moving towards some kind of recognition of Hamas. However much the relevant officials may say that they were only speaking about issues of local government, expectations or fears about this are inevitably raised on one side or the other. Israel is naturally and understandably cautious and fearful of the possibility that another government will recognize a group such as this with which it is in conflict. When the same people are met by relief agencies or development groups, by church leaders or other faith leaders, there is little or no such attention paid. In 2002 Canon Andrew White in the Alexandria Process brought together a number of senior figures from the religious and political world in Palestine and Israel. A meeting, which had it been held under the auspices of the British or American governments would have attracted great attention, was almost completely ignored by the media.

As well as the status, the sheer determination of the reconciler reduces risk. Determination comes in seeking to ensure that equal contact is made with both sides, despite personal preferences, and also that the 'scandal' of talking to evil people is accepted and endured. It is often said, when one is challenged about meeting those who have committed crimes against individuals and groups, 'why do you meet bad people?' to which the answer is 'it's the bad people who are causing the trouble'. However, the risk of being drawn into damaging relationships with powerful figures, who manipulate and deceive the reconciler is very great. Constant accountability and a willingness to report and to be questioned are both essential in managing this risk.

Another risk is that of failure and thus of accelerating the conflict. We saw earlier that conflict is dynamic and not static. It will either be going up or down. Failed reconciliation usually forces people back towards an approach that involves violence, as the only alternative which they can see. Failed reconciliation also deepens hatred in a way that even low levels of violence do not manage to achieve.

The importance of continually reviewing risk cannot be exaggerated. However, without risk there will be no reconciliation. In the parable of the Prodigal Son the older brother takes no risks. He will not even risk meeting his younger brother but stays outside, further demonstrating his independence and self-will. By contrast, the father risks everything. He risks his dignity in running publically to meet his son. He risks rejection by offering him forgiveness. He risks economic and financial loss by re-establishing him in the family (it is not clear from the parable whether there is a happy ending to this with the younger brother accepting his reinstatement). He risks conflict with his elder son, and again risks losing public respect by going out to meet the older son rather than by summoning him to his presence.

FRAMEWORK ENABLING CONFLICT TO be Pursued Safely utilising mediation, & ARBITRATION &/or Conflict Resolution.

Reconciling → STRUCTURES Created & SUSTAINED INC App. JUSTICE, & PROCESS; Restoration of Confidence; Forgiveness; TRUTH; Hold VISION of Peace

A very high proportion of reconciliation projects do not succeed. The reasons for this may vary from the incapacity of those involved in the reconciliation to the unwillingness to those involved in the conflict to be reconciled. Reconciliation is something that is achieved by parties to a conflict, not just by outsiders. Because, by definition, there will be pre-existing hatreds and often histories of violence, there is a deep resistance to genuine reconciliation which involves building long-term and sustainable relationships with those who are enemies. In the majority of cases, where this happens at all, it is only after the defeat of one side or the other and the passage of an extensive period of time. It could be argued that a week of conflict creates a generation of reconciliation work, because the memories of violence and killing done to parents and siblings take many years to fade.

Comment

The illusion that reconciliation can be quick is fostered in the media, and by the cynicism that appears once a short period, often of only a few months, has passed and it is not evident that the parties to the conflict have put aside their differences. It is in the reconciling, the meeting and building of relationships and the creation of structures to sustain those relationships in a non-violent way that issues of justice first begin to emerge. Justice must come from an objective assessment of harm done and the necessary means for bringing restitution and the restoration of confidence in law and order. Ideally, it also comes from the forgiveness of the perpetrator by the victim. However, this will often be withheld and it often ends up becoming the forgiveness of the perpetrator's descendants by the victim's descendants. It is as reconciliation begins to find its foundations, that Tribunals can be established for the purpose of clarifying events, and determining consequences. Truth and reconciliation commissions are also often called on, they tend to work in very restrictive circumstances indeed. They need the exceptional leadership of characters such as Archbishop Desmond Tutu and President Nelson Mandela. They require a society to recognize in general that the alternative to reconciliation is destruction, as happened in South Africa in the early 1990s. There needs to be a genuine desire for peace within the society. Finally, it should be noted that the truth and reconciliation in South Africa was not called 'truth, reconciliation and justice commission', Archbishop Tutu recognized that justice was too emotive a word, and in the end justice was served by confession and amnesty more than by punishment or even restitution.

Notwithstanding all these negatives, it is essential to hold to the vision of reconciliation and the process of reconciling because of its huge capacity for individuals and society. Reconciling is a process, and never an event. Signings of peace agreements and meetings of leaders are often portrayed as events of reconciliation, but do little except create momentum in the long term process. For that reason alone they are necessary but they are never sufficient. The psychological uncertainty of the reconciling process is brought out profoundly in the parable of the Prodigal Son. The younger brother chooses to return as one of his father's hired servants. His father rejects this choice and insists that he return as a son. Within the culture of the time, there were at least three types of servant. First, a slave who was the property of the owner. Second, a form of indentured servant who did not receive pay but was kept and could have the opportunity to leave. Third, the hired servant who was an employee and could move on at any time, with both the insecurity but also the liberty that came from that rather different economic relationship. The younger brother chooses the third to offer to his father, leaving open the question as to whether he was not seeking to keep a certain amount of the distance that he had put between himself and the family, while having the advantage of the father's generosity and protection. After the feasting was over, how would this relationship have developed? To be a son locked him into the family, with a hostile elder brother, and obligations of family duty. The elder brother, whose duty it was to be the reconciler, is in fact the spoiler and seeks to worsen the conflict. At the end of the story we have no idea whether he responds to the father's plea, or whether he chooses to remain outside seeking to cause trouble.

Reconciliation, as we have been seeing, is neither easy nor quick, but it has the promise of the blessing of God. It is, therefore, a responsibility of the church to demonstrate the overflowing of the reconciling power of God both to individuals and to societies. The generosity of God means that there is much more reconciliation than can easily be confined within the church (despite the church's best efforts). A healthy church will be a point of healing and reconciliation for the society in which it is situated. It is very noticeable that across Africa, with one or two exceptions, faith groups and especially churches have been among the leaders in reconciliation. They provide networks that can continue to function when all forms of civil government have collapsed. They also tend to be less penetrated by corrupt motives.

Resourcing

It has already been said that reconciliation is something achieved by the parties to a conflict and that it cannot be done by outsiders, although outsiders can facilitate and make possible contacts that would not otherwise have occurred. For reconciliation to become sustainable, it is absolutely essential that the outside agency provides the financial means for its continuation by local societies and individuals. To do the initial work, and then to leave is merely to create dependency followed by failure. One of the key parts of researching, as it continues through the entire process in a series of endless iterative cycles, is to discover the natural resources for reconciliation in the life of the society concerned. Very often it will be found that groups of elders exist who are capable of carrying out such work, and in fact they did so where there were civil disputes before the Colonial period. They were suppressed as potential rival leaders to Colonialism during much of the first half of the twentieth century. This has been found to be true both in Rwanda and Burundi.

Resourcing begins by enabling people to work out a model of their own with clear structures and processes that will address their conflict easily and naturally. Those involved need to be aware of what they are involved in and to understand the process that they have developed and why these belong to them.

External agencies need to maintain relationships through recurring contact, but not by dominance or direction. Local expertise should be built up using natural skills giving local people a capacity to repeat training and reconciliation for others and thus spread it through the society.

Above all issues of justice must be, at last, addressed, and the means found to face the enormous challenges that they will present. It is likely that the costs of resourcing ongoing local reconciliation will be insignificant compared to the intervention of external agencies. For this reason alone, resourcing is the only way of permitting reconciliation agencies to work extensively without being bogged down in ever more expensive operations in a local area at the expense of greater needs elsewhere.

One of the faults in many models of reconciliation is the absence of a sense of spirituality and a neglect of the holistic approach to the human person. The re-establishment of spiritual life and common prayer will be a major force in the healing power of reconciliation between individuals and in societies. As the militias left the Niger Delta in 2005 many of them sought church services where they could confess their sins and find a sense of forgiveness from God to enable them to restart their lives outside the swamps. The vocation to being reconciled is the most powerful force in resourcing the desire of participants in conflict to persist in what often seems the less attractive path to confrontation.

Resourcing is also an issue of justice. It draws on the idea in Catholic social teaching of subsidiarity, releasing power to the lowest possible level, while maintaining a sense of solidarity with the wider world through recurring contact with the facilitator.

Conclusion

The leading Italian politician and former EU commissioner Emma Bonino set up an NGO in 1994 called No Peace Without Justice. This title exemplifies the tensions of reconciliation work and brings to the foreground the theological questions that must be raised. If there is no peace without justice, can there ever be peace? Is God just in permitting reconciliation with human beings who have done what is wrong? The grace of God overwhelms human sin, and the justice of God comes inevitably through allowing those who have gone wrong to bear the consequences of their own choices. Reconciliation in the Christian tradition is seen above all in the cross of Christ. It stands as a judgement on humanity. It requires the response of obedience. Such obedience is at the heart of the work of reconciliation. This is why reconciliation in the Christian tradition transforms individual human beings and human societies alike, giving them both an opportunity for flourishing which is impossible where conflict and hatred divide.

R. JOHN ELFORD

Andrew White in Iraq

Peacemaking is, of course, best made between parties before they resort to violence to settle their differences. This is why reconciliation activity should not just be thought of as something which is called in when or just before violence is ceasing. People who work on the ground in these activities need to be there throughout. It is a long game. Hopefully these peacemakers will often prevent violence occurring in the first place. If they fail at this and violence breaks out, they need to be constantly at hand maintaining contacts and seeking ways of effecting reconciliation. All this presents what they do with a seemingly insuperable initial hurdle. People who hate, persecute and bomb each other are not natural candidates for reconciliation. They do not like sitting around being nice to each other. Quite the reverse, their natural disposition is to carry on as they are and for the conflicts they are in to get progressively worse as a result.

All this is, sadly, too familiar in countless theatres of conflict around the world. However, the powerful point is being made throughout this book that such conflict is not irresolvable. There can be hope. Evidence for this, however slender it might be to begin with, comes whenever warring parties can begin to talk to each other. Initially, they will probably have to do this in the utmost secrecy and even by proxy, lest their actions are misconstrued and exploited by any opposed to such initiatives. It is only long after conflicts are resolved that we occasionally even begin got hear that such initiatives ever took place at all. Above all, they are fraught with danger for all those involved. Lives are put at risk and only those possessed of great courage even dare take part. Hope amid all this despair comes from the now increasing body of evidence that shows that progress in reconciliation can happen and lead to peaceful results. The extensive resolution of the former conflicts in South Africa, Northern Ireland, Kosovo, Bosnia

and elsewhere are powerful examples of this. The work of often a few pioneering individuals in establishing near impossible communication and
reconciliation is invariably a key to this. They are most effective when they
are not aligned with any of the warring parties. They may not initially be
welcomed by any of them. They will often be lonely figures. They will seek
to work in secrecy. And, above all, they will possess incredible patience and
fortitude as they seek to achieve what to others will look like impossible
odds against them.

The now amazing thing is that such initiatives can, have and will continue to succeed. They will only do this, however, if we are all take the
trouble to understand and support them. More to the point, this support
must, as argued elsewhere in this book, become an integral part of planning
and provision before military interventions are carried out. None of this
should any longer be left to chance and happenstance. Pioneering individuals will invariably play key roles in this, for reasons we will discuss below.
As is argued elsewhere in this book, they should no longer be expected to
do so at their own expense and without logistical and other vital support.
Invariably, their needs are miniscule compared with the often incalculable
expense incurred in the continuation of conflict.

For obvious reasons, pioneers in these areas will be often be independent of governments and alliances. They will, therefore, have their
own motivations for acting as they do. One such is the motivation some
Christians feel when confronted with violence. Peacemaking is a central
part of their faith and the activity it requires of them. An example of this
is found in the remarkable ministry of The Revd Canon Andrew White,
the Anglican Chaplain (more commonly known as Vicar) of St George's,
Baghdad, and Director of the Foundation for Relief and Reconciliation in
the Middle East. He has been working in Iraq on and off since 1998 and is
the longest-serving foreign national peace worker in the country. He has
also written extensively about his work and engages widely with the media
and in public debate.[1] For all these reasons, his example of peacemaking
deserves close attention.

---

1   See: Andrew White, *Iraq: People of Promise, Land of Despair* (Tonbridge: Sovereign
     World, 2003); Andrew White, *Iraq: Searching for Hope* (London: Continuum, 2005);
     Andrew White, *The Vicar of Baghdad* (Oxford: Monarch Books, 2009).

In what follows we will look at seven aspects of White's ⌐
are: (a) his belief that in Christ evil was vanquished on the Cro
spirituality, (c) his understanding of religions, (d) his understa____ ⌐₁
Christian love, (e) his radical realism and non-pacifism, (f) his practical
and organizational skills and (g) his gift for friendship and love of children
and (h) his experience of the imperative of the Gospel. These topics will
not exhaust an understanding of his work, but it is intended that they will
provide sufficient insight to show why it deserves proper study.

The Triumph over Evil on the Cross

No small part of the profundity of Christianity is expressed in the practi-
cality of its understanding of evil. This is derived from what Jesus achieved
on the Cross. In his death, all separation of humans from God came to an
end. By it they were atoned; made one with God. In their newly created
relationship to God in Christ, Christians secured access to perfect unsul-
lied goodness. In more colourful language; the Devil and all his works were
triumphed over. A new order came into existence and expressed itself in
one of the most powerful beliefs history has ever witnessed. This was the
belief that good had triumphed over evil for all time. That the confrontation of good and evil was no more. Evil, as such, ceased to exist. This meant
that Christians did not have to suffer evil, as the Stoics believe, nor seek to
escape from it, as the Buddhists later sought. Nor did they have no satisfactory way of understanding it as Western secular philosophy has repeatedly
demonstrated. Nor did they have to become helplessly resigned to and
enervated by it. Leading the Christian life after the Cross meant living out
the triumph of good over evil which was there achieved.

Put like this, the Christian understanding of the triumph of good over
evil can look pious and facile. It most certainly is not. It is profound in the
sense that it enables Christians to face contemporary evil, even radical
evil *and* believe that it can still be overcome by the power of God's love in
Christ as it initially was on the Cross. This does not mean that they do not
take evil seriously. They know that the complete triumph of good over evil

will not be complete this side of the Kingdom of God. But in Christ, they
know what that triumph looks like and know, above all, what to they have
to *do* about it in the here and now. In short, at their best they work tirelessly
to confront evil and thereby continue the work of vanquishing it which
was begun on and made continually possible by the Cross. All this is the
polar opposite of lying down in the face of evil. It is the spring of nothing
less than the most effective practical understanding of evil the world has
ever seen. Its great strength lies not in its ability to 'explain' evil, but in the
profundity of its understanding of what must be done about it.

For White, all this means that even the most atrocious of evils never
destroy hope. He has and still does witness them at first hand. The deaths
of children and other friends, the privations of hostages, the suffering from
debilitating injuries, the deaths caused by lack of medicines and the widespread hunger which is sadly so common in war zones. All these horrendous experiences and more are part of the daily lot of the people he loves,
ministers to and cares for. He says repeatedly when times are hard in Iraq
that things can and will change. His sheer continued presence there after
such a length of time is, literally, the embodiment of his conviction that
good triumphed over evil on the Cross. This is the bedrock of his belief
that everything can be done in the name of Christ to redeem despair and
keep hope alive. The Christian theology of the Cross could not be more
eloquently or courageously embodied than it is in his ministry.

White's Spirituality

The word spirituality is now much bandied about. As would be therefore
expected it is used in different ways to mean different things. Traditionally,
it has been used by Christians and other theists to refer to the relationship
between believers and God. More recently, however, it has been widely
used to refer to the relationship of believers and non-believers to the wider
world and to what they do therein. In this sense the word has acquired
and additional and secular meaning. Use of this duality of meaning will

help in understanding White. He is unequivocal about his relationship to God in Christ. He writes 'I give thanks to God that I have never doubted him.'[2] Again and again he stresses that the greater the agony and suffering the greater he is aware of God's glory. In the face of despair he repeats his belief that it is only the glory of God that sustains. He writes: 'There have been times when everything has gone wrong, when friends and colleagues have been killed and there has seemed to be no hope. It is at times like this that I ask God to show me his glory.'[3] This clear faith conviction was originally derived from White's Anglican evangelical background. He was part of the Cambridge Intercollegiate Christian Union and trained there for the ministry at Ridley Hall. These institutions are noted for the clarity and conviction of their faith-professions. They are not given to self-doubt. That, in fact, is why they appeal as they do to so many. White flourished in all this. It provided the foundation for the first part of his spirituality; his relationship to God. He is a naturally religious person whose life is grounded in prayer and worship. Throughout his writings he refers to numerous religious experiences, many of them occurring whilst singing hymns. All this evidences his personal capacity for religion. It comes naturally to him. He is clearly recognisable to others as a distinctively religious person. This is, of course, why he is so readily accepted by those of other faiths who recognize religious integrity for what it is. Not all Christians are so distinctively religious as this. Many, for example, are much more liberal and their views more akin to humanist ones. Not so White. He is a religious person *per se*. It is immensely to his credit and to be admired by those (as here), who do not share his particular religious tradition. This aspect of his person and work cannot be overstressed. It enables him to be unwavering in his convictions even and perhaps particularly, in the face of suffering, despair and death. This is something which is repeatedly recognized and valued by those he deals with of other faiths and sects as well as by his co-religionists. He is, for all these reasons, not a secular priest. He often appears more akin to the sort of priests found in the religious orders.

2   White, *The Vicar of Baghdad*, p. 171.
3   Ibid.

Many Christians who come out of the evangelical tradition we have just described never move beyond it. They may be none the worse for that of course. This is not so for White. He takes this tradition with him, but he moves beyond and complements it. When challenged, in fact, he protests that he is 'not an evangelical' and adds that he is also Catholic and Orthodox. In other words, he moves freely among these other Christian traditions sharing their beliefs and styles of worship. His ability to do this arises from the second aspect of his spirituality. This can be observed in the way he goes about his peacemaking and reconciling.

Nothing White says or does is designed to encourage others to be like himself. This is his credential for 'not being an evangelical'. Mainstream evangelicals manifestly want others to be like themselves. They want others to join their circles, styles of worship and beliefs. Not so White. He is content to witness to the love of God in Christ and *accept others for what they are*. The italics here are important. White's peacemaking is not covert evangelism. When asked by an earnest young mainstream evangelical Christian why Muslims will not come to Christ, White replied that he did not know and was not interested. His claim not to be an evangelical could scarce come more evidently than this! A metaphor will help make this clear. Many Christians, evangelicals included, carry about with them huge amounts of 'baggage'. This is; their beliefs, testimonies, styles of worship and most anything else they can carry about which announces to all who they are. White could not be more different. He travels baggage-free. In doing so he accepts other people for what they are and, this is important, requests only that they accept him for what he is. Simple as that. It is also unusual. Most Christians would not have the self confidence to do this. White is also confident that the work of peacemaking can be left to the grace of God. He simply gets on with it in God's name. His objectives are to relieve suffering, assuage hunger, cure disease and bring peace. This is the work of his faith in action, the secular part of his spirituality. It comprises what he actually *does*, day in day out, to confront the joys sorrows needs and evils in the lives of people in a place like Iraq. Understood in this way, the word spirituality denotes something like 'common decency', sheer humanitarian goodness. This is not the sole preserve of religious people. It is what people from all faiths and none can aspire to as they work together towards achieving common aims. If a common meaning is emerging in the modern use of the word, then it might well be something like this. It is the name for what people at their best can achieve together for the good, regardless of the several and differing reasons they might have for doing so. They just keep quiet and get on with it. Religious people do not usually take to this at all naturally. On the contrary, they invariably make a virtue out of proclaiming their faith and the reasons for acting as they do at any and every opportunity. That is say, using the baggage metaphor, that they carry the baggage of their faith, or whatever, into action with them. To this end their actions, however kindly and well meant, are but covert means of proselytizing. Their real aim and motivation is to convert others to their religion. In all this they feel entirely justified, virtuous and, often as we all know, smug. More seriously, in acting in this way their common decency is often compromised. They are acting in their own interest as well as ostensibly in that of others.

We have now considered briefly where White's spirituality originates, how it manifests itself and how it structures everything he does. He is, of course, not unique in this. Countless Christians quietly go about pursuing the good of others in similar ways as they pursue works of love often to their own and even ultimate cost. What we have done is try to be clear about is why White goes about his remarkable work as he does. One more consequence of it is worthy of note. It gives him ease of access. This is a proverbial jewel in areas of conflict and mistrust where there are so many barriers to communication and travel. White moves freely where others cannot tread. This often demands of him, of course, great courage in the face of horrendous dangers, but he summons that in great and unflagging measure. As a result, warring parties can be seen to want to talk to him, as Tariq Aziz did so often in the days leading up to the 2003 invasion of Iraq. They developed a mutual bond of affection and respect for each other. That White achieved this under such dire circumstances is nothing less than remarkable. For the reasons we have briefly considered, however, it is not inexplicable. White is able to work as he does because of the grounding of his Christian faith and equally because of the way in which he puts it to work in the way he does.

White's Understanding of Religions

White's understanding of relationships between the religions is derived
from his spirituality as we have described it. He is content in the field
with proclaiming the love of God in action. In doing so, he makes no even
implied judgements about the superiority of his own religion over that of
others. He is, in fact, clearly content to accept others, be they Jews, Muslims or whatever for what they are. Nothing he says or does is intended
to restrict them in any way. In fact, he seems to go out of his way to help
others to affirm their own faiths as he affirms his. He never engages in so
called inter-religious dialogue. The time he spends with people of other
religions, which is a great deal, is entirely taken up with pursuing common
goals in the interests of others. This is refreshing, to say the least. So much
labour is lost among religious people by dialogue between them about
their faiths. It seldom, if ever, makes any progress. What it, in fact, does
provide is the opportunity for people of different faiths to reinforce their
prejudices against each other. Although such dialogue may well map out
important common grounds among religions, what it does for the greater
part is to leave them as they are with all concerned happily justified in
their differences.

In understanding the relationship between religions in this way, White
does more than simply accept people of other faiths for what they are. He
goes on to try and understand why they act as they do, particularly when
it inspires them do to atrocious things. He writes:

> I have learned that the established strategies for resolving conflict – working through
> political issues, restoring civil society, supporting the moderates, involving women
> – are mostly ineffectual. What is more productive, I have found, is to gain an under-
> standing specifically of the people who are responsible for the violence of their
> culture, religion, traditions and everything that shapes their expectations. These are
> the influences that propel people into conflict, these are the factors that complicate
> its resolution.[4]

4   Ibid., p. 123.

For this reason, in his dealings with administrators in Iraq such as Paul Bremer, White has repeatedly insisted that religious problems should be given priority treatment. Unless they are resolved to some degree at least, all else will be thwarted.

Implied in all this is the fact that Middle Eastern societies are religious in ways which Westerners, even Western Christians, can scarce understand. No one sees this better than White. He also knows how difficult it is to get Westerners to accept it and act accordingly in their endeavours for peace. As we shall see below, he is not only accepted by members of other religions, he is trusted by them. This is simply because he proffers them respect for what they are. They, in turn, then do the same to him. This is undoubtedly the reason why he is able to dialogue so freely and so creatively among them.

This approach to understanding other religions achieves something which is vital to White's work. It establishes mutual respect. Simple as that. In this there is no room for hidden agendas. People are accepted for what they are even, and importantly, if they are something that would make them enemies. With characteristic humour White writes: 'Contact between the leaders of different religions and sects in Baghdad is a very different matter from sitting down with cups of tea and smoked salmon bagels in London. In Iraq, where politics and religion are inextricably linked, it is often a matter of life and death.'[5] This respect creates a foundation for other and even more important things to be achieved.

The Importance of Love

White is motivated not just to respect others, important though we have seen that to be. He is even more motivated to love them. More specifically, he seeks to show them the love of God in Christ. His understanding of

5   White, *Iraq: Searching for Hope*, p. 95.

this is derived from the beatitudes in the sixth chapter of St Luke's gospel. 'But I say to you that hear, Love your enemies do good to those who hate you, bless those who curse you, pray for those who abuse you. To him who strikes you on the cheek, offer the other also; and from him who takes away your cloak, do not withhold your coat as well' (Luke 6:27–9).

All the gospel writers repeat these words in similar ways. They are fundamental to Jesus' teaching. Scholars have generally agreed that they take us back to the original and authentic teaching of Jesus.[6] Moreover, they are in the form of an injunction, something that must be done. The reason given for this is because God loves those who despise God. The love of God is, therefore, unconditional and universal. For this reason, it includes the requirement to love even enemies. White understands this rightly as something central and even unique to Christianity. It is not something which appears is such stark form in either Jewish or Muslim teaching. The unconditional nature of God's love is, of course, reflected throughout Jesus' teaching. It is prominent in the parable of the Good Samaritan which can be read as a polemic against the religious restriction of both the sources and objects of God's love. The giving of this love requires nothing, not even repentance. No one can do anything whatsoever to make themselves ineligible to receive it. It is nothing less than the earthly expression of God's eternal and universal love for all creation.

All this is so powerfully central to the Christian Gospel that by repetition it can become a cliché. Christians can often be seen to behave as though they think that loving in this way is easy. Not only Christians, writers of pop songs as well 'All you needs is love.' This can reduce love to a disposition, a requirement only to be disposed to others in a certain sort of way. A way that will solve all problems without further thought or concern. White rightly knows better than this. He knows that love is tough and demanding in its requirements. To understand this more clearly we need to break down the works of love. It can be seen to do three things. First, it inspires action. This is no small thing when most of us want to walk past on the proverbial other side of the road. Love does not allow

6   Victor Paul Furnish, *The Love Command of the New Testament* (London: SCM, 1973), p. 61.

that. Passers-by do not love. Second, it sustains the endeavour of love when
things get difficult as they invariably do. It enables people to aspire to and
achieve heroic self-sacrifices in the love of others. But even these are not
the whole of its requirements. There is more, much more and it is tough.
It requires, also, that we think out love's requirements for ourselves in each
and every situation. These requirements, moreover, have to be specifically
identified. For White they translate into specific, for food, medicine, and
safety from harm. A great deal of his work and energy is expended on
providing for these needs. The Foundation for Relief and Reconciliation
in the Middle East, is not casually named. It embodies his understanding
of the requirements of love.

White's Radical Realism and Non-Pacifism

This is derived for the reasons we have considered, from his understanding of love. It is not something remote or delivered by proxy. It demands
nothing less than actual hands-on day in day out involvement with the
needy. St George's Church in Baghdad is White's central expression of
this. He writes:

> I will never forget the first service held there after the liberation of Iraq. The con-
> gregation of about fifty consisted mostly of military personnel and diplomatic staff,
> though the Patriarch of the Ancient Church of the East (Old Calendar) turned up
> as well. The building was ringed with tanks and armoured personnel carriers and
> helicopters clattered overhead like noisy angels. The security was so tight because
> there was reliable intelligence that someone was planning to blow the church up.[7]

From these beginnings the congregation has become predominantly Iraqi
and its numerical growth is exponential. Its services are mainly in Arabic
and it attracts people from different religions and sects. They have to be
held throughout two days at the weekend. The church carries out daily

7   White, *The Vicar of Baghdad*, pp. 145–6.

relief work providing food, medicine and education. It also has a large and
flourishing Mothers Union which releases and focuses the energies women
in the extended relief work of the congregation. A central sadness is the
significant number of members who are killed and mourned for. All this is
nothing less than life on the edge. But it is a beacon of hope amid despair.
White calls it 'the most wonderful church in the world'.[8] Clearly, they key
to the phenomenal success of the church lies in the way it meets the actual
daily spiritual and material needs of a people under siege. Practical realism
scarce comes in more effective ways than this.

White's realism is also reflected in his non-pacifism. This is not something he goes out of his way to explain. He takes it for granted that there
are states of affairs that are worse than war. Peace has to be fought for, as he
expresses in the subtitle of his book, *The Vicar of Baghdad: Fighting for Peace
in the Middle East*. He arrived at this conclusion not by way of theological
argument, but simply and importantly out of compassion for the people
of Iraq. When he returned to London in 2002 he reported the words of
the people of Baghdad: 'We have had enough.'[9] He also believes that the
infamous weapons of mass destruction actually existed. He writes:

> They were never found because they were moved out of the country before the UN's
> weapons inspectors arrived. (In his 2006 book *Saddam's Secrets*, Georges was more
> explicit: there were chemical weapons in Iraq as late as summer of 2002, which were
> then spirited away to Syria.)[10]

White also came to accept from the Iraqis themselves that they tyranny
they were suffering under the Ba'athist regime was intolerable. Something
had to be done.

White supported the invasion of Iraq and still does so. This is a powerful testimony, coming as it does from one so close to the action there for so
long. As well as believing that the fabled weapons did exist, as the military
intelligence claimed, but has never been able to verify, he also accepted

8   Ibid., pp. 143ff.
9   White, *Iraq: Searching for Hope*, p. 38.
10   White, *The Vicar of Baghdad*, p. 72.

from the Iraqis themselves that their situation under Saddam Hussein had become intolerable. Such peace and prosperity that they did enjoy, was wrought at the terrible price of tyranny and death. This was nothing less than a situation that was worse than a limited war of liberation which was earnestly desired by the people themselves. All this is a powerful witness, given the opposition to the invasion by people who were unaffected by the suffering and often had no such intimate experience of the country.

White is under no illusions about war. He had witnessed more than his share of it at first hand and for so long. He writes:

> All war is dreadful. There are losers on all sides. Death and destruction become the norm. 'Collateral damage' is merely a euphemism for the killing and maiming of real people. Modern technology may try to make war clean, but it can never succeed. The Third Gulf War was no exception. It may have been quick, but it left thousands of people dead and injured.[11]

The Iraqis, White was convinced, were aware that this was going to happen but were prepared to face the consequences. Those of us who are older can still remember the horrors of the Second World War, but a situation like this is unimaginable to those of us who have not experienced it. It was desperate, getting progressively worse and showing no sign of resolution by any other means. The Iraqis saw it as a last resort in contrast, again, to those critics from afar who still wanted to continue with the sanctions that had already been in place for thirteen years and had failed to bring down Saddam.

In these situations Christians such as White resort to the tradition of the Just War. This is not specifically a Christian tradition. Its origins lie deep in Classical pre-Christian history. Christians became engaged with it in earnest after the conversion of the Emperor Constantine and the Christianization of the Roman Empire. All this is discussed elsewhere in this book. White's reflections on the applicability of this tradition to Iraq are a continuation of this tradition. He focuses on the following aspects of it. The justice of its cause, the authority to carry it out, its limited objectives,

---

11   White, *Searching for Hope*, p. 38.

possibility of success and the right intention which lay behind it. He was in no doubt that Saddam had to be dealt with and that the cause was just. He regrets that the UN did not explicitly sanction the war, but notes the present weakness of that institution. That authority, White believes, came from Britain and America and the forty or so other states which supported it, including most of those adjoining Iraq.

White writes: 'The Coalition supporting the war in Iraq can therefore be said to have had competent authority even without the sanction of the UN.'[12] This point will be endlessly debated and it needs to be. The criterion of lawful authority is a central one to the tradition. What White did was to have the courage to come to a view on the matter from the front line and to the best of his ability. He also believes that the objectives were limited, though they were less clear. All those involved wanted the removal of the weapons of mass destruction. They were divided about whether the Iraqi desire to remove Saddam was also justified. In fact, this came sooner than expected and occurred on 9 April 2003. Just over a year after this sovereignty was handed back to the Iraqi people. This limited objective had been achieved. The reasonable hope of success criterion, White believes, was the easiest to meet. No one doubted but that the action would be swift. It turned out to be more so than most any had expected. White also believes that the intention was just and that the implication of covert motives, such as acquiring the oil reserves, were unfounded. White also believes that the invasion met the requirements in the tradition about proportion and discrimination. The action was limited, compared to that taken in the 1991 Gulf War, and military and related targets were effectively distinguished from civilian ones.

White's detailed analysis of the 2003 Gulf War is that it did broadly meet the criteria set out in the Just War tradition. This is the central example of his non-pacifism in action. It is also witnessed by images of him in military protective uniform in the battle zones. He moves among and is respected by the military, many of whom worship in St George's. White is, in this way, hard-headed about not being a pacifist. He faces the

12   Ibid., p. 41.

consequences of his choice in the responsible way that Christians have done since the fourth century. All this requires in him and others hands on involvement and engagement. Of course, there are many pacifists who do the same working in battle zones in non-military capacities. They also are to be respected for the same reasons.

There is no doubt that mistakes were made by the coalition forces after the surprising, probably even to them, speed of the success of the invasion. The task of reconstructing civil society in Iraq is also taking longer than expected. White is characteristically hard-headed about this. He notes that things are alleged to be getting better, but notes that he has not noticed them. Meanwhile, his work there continues unabated.

Practical and Organizational Skills

It has already become more than clear that Andrew White is a realist in the sense that he is able to face situations for what they are, however dreadful they may be. This contrasts, as we have seen, with his faith which is idealist. Both are indefatigable. This duality lies at the heart of his work. We have also seen that he lives with the belief that things can and will get better. There is one other vital element in his work at this point. He believes that he has a responsibility under God for helping to bring that improvement about. He also believes that this must be sustained, no matter how hard the going and remote the chances of success may be. This, again as we have seen, is where he is sustained by the unfailing love of God. These observations are all essentially simple but they bring us close to understanding why he works as he does. But, again, there is more. White seemingly instinctively knows that his realism requires practical action. He carries this out all the time in his pastoral and relief work. But again there is more. He is not simply an activist who is into what he does for self-gratification. His activism is part of a greater picture and that includes nothing less than the pursuit of peace. In all this, practical action is always bound up with greater

and noble ambitions. As would be expected of one so driven, White often
meets with criticism and opposition. This comes from those who claim
that his methods are sometimes abrasive and not always successful. It is
sometimes observed that he is not always the easiest of people to work with.
Such criticism, however, is perhaps to be expected of someone so driven
and determined. It does not deter him.

The establishing of Religious Accords has played a major role in the
pursuit of these ambitions. There have been two major ones; the Baghdad
Religious Accord in February 2004 and the Dokan Religious Accord in
July of the same year.[13] Both of these arose from meetings of the majority of Iraq's religious leaders. These were brought about because of the
extent of White's contacts and trusts he engendered. (We will examine
more closely below.) In this he was crucially assisted by the *de facto* Head
of the British Embassy, Christopher Segar and Prince Hassan of Jordan.
Colleagues from Coventry Cathedral and elsewhere were also involved,
most crucially the Archbishop of Canterbury George Carey. At a crucial
stage White was able to harness and build upon nascent desires among religious people to do more than tolerate each other. They wanted to move to
tangible mutual respect and trust. To this end he assembled a team which
he led with vigour and the usual determination. Clearly, without him this
could not have occurred.

The initial meetings were difficult and White was even suspected of
being a CIA spy. However, as it became clear to the reluctantly participating people involved that he was genuine; had been working in Iraq for a
long time and created a network of trusts, the process began to move forward. In his own records of this there are moving accounts of friendships
emerging and trusts being created. An awareness was emerging that Iraq
was changing and for the better. By January 2004 the team had produced
a ten point head of agreement. No small part of getting people to sign up
to it resided in the fact that Christians were reluctant to get involved for
fear of getting caught up in hostilities between the Sunni and Shia Islamic
groups. When the time came for them to meet in Baghdad many of them

13   Ibid., pp. 171ff.

had never met before. The meeting was chaired by Dr Mowaffak, an old friend of White's and Iraq's National Security Adviser. First, agreement was reached that the assembled religious leaders needed to commit themselves to playing key roles in the pursuit of peace. After that attention turned to the details of the drafted accord.

Throughout this discussion, White and his British colleagues kept a low profile. This ensured that it was totally Iraqi in character. When it concluded, 39 signatures were appended to the Accord. The following sense of general relief was tempered, for White, by the realization that his work in all this was, effectively, just beginning. He had cleared the way for what he had been trying to achieve. This was the creation of practical steps towards peace which were supported by all the warring religious factions.

To further this the Iraqi Centre for Dialogue, Reconciliation and Peace was founded. It immediately set up six working groups to oversee activities with; women, youth, the media, religious freedom, interreligious dialogue and conflict prevention and resolution. In this way in February 2004 White's work was well established and structured. It led to the Dokan Religious Accord being signed in July of the same year. This extended the agreement beyond Baghdad.

The story leading to these Accords is, of course, much more detailed and interesting than these few descriptions indicate. It centrally includes the overcoming of mistrust and the creation of friendships around and through White himself. We will examine these briefly below. This story illustrates White's instinct for under-girding agreements with practical action and support. Without this it would be palliative and lead nowhere. For him everything he does is of a piece. No effort is wasted, however long it might take to achieve its aims. Central to this has been his work, with others, to help negotiate the release of hostages. This tries patience and energy to the extreme, but it is central to his continuing work.

To say that all this demands of White considerable leadership skills, is but to state the blatantly obvious. Without those skills all his faith, determination and well-meaning would be lost is a sea of activism. They are emphatically not. He uses every resource around him, mainly of people, to achieve his noble ends. Moreover he also seems to know when to lead and when to stand back, as in the meeting leading to the Baghdad Accord. Writers of Manuals of leadership would do well to study his instinctive methods. There is more to learn from them than these few observations have even begun to uncover.

The Iraqi Institute for Peace has now been superseded by White's Foundation for Relief and Reconciliation in the Middle East (FRRME). This is a UK-registered non-profit-making charity. It specializes in the resolution of conflict where there is a religious component. Its work is international and includes humanitarian relief and economic regeneration.

White's Gift for Friendship

In all that has preceded, it will have become abundantly clear that White has a remarkable gift for friendship. His writings abound with the joy he takes in making and keeping friends. It must be said that his striking personal appearance and personal style are central to this. He is not the sort of person you ever forget! He is tall, has the ability to give rapt attention, is generous in his physical expressions of friendship, does not take himself seriously and possesses a ready sense of humour. All this is enhanced, rather than detracted from, by his slight speech impediment which is a consequence of his multiple sclerosis. He is a compelling public speaker.

The key to White's gift for friendship is his conviction that Christians are bound to love their enemies as a matter of spiritual obligation. He studied in Jerusalem as part of his theological training and there developed his studies in Judaism and Islam. In 1998 he became the Canon in charge of International Ministry at Coventry Cathedral. This remarkable initiative, rose from the ashes of the bombing of Coventry's old cathedral. It has a fine record of peacemaking and reconciliation around the world. From there his engagement with Iraq began in earnest.

Jesus' command to love enemies is found principally in the Sermon on the Mount in Matthew's Gospel, the Plain in Luke's Gospel. In this passage 'enemies' are explicitly identified as 'those who persecute you' (44b). They are people who are also identified as being evil and unjust. In Matthew's gospel readers are enjoined to do this so that their love exceeds that of the Scribes and the Pharisees. In the radical teaching of Jesus this is what love requires. It is probably the most difficult thing required of the Christian disciple. Many devout people have to admit honestly that they cannot do it. When people do so in public after suffering personal loss and affliction, it is moving in the extreme. For Christians it is the way that they participate in the providential love of God which cares for the unjust as well as the just. It is as simple and as difficult as that. It means that no one, whatever the extent of their atrocities, is beyond reach by the love of God. All this is part of the cutting-edge of Christian spirituality. Of what makes it so demanding and so revolutionary.

For Andrew White this requirement to love ones enemies is not an option. It is imperative. We have seen why he knows that it is dangerous, all demanding and, at times, defeating. He also knows that it cannot be given up. It is the ultimate test of love. It also expresses something we pointed out at the beginning of this chapter. Namely, that there cannot be any evil situation or person that is beyond redemption by the love of God.

White literally embodies all this as he goes about his work. It is central to everything he does. And, moreover, it shows. It is evident to all. This is why he is received and trusted so readily. He accepts people for what they are. This does not threaten them and is the basis of all his friendships. His writings abound with marvellous accounts of them. But there is more. He seems to have an incredible capacity for enabling others to emulate what he does. Time and again you can observe enemies making friends with each other in his presence. His example is clearly infectious. When combined with his other many talents, some of which we have discussed, it achieves results.

White's Work with Children

As we have seen, White works with the conviction that things can and
will get better in Iraq. He is modest about the contribution his own work
makes to this to the point of saying that he does not even know if it will
bear fruit. He is motivated to keep going in large measure by his delight
in the company of children. They inspire him and give him hope. His own
sons, Josiah and Jacob, are the foundation for all this. He uses the phrase
'my children' primarily but not exclusively for them. It includes the children
he has worked with in Iraq, Israel, Palestine and America. His charismatic
presence which is so important in all his work, is attractive to children,
particularly those who have lost their natural fathers. Many of these are to
be found in the congregation at St Georges. He movingly tells of a young
boy whose own father had been executed asking him if he would be his (the
boy's) new father. When Andrew agreed the boy was overjoyed because, as
Andrew realized, the boy wanted to tell everyone that he had a father again.
There are countless examples like this in Andrew's ministry. Mention of just
this one illustrates how immediate and effective all this is. Children literally flock around him. At times they even act as his physical body guards.
There is undoubtedly more to this that a natural affinity with children.
Andrew, as we have already seen, is totally unselfconscious. As a result he
does not seem at all affected the myriad of inhibitions that afflict most of
us in one way or another. Most people readily sense this when they meet
him. Children do it instinctively.

Again, there is a Gospel imperative for all this. It is in the many accounts
of Jesus' work with children. Andrew quotes them throughout his writing.
A point he stresses is that children are not just to be loved. They are also to
be appreciated for the love they show, the love of God. Jesus wanted people
to pay attention to children for this reason and, above all, to see what they
could learn from them. They are not just adults in waiting. They serve part
of the divine purpose in their own right. Part of that, as is well known to
all parents, is found in their ability to break down barriers. In Baghdad the
barriers they are good at breaking are the religious ones. There are only three
Anglicans in St George's and Andrew is one of them. The children that

surround him there are mostly Muslims and many different sorts of Muslim at that. They show a remarkable ability to exercise joy and freedom in the midst of horrors which debilitate adults. This is so marked that they even seem impervious to the dangers of the moment. It is difficult for those of us not immediately involved to comprehend this. How is it that children can rise so obviously and so often above horrors that debilitate the rest of us? The smile of a child in the wake of disaster is worth a thousand words. All these are the things about children which Andrew knows so well. This knowing is not, of course, just cerebral. He knows how central children are to seeking and maintaining hope. He literally experiences them as a gift of the spirit, bearers of the supernatural.

The Imperative of the Gospel

Andrew does not write much about this, but it is implicit in all that he writes. The imperative with which the gospel must be proclaimed is something emphasized by all the Gospel writers. Initially it took the form of it being imperative for believers to prepare themselves for the imminence of the arrival of the kingdom of God. Of course, as it became progressively clear that that arrival was delayed the Gospel writes explored others ways in which the Gospel imperative had to be lived out. St Paul turned this into an imperative to evangelize the known world. This was a world which embraced gentiles all of which was to be addressed. Much of St Paul's ministry and writing can be understood in this light. He was a driven man. 'Go forth...' has been and remains the rallying call for many Christians. For Andrew this does not mean, as we have seen, go forth and convert. It most certainly does mean go forth and proclaim the love of God to the afflicted. It also means the seeking peace and hope in places where others have despaired of doing so. What therefore appears as something superficial in Andrew's demeanour is anything but. It is an integral part of the outworking of his spirituality.

Andrew White is outstanding at what he does but not, of course, unique in it. Thankfully, there are others who share his spirituality and engage in similar endeavours. These people come from other religions and from none. They bring hope to despair in a world which is in seemingly infinite need of their ministrations. White's work deserves the attention it sometimes receives because of its longevity and determination. It is also deserving because it is consciously a part of a wider whole in the endeavour for peace. He ensures this as he works with all and sundry to achieve his goals.

As we have already observed in passing, those who study the processes of peacemaking should take proper notice of what individuals such as Andrew White can achieve. Their very independence and clarity of religious motivation makes them special, if not at times, unique. For all these reasons, their work should receive the recognition and support that it deserves. More than that, even. Their lives and work should be carefully studied for the important clues it gives to all who work seek and care about peace.

Religious people like Andrew White are, of course, an example to their co-religionists. But they are more than that. Because what they achieve is wrought from the actual circumstances of dire conflict, they stand as an example to all of us whether we are religious or not. As he says repeatedly, religion cannot be ignored in conflict zones. Nor can it be ignored by any who seek peace with integrity. This does not means, of course, that it does not have its limitations and serious perversities, nor that it is not blatantly so often the cause of conflict itself. For all this, we need always to remember that the religious life lived by someone like Andrew White is also a source of hope and inspiration.

MARC H. ELLIS

Jews of Conscience and a Just Reconciliation in Israel/Palestine: Reflections from a Jewish Theology of Liberation

What everyone knows, few will say: that no matter what proclamations and agreements are signed, the contours of Israel and Palestine have already been set. The map of Israel and Palestine as we know it today – Israel within its pre-1967 borders, Jerusalem as its capital; Israel occupying major areas of the West Bank; Gaza safely surrounded by both Israel and Egypt – is permanent. Though the yard markers may be moved here and there, slight adjustments to placate this or that constituency, the map of Israel and Palestine has been drawn. Since the 1967 War, with Israel's conquest of East Jerusalem, the West Bank and Gaza, this map has been in place; the years after have been spent only filling in the details. It may be that this map was already in Israel's future from the time of its birth in 1948, a birth that saw over 700,000 Palestinians expelled from their land.

Israeli commentator Meron Benvinisti and historian Ilan Pappe have called this expulsion the 'ethnic cleansing of Palestine'. Others have called it Israel's 'original sin'. Whether calculated or accidental, a sign of Israel's superiority or the Arab world's weakness, is less important now than the facts we face on the ground: Israel controls from Tel Aviv to the Jordan River with millions of Palestinians in between. Though it seems that such a political and human rights arrangement would be impossible to maintain for any length of time, the only possibility of fundamentally reversing this situation is a war that leads either to Israel's defeat or the Palestinians being driven out of the land altogether. A more likely scenario is a catastrophe of unimaginable proportions where either side may face mass death or a destruction that consumes both.[1]

What nation-state wasn't born through ethnic cleansing in one form or another? Is there any political entity without an original sin? If history, as it seems to be, is a cycle of violence and atrocity, is there any reason to lament the birth and expansion of any political entity, especially those who are the chroniclers are riding the crest of victory? The difficulty is compounded if, as with Jews, an original homeland was lost and a recent cataclysm had just overtaken a people. The exercise of conscience as a judgment on contemporary history is always available and usually difficult. After their long and difficult sojourn, should Jews now exercise their conscience, especially when many see a new Holocaust threatening the state of Israel?

Caught between an original and continuing sin – a sin that seems institutionalized and with the wholesale support of normative Judaism – what is a Jew of conscience to do? In fact a group of Jews – I have called them Jews of Conscience – do exist, though on the margins of the Jewish community. These Jews carry the indigenous of the people Israel, the prophetic, into an uncertain future. Much maligned, even persecuted, and certainly in exile, Jews of Conscience seek a just reconciliation for Jews and Palestinians in the land. Moreover they seek a renewal of the Jewish ethical tradition in a turbulent time. Engaging rather than seeking to transcend the reality of Holocaust, Israel and the Palestinians, Jews of Conscience work toward a world beyond injustice and where Jews, with others, especially Jews and Palestinians, can enjoy a mutually interdependent empowerment.

As is often the case, the devil is in the details, or put another way, reality is a test of ideals. Even Jews of Conscience are caught in between their ideals and the reality on the ground. Still the Jewish question is even more complicated, perhaps uniquely so: chosenness, peoplehood, history, tradition, the covenant, God and the prophetic are all involved so that the movement of conscience one way or another is either buoyed or constrained. Though a way seems clear, an obstacle may yet appear. That obstacle can be

1   See Ilan Pappe, *The Ethnic Cleansing of Palestine* (London: One World, 2007) and Meron Benvenisti, *Sacred Landscape: The Buried History of the Holy Land Since 1948* (Berkeley: University of California Press, 2002).

self-involved and in need of critique; it can also be a legitimate constraint on individuality and hope. Can the prophetic demand that the people Israel move into back into danger? After the Holocaust, can the Jewish people afford conscience?

Even the prophetic is limited and, at least historically, is tainted. If after the Holocaust the question of the God of History is difficult, if not impossible, to affirm – Where was the God at Auschwitz? – and the prophets were called by God, how do Jews of Conscience affirm the prophetic? After the Holocaust, the Jewish covenant itself is called into question. After all, the covenant is a mutually binding contract of responsibilities and obligations. For most of the Jewish tradition Israel's suffering was understood as punishment from God for straying from God's commandments. Few if any Jewish theologians affirm this traditional understanding today. Rather the opposite is the case: much of post-Holocaust theology is a confrontation with God. If through most of Israel's history, at least from the perspective of God, Jews are on trial, a monumental reversion has taken place in our time. For the first time in Jewish history the initial and most difficult theological move is to assert a God of History. That is why even those who affirm the continuity of Jewish life in the post-Holocaust era start with the people Israel rather than the God of Israel.

Here Emil Fackenheim's 614th commandment is instructive: 'The authentic Jew of today is forbidden to hand Hitler yet another posthumous victory.' According to Fackenheim, this commandment, issued in the days before, during and after the 1967 War was a response to the Commanding Voice of Auschwitz rather than the Commanding Voice of Sinai. Since the Commanding Voice of Sinai had been lost in the Holocaust, there was only one voice that Jews can hear today, that of survival. This 'survival' voice is a response to the absence of God to ensure Jewish continuity after the attempt by the Nazis to annihilate Jews and Judaism. If God and humanity has abandoned us, Jews have only ourselves to command and obey. After the Holocaust, and in the form of Israel the state, Jews have committed themselves to survival. Therefore any action in service to that cause is raised to the highest level of communal obligation; survival becomes a religious commandment. Coupled with Rabbi Irving Greenberg's admonition that the Jewish critique of power, issued when Jews were out of power and in a unique and devastating way, could diminish Israel's power and thus even unintentionally weaken Israel to the point where another Holocaust could become possible, the prophetic exercise of conscience is relegated to the corners of contemporary Jewish life. Who dares speak truth to power when the result, even unintentionally, might be another Holocaust?[2]

On the other hand, Irving Greenberg issues a command of his own in relation to speech about God that ultimately challenges his own restraint: 'After the Holocaust, no statement, theological or otherwise, can be made that is not credible in the presence of the burning children.' While this statement refers to the burning children of the Holocaust, the prophetic implications and extended reach of this statement are difficult to limit. All speech about God is disciplined to the point of near impossibility. Greenberg's 'theological or otherwise' points to statements that come with other religiosities, ideologies and political, economic and military policies that impact 'burning children' everywhere. Is it possible to resist extending this to 'all' burning children, including Palestinian children? While not specifying the Palestinians, Greenberg leaves this open with two other statements: 'The victims ask us above anything else not to allow the creation of another matrix of values that might sustain another attempt at genocide'; 'The Holocaust cannot be used for triumphalism. Its moral challenge must also be applied to Jews.'[3]

On the matrix of values leading to another genocide, Greenberg does not specify the Jewish people in particular. Rather the lessons of the Holocaust apply to the future, for all. To the moral challenge of triumphalism, Greenberg applies this directly to Jews and the state of Israel: 'Those Israelis who place as much distance as possible between the weak Diaspora victims and the "mighty Sabras" are tempted to use Israeli strength indiscriminately (i.e. beyond what is absolutely inescapable for self-defense and survival), which is to risk turning other people into victims of the Jews. Neither

2   For my analysis of Holocaust Theology and its early emergence see *Toward a Jewish Theology of Liberation: The Challenge of the 21st Century*, 3rd expanded edition (Waco: Baylor University Press, 2004), pp. 15–74.

3   See Irving Greenberg, 'Cloud of Smoke, Pillar of Fire: Judaism, Christianity, and Modernity after the Holocaust', in *Auschwitz: Beginning of a New Era? Reflections on the Holocaust*, ed. Eva Fleischner (New York: KTAV, 1977), 29.

faith nor morality can function without serious twisting of perspective, even to the point of the demonic, unless they are illuminated by the fires of Auschwitz and Treblinka.' Then to make statements about faith and political reality even more complex, Greenberg comments on the possibility of faith after the Holocaust: 'After Auschwitz we now have to speak of "moment faiths," moments when Redeemer and vision of redemption are present, interspersed with times when the flames and smoke of burning children blot out faith – though it flickers again.'[4]

Fackenheim posited the 614th commandment in 1968 while Greenberg wrote of burning children, issued his warnings and posited 'moment faiths' in 1974. Nowhere is there a reckoning with Israel's original sin and though Greenberg tempers Fackenheim's 614th commandment, his call for Jews to recognize the 'normalization' of the Jewish condition in the wake of Israel's crushing of the Palestinian uprising in 1988 – that is though Jews are called to a higher level of morality than others, that 'higher' level is dangerous and must be limited lest Jewish morality overwhelm the need for Jewish power – diminishes his own earlier warnings. In Greenberg we see the post-Holocaust Jewish world caught in its own double bind, projecting the lessons of the Holocaust onto Jews and the world, infusing them with Jewish power while applying them and then blocking their application internally and more. Contemporary Jewish life exudes a conscience that is assertive, even militaristic, while reserving a naiveté about Jewish power and it emergence as an empire reality in the Middle East linked with the empire realities of Europe and America.

In this bundle of deep thought and contradiction, where can Jews and others venture in the realm of justice and reconciliation? What is a just reconciliation after the Holocaust and after Israel? Who has the first and last word on a just reconciliation? Do Jews? In this search, do Palestinians have anything to say on their own behalf, independently? Do Palestinians have anything to say to Jews and possibly within Jewish life? What do Western Christians have to say, they being the primary source of anti-Semitism in Europe that historically laid the groundwork for the Holocaust? Is the history of ant-Semitism primarily an internal question for Western Christians? Do Jews and Palestinians have the right to enter

4   Ibid., p. 27.

this Western Christian problematic? If Jews and Palestinians speak truth
to Christian support for Jews after the Holocaust, including in the empow-
ering Holocaust narrative in relation to Israel, does this just confuse the
question of Christian complicity in the historic destruction of Europe's
Jews and ongoing destruction of Palestine?

Beyond Innocence and Redemption

As I wrote *Toward a Jewish Theology of Liberation* in the 1980s, I imag-
ined reconciliation between Jews and Palestinians within a two-state con-
figuration – Israel within its pre-1967 borders and Palestine as including
East Jerusalem as its capital, the West Bank and Gaza. During the 1990s
I wrote about the possibility of revolutionary forgiveness between Jews
and Palestinians that would begin in Jerusalem with a confession from the
prime minister of Israel to the leadership of the Palestinians, a confession
that included a specific – and political – path toward equality and justice
between Jews and Palestinians. This would involve a shared Jerusalem –
the broken middle of Israel and Palestine – a designation of other areas of
Israel/Palestine where Jews and Palestinians would share citizenship and
governance, a place where those Jews and Palestinians who wanted to live
separately could do so and indeed a competition over time as to which areas
would flourish and which areas would ultimately attract creativity, capital
and population. Such a move would lead to a demilitarization of Judaism
and Islam, thus allowing both religions to become agents of change and
inclusion rather than harbour a static sense of oppressor and oppressed,
victor and victim – all the while pretending to innocence and redemption.
My thought was that if the political could be demilitarized, religion would
follow suit. Together politics and religion could defuse injustice, bitterness
and aggression. In the end the seemingly unending cycle of violence and
atrocity could be mitigated if not ended.[5]

---

5   For my ideas on here and in the rest of the essay see my *Revolutionary Forgiveness: Essays
     on Judaism, Christianity and Religious Life* (Waco: Baylor University, 2000).

Though I knew that Jews needed to confess to Palestinians for the historical wrongs done in and through Israel, at that time I did not envision Israel's original sin as demanding a reversal of the situation of Israel as a state; the two – state solution would suffice. Was there anything more to be contemplated? The revolution that characterized forgiveness had to do with the end of the occupation of the Palestinian territories, the granting of a full state for Palestinians, a confession of wrong doing and even reparations for the damage down to the Palestinian people. Yet even with this moderate political path I proposed, the internationally agreed upon two-state solution, there was criticism directed toward me among conservative, moderate and progressive Jews. The criticism among the conservatives is easily understood, since even mentioning a full Palestinian state limited Israel's expansion and might, from their point of view, damage Israel's security. Yet it initially the criticism from moderate and progressive Jews was more difficult to understand, in the end it was more telling.

My first taste of the moderate/progressive criticism came in response to the book I published after my work on a Jewish theology of liberation. Published in 1990, *Beyond Innocence and Redemption: Confronting the Holocaust and Israeli Power*, languished in bookstores. An influential review in the Christian journal Commonweal, written by a known Jewish progressive, Leonard Fein, carried the title, 'Thanks But No Thanks.' When Edward Said, the prominent Palestinian intellectual asked if he could review my book along with one they had requested for review, the *Washington Post* declined his request. In the end I understood there was something in my book title that carried ominous tones for many Jews and those who sought to be on good and proper terms within the parameters of acceptable thought. Confronting the Holocaust? Confronting Israeli power? That Jews aren't innocent? That Israel is not redemption for the Jewish people?[6]

Fein's review stated explicitly that the trajectory of my writing was one-state and that Israel would therefore cease to exist. The implication was there couldn't be any more anti-Jewish or self-hating Jewish analysis to be had anywhere, except possibly among Palestinians. Such Jewish analysis was even more pro-Palestinian than Palestinians were and more dangerous since it came from within the Jewish community.

6   Leonard Fein, 'Thanks but No Thanks', *Commonweal* (January 1991).

Defining such thought as outside the Jewish community from Fein's perspective was important for everyone involved, Jews and Christians. It might even be better for Palestinians. Why encourage Palestinians to hope for something they wouldn't get and shouldn't desire? The Palestinians were better off to drop their grievances, take what was being offered and accept Israel as the achieved goal of Jews everywhere. In the end only misguided and anti-Semitic Palestinians were intransient. Perhaps it was due to their leadership. Palestinians were probably descent folks who were being led astray by abhorrent politicians, especially Yasser Arafat. Should self-hating Jews also help keep Palestinian misguided hopes alive?

There is no mention of a one-state solution in *Beyond Innocence and Redemption* as there was none in *Toward a Jewish Theology of Liberation*. As it turns out, Fein anticipated arguments that would flourish in some Jewish and international circles a decade or so later. Rather than the mention of such a one-state destination – a thought that hadn't even occurred to me at the time of my writing – I wonder if it was the radical questioning of the founding and subsequent history of Israel that fast-forwarded Fein's imagination. In this line, three central themes of the book come to mind; my chapters on different ways of looking at the Holocaust, a substantial and evolving tradition of dissent regarding Israel and its policies, and the continuation of a homeland and spiritual Zionism that battled – and in fragments continues to live on – the state Zionism that emerged victorious in 1948.

In all of these themes I catalogued, what had happened and what was ongoing within the Jewish world had either dropped from sight or was being neglected. Certainly from the beginning of the state of Israel there were reports from the front line on the atrocities of war, massacres, expulsion and terror, part of any war to be sure but aspects of the birth of Israel that present-day Jewish commentators wanted buried. Among the reports in 1948 and beyond, including in articles published in Israel's leading newspapers during the Palestinian uprising of 1987, there were consistent references to the Nazis and Jewish behavior in war. Though I stressed that such terminology was not used as a tool of direct comparison, for they pointed to something much deeper, often they were taken as such. Instead I called them historical analogies that contained warnings that Jews were transgressing boundaries that could not be transgressed to right historical wrongs or for ideological reasons of the emerging state. Something was amiss relating to Jewish history. The historical analogies were making it difficult for the participants and observers to elucidate within a Jewish framework. They were facing a choice: either to commit these acts and cease to be Jewish or refuse these acts as Jews.

Of the many encounters with this dissenting material, three stand out. The first is from the 1948 war recalled within the context of the first Palestinian uprising. The others are from the uprising itself.

After the first Palestinian uprising began, Amos Kenan, a columnist for the Israeli daily, *Yediot Aharonot*, wrote an essay titled 'Four Decades of Blood Vengeance.' The article presents a dialogue with George Habash, head of the Popular Front for the Liberation of Palestine, whom he met in 1948 when the Israeli army conquered Lydda.

Kenan was a soldier who, as a part of the invading and occupying force, kept Palestinian Arabs at a distance. Habash, whose ailing sister lived in Lydda, managed to avoid security and visit her. Habash's sister was thirty years old, married, with six children, and at that point dying. A medical doctor, Habash diagnosed her disease and prescribed the appropriate medicines, but because Lydda was under curfew with no local pharmacies and no access to the outside, his sister died three days later. With the curfew in effect, it was impossible to bury her properly, and so Habash dug a grave with his own hands and buried his sister in her own backyard. When the curfew was lifted, the survivors of the village, Habash and his sister's six children included, were transferred to temporary prison compounds and later expelled to Jordan.

Kenan recalls his days of guard duty in Lydda as essentially uneventful and in some senses comical, both because of the lack of military preparedness of many of the military personnel, some of whom had recently arrived from Eastern Europe, and the quality, or lack thereof, of the weapons. Since most of the inhabitants of Lydda had fled before the occupation by Jewish soldiers, there were few people to guard the Arab villagers who remained. In short, they had a typical military life with much standing around, gossiping, and the inevitable boredom. And it was typical in other, more horrifying ways as well:

In the afternoon, those of us who couldn't take it any more would steal off to Tel Aviv
for a few hours, on one excuse or another. At night, those of us who couldn't restrain
ourselves would go into the prison compounds to fuck Arab women. I want very
much to assume, and perhaps even can, that those who couldn't restrain themselves
did what they thought the Arabs would have done to them had they won the war.
Once, only once, did an Arab woman – perhaps a distant relative of George Habash –
dare complain. There was a court martial. The complainant didn't even get to testify.
The accused, who was sitting behind the judges, ran the back of his hand across his
throat, as a signal to the woman. She understood. The rapist was not acquitted; he
simply was not accused, because there was no one who would dare accuse him. Two
years later, he was killed while plowing the fields of an Arab village, one no longer
on the map because its inhabitants scattered and left it empty.[7]

Kenan then begins to write about blood vengeance, and about how difficult
it is to square accounts. What he does know is that many have sought and
taken revenge, and, to his mind, all the vengeance has already come:

Both you and I, George, have already taken vengeance – before and during and after
the fact. And both you and I have not taken pity on man or woman, boy or girl,
young or old. I know that there is not much difference between pressing a button
in a fighter plane and firing point blank into the head of a hostage. As if there is
no difference between a great massacre that was not meant to be and one that was
meant to be. There is no distinction between justice and justice or between injustice
and injustice, as there is no difference at all in what people – weak, transient beings,
assured of the justice of their ways and their deeds – are capable of doing to people
who are in sum exactly like themselves.

Tears filled my eyes, George, when I read for the first time in these forty years
how your sister died. How you dug her a pit with your own hands in the yard of her
house in the city of Lydda. I reach out with an unclean hand to your hand, which
also is not clean. You and I should die a miserable natural death, a death of sinners
who have not come to their punishment, a death from old age, disease, a death weak
and unheroic, a death meant for human beings who have lived a life of iniquity.[8]

7   Amos Kennan, 'Four Decades of Blood Vengeance', *The Nation*, February 6, 1989,
     155.
8   Ibid., p. 156.

Two other events from the Palestinian uprising make this connection between Palestinian and Jewish history in relation to the Holocaust. The first dates from January 1988, one month after the Palestinian uprising had begun, when an Israeli captain was summoned to his superior. The captain was given instructions to carry out arrests in the village of Hawara, outside Nablus. The arrest of innocent young Palestinians is hardly out of the ordinary. However, the further instructions provided to the officer as what to do to those Palestinians after their arrest was disturbing. His conscience would not allow him to carry out these instructions unless he was directly ordered to do so. Having then received the direct order, the captain, with a company of forty soldiers, boarded a civilian bus, arriving at Hawara at eleven o'clock in the evening.

The local Muhktar was given a list of twelve persons to round up, which he did, and the twelve sat on the sidewalk in the center of the village, offering no resistance. Yossi Sarid, an Israeli political analyst, describes what followed.

> The soldiers shackled the villagers, and with their hands bound behind their backs they were led to the bus. The bus started to move and after 200–300 meters it stopped beside an orchard. The 'locals' were taken off the bus and led into the orchard in groups of three, one after another. Every group was accompanied by an officer. In the darkness of the orchard the soldiers also shackled the Hawara residents' legs and laid them on the ground. The officers urged the soldiers to 'get it over with quickly, so that we can leave and forget about it.' Then, flannel was stuffed into the Arabs' mouths to prevent them from screaming and the bus driver revved up the motor so that the noise would drown out the cries. Then the soldiers obediently carried out the orders they had been given: to break their arms and legs by clubbing the Arabs; to avoid clubbing them on their heads; to remove their bonds after breaking their arms and legs, and to leave them at the site; to leave one local with broken arms but without broken legs so he could make it back to the village on his own and get help.[9]

The mission was carried out; the beatings so fierce that most of the wooden clubs used were broken. Thus was born the title of the article detailing this action, 'The Night of the Broken Clubs.'

9   Yossi Sarid, 'The Night of the Broken Clubs,' *Ha'aretz*, 4 May 1989.

The second event occurred just months after the beatings had begun, when Marcus Levin, a physician, was called up for reserve duty in the Ansar prison camp. When he arrived, Levin met two of his colleagues and asked for information about his duties. The answer: 'Mainly you examine prisoners before and after an investigation.' Levin responded in amazement, 'After the investigation?' which prompted the reply, 'Nothing special, sometimes there are fractures. For instance, yesterday they brought a twelve-year-old boy with two broken legs.' Dr Levin then demanded a meeting with the compound commander and told him, 'My name is Marcus Levin and not Josef Mengele, and for reasons of conscience I refuse to serve in this place.' A doctor who was present at the meeting tried to calm Levin with the following comment: 'Marcus, first you feel like Mengele, but after a few days you get used to it.' Hence, the title of an article written about the incident, 'You Will Get Used to Being a Mengele'.[10]

References in these articles to the Night of Broken Glass, 'Kristallnacht,' and to the Nazi physician Mengele, as ways of seeing contemporary Jewish Israeli policy and activity, startled me. The resistance on the part of the Jewish community to what one might call the Nazi analogy is understandable and so strong as to virtually silence all such references. Yet, during the brutal attempt to suppress the Palestinian uprising, in fact, from the very beginning of the Jewish struggle for statehood in Palestine in the 1940s and continuing to the present, the connection between the Jewish experience of suffering in Europe and the Palestinian experience of suffering at the hands of the Jewish people in Palestine and Israel has been, and continues to be, repeatedly made by Jewish Israelis.

10   Gideon Spiro, 'You Will Get Used to Being a Mengele,' *Al Hasismar*, 19 September 1988.

What are we to make of these references?

First, it is important to see that they are not primarily comparisons between Nazi and Israeli behavior, though some of the behavior may in fact be comparable. Second, these references are not attempts to further political objectives, such as promoting one political party over another or challenging the legitimacy of the state of Israel, though clearly they subvert both partisan and bipartisan policies of Israel that lead to these incidents.

Rather, the force of the Nazi reference involves and moves beyond comparison and politics to represent an intuitive link between the historic suffering of Jews and the present suffering of Palestinians. It further represents an implicit recognition that what was done to the Jews is now being done *by* Jews to another people. At the same time, the connection of Jewish and Palestinian suffering is pre-political and pre-ideological; that is, it operates in a terrain filled with images of Jewish suffering, which remain untouched by the 'realities' of the situation, with the need to be 'strong,' or even in the face of communal penalties for speaking the truth.

We might say that the Nazi reference represents a cry of pain and a plea to end a madness that was visited upon Jews for millennia and now is visited by Jews upon another people; thus, the vehemence with which such analogies are met when spoken, as if a blunt instrument is needed to repress the memories and aspirations of the Jewish people to be neither victim nor oppressor.

Could it be said that it is impossible today to understand the Jewish liturgy of destruction, the burning of the Temple, the death of the martyr, and the pogrom, the events of exile and Holocaust, unless Jews include as their intimate partners, those expelled, tortured, and murdered, those who, for most Jews, exist without name and history, the Palestinian people?

Here, in an inclusive liturgy of destruction, lies the possibility and the hope of moving beyond the peripheral and superficial into an engaged struggle on behalf of the distinct and common history of the Jewish and the Palestinian peoples. Might Jews be liberated from policies and attitudes that, when understood intuitively, betray Jewish history, but have been seen as weakness, lack of political maturity, or even self-hate? Jews would then be released from theologies that now serve as ideologies to close off critical thought and favor the powerful at the expense of others.

Could these point toward a just reconciliation? Indeed, in the first instance Amos Kenan is addressing his 'enemy' George Habash in frank terms. There are no lies, complicated arguments, protestations of innocence or pretense to heroism. In Kenan there is no way back, only a way forward, a confession that might bring something in the future beyond the life of 'inequity' they have lived. What was, still is. Could a mutual confession and solidarity rescue the dead and pillage – indeed rape – of that war from infamy or oblivion? Kenan's life is without a happy ending. Still there is history to atone for and more time to live in a different way.

Revolutionary Forgiveness

The heady times of the early 1990s are very far behind us now. During the first Palestinian uprising there was hope for a two-state solution and a mutual respect even between those who were clashing. Across border and boundary solidarity between Jews and Palestinians flourished as never before – and never since. There are those who see this former hope as naïve; regardless it was there, in the air, the possibility of revolutionary forgiveness.

Revolutionary forgiveness has at its heart justice. With confession and the willingness of the oppressor to cease his oppression, and with the path toward equality opening before us, memory, drenched in the blood of dislocation, atrocity and death, may have a space to breathe, reconsider not the past but what it means, or, depending on the future what the past *might* mean retrospectively. No matter the future, the pain of suffering and loss remains; its memory is crucial to the understanding of past sacrifice. Though no future can justify, can transcend, past injustice, the possibility of a different future allows meaning to that suffering. When meaning can be attached to suffering, forgiveness is then possible. Not forgiveness for the deeds themselves, but for the tragic circumstances that oppressor and oppressed alike were caught up in. With Palestinians a new life is created: can their memory of suffering change in this new context where, once anchored in solitude and vengeance, may now become rooted in a just and compassionate order that binds Jews and Palestinians? A shared life in community and equal citizenship binds old wounds together in a new fabric. Sometimes, especially as the generations pass away, old wounds are forgotten or rewoven to such a degree that a joint history is recognized from the beginning. Though injustice was at the heart of the old, reconciliation allows both the former oppressors and the former victims to view that history as a mutual evolution. By that time they are bound together in a way that could not have been foreseen, and in this new time, will not be unbound.

I have seen this in my teaching of the Holocaust in various settings, including among Christian conservative and evangelical students. The introduction of Christian history regarding Jews is enormously difficult for them for a variety of reasons, the first being their naïve view of Christian history itself. Yet even with this caveat, the idea that Christians despised, denigrated, harassed, ghettoized and murdered Jews throughout European Christian history, the history to which they are heirs, is too shocking, too disconfirming of their own upbringing and thoughts about Jews to be coherent to them. Though once naiveté is dispensed with, denial remains, and the reality is that there has been a decade's old process of revolutionary forgiveness in the West that these students inherit. Even the desire for Jews to become Christians, an age-old Christian desire, and today considered in many Jewish and Christian quarters as a holdover of anti-Semitism, may be functioning on a different plane. It may be less a disdain for the limits of Judaism than a positive sense of Christian redemption.

What happens when the prospects of revolutionary forgiveness fail or become so distant as to be relegated to another historical horizon completely? In that case, is revolutionary justice still called for?

Certainly in the case of the death camps, a revolutionary justice was needed. It is only after justice that revolutionary forgiveness can be contemplated. In the case of Israel and the Palestinians, now rather than in the 1980s, can we say that the prospect of confession and justice is so distant that only the defeat and dismantling of the state of Israel should be envisioned, if not at least hoped for? If this is the case, does this mean that Jews who won't argue for the dissolution of Israel can be trusted when they proclaim to be on the side of justice for Palestinians?

When discussing revolutionary justice as a way toward a mutual and interdependent empowerment, the question is first whether interdependence is indeed a desired result. Clearly the position from which one is arguing is crucial here. If, for example, Palestinians want a Palestine – here defined as historic Palestine rather than the limited land of the idealized two-state solution, let alone what is left of Palestine – devoid of Jews, who could argue against their case? Of course, if that could be achieved, it is unlikely that the resulting state would live up to the ideals of the Palestinians that might legitimately argue this point. In the free-for-all that would result from the fall of Israel, it is impossible to predict what government would survive or be established. Though some Palestinians would be involved in the ensuing governing power, it is likely that a power struggle would commence that would hardly be limited to the various Palestinian factions themselves. Outside actors and influence should be expected and the forces that would be unleashed in the Middle East are unpredictable.

So revolutionary justice might become injustice within the Palestinian community itself. Would at least justice have been meted out to the Jews of Israel who caused so much havoc, taken so much land and so many lives in building their state over and against Palestine and Palestinians? Would that reversal be enough to justify revolutionary justice no matter the outcome?

If in fact Jewish anti-Zionist groups are correct, that Israel is a colonial project and as such must be dismantled and replaced with Palestinian sovereignty, does that mean that any Jew who recognizes Israel's original sin must *per force* become anti-Zionist? The situation becomes even more complicated when Jews of Conscience recognize that Israel's victory itself has made a two-state solution impossible and that *de facto* a one-state solution has been imposed on the Palestinians by Israel. If Jews keep arguing for a two-state solution that will never arrive, isn't that perpetuating a lie, one that allows Israel's oppression of the Palestinians to become even stronger? Here Jews of Conscience are caught in the conundrum of Jewish history and power. Are not Jews of Conscience thus in the same vice as those Jews who use Holocaust and Israel as a lever of power?

This was another discovery I made as I researched the Jewish tradition of dissent regarding the formation of Israel and its subsequent policies toward Palestinians. Even Martin Buber and Hannah Arendt could not escape their Judeo-centric and – much more troubling – Orientalist perspective when it came to Palestine and Arabs. Though both argued for a bi-national state in Palestine, Jewish homeland for Jews alongside a homeland for Palestinian Arabs in one unified Palestine, thereby opposing the formation of a Jewish state, Buber and Arendt were Western in their views toward Arabs. One of their arguments for Jewish settlement in Palestine is that Jews would help a backward Arab region, develop technology and social structures for the modern age. As agents of development, Jews should be welcome in Palestine as partners rather than being seen as the last vestige of a colonial age. Unlike Arendt, Buber also argued for the Jewish right to settlement based on ancient Jewish history. In that sense, the economic and political development of Palestine would also escalate with the Jewish 'native' presence having returned to their land. For Buber the land responded to Jews because of this indigenous connection.

There are so many twists and turns in the Jewish connection to Palestine historically, to Jewish history in the present and in the complexities of Israel as a state with now close to five million Jews, that it is difficult to see an argument about the future of Israel and the Palestinians being untainted with Jewish bias. Can there be a just reconciliation of Jews and Palestinians with that bias intact? Of course, Palestinians also have their bias; all arguments and struggles have biases attached. But here the Jewish bias is shored up by the superior power of Israel, the backing of the United States, and with the decided advantage of a Western narrative that twins the Holocaust and Israel. If the power shifted toward Palestinians, they would have a similar array of powerful levers at their fingertips, though coming from a different direction, that of the narrative of a decolonizing Pan-Arab world, Islamic attachments to Jerusalem and a more than fifty year long negative experience of Israeli power. Without specifying the details, this may have been exactly what Greenberg was arguing when he wrote about even unintentionally undermining Israel's power as an invitation to another Holocaust.

Is there a time when partisans on one side of a dispute lose their right to speak about 'solutions' to questions of justice and injustice? Clearly if an objective observer looked at the maps of Israel and Palestine – over time and now – they would see a seamless and relentless pattern of Israeli expansion and Palestinian diminishment. That same objective observer would see the ongoing peace process as having failed to halt this movement and perhaps even providing cover for it. They would also judge Jewish normative discourse about Israel and the Palestinians as part of the reason for the ongoing problematic; even progressive Jewish discourse would be judged as seeking to halt aspects of Israeli expansionism while covering up other aspects of Jewish hegemony in the area. In defining what it is and what it is not possible to say and advocate by defining the acceptable and unacceptable parameters of discourse on the issue of Jews, Israel and the Palestinians, progressive Jews would be judged harshly. What seems to be obvious from a Palestinian perspective – that Israel is a colonial project bent on the destruction of Palestine with the backing of the American empire and an empowered Jewish discourse within the United States – is obviously unacceptable speech in the West still dealing with the legacy of anti-Semitism and the Holocaust. If one side's speech about what it would take for a just reconciliation is declared *ipso facto* as out of bounds – and is seen as a genocidal assault on a people just emerging from the prospect of annihilation – can there be a way forward? And where should Jews of Conscience stand on the issues of speech, bias and power?

Jews of Conscience Journey into their (un)Jewish Future

Jews of Conscience journey into a future defined by a violent Constantinian Judaism. In many ways the time has already arrived. In a deep sense, Jews of Conscience are defined as (un)Jewish, at least in the normative definition of the term. However, Jews are not alone. Many Christians and Muslims are also defined as normatively (un)Christian and (un)Muslim. In this grouping, there are also Israeli and Palestinians who are in exile from the normative definitions of what they should be and what future they should work toward, and also struggle within a variety of religious and national Constantinian formations. In the larger arc of history, should these sub groupings be seen as disparate or aligned? Do they belong to the communities that define them as outside, or are they themselves a community? Here we can see the Constantinian formations of various peoples and nations as joining together. Should we not also see people of conscience from wherever they hail as belonging to a distinct community?[11]

Those in exile always feel alienated and separated from their birth identities, as indeed they are. But since identities are constructed and reconstructed over time, should Jews and others be reluctant to construct their identities anew or accept the new construction as they find it? The question of what it means to be Jewish at any particular time lies with historians; the challenge for Jews of Conscience today is to live their Jewishness with others who are also in exile. In this lived exile, another way of being Jewish – and Christian and Muslim – is being forged. What these new identities will be called and who will recognize them as heirs of previous identity constructions or as pioneers of a new identity is also for historians to trace. What Jews of Conscience need to do today is live their reality with other people of conscience wherever they are found. The essence of Jewish fidelity today is to embrace the Jewish prophetic as a particular *and* universal identity. What the children of these Jews of Conscience will call themselves and how they will identify themselves is anyone's guess. If they embrace the indigenous of the people Israel, the prophetic, can they be far off the mark?

At the heart of revolutionary forgiveness is the prophetic tempered with compassion. The prophetic judges injustice; it also provides a way back to right relation. In Israel/Palestine we have some sense of a past within Palestine before the birth of the state of Israel where over hundreds of years and more Arabs and Jews lived ordinary lives together. Of course we also have the witness of Jews who are Arabs, within and outside of the contemporary state of Israel. This past is very different than the sojourn of European Jews, and yet it might provide a model of a future in a reconfigured Middle East.

---

11   I develop these understandings of Jews of Conscience more fully in my *Israel Does Not Equal Judaism* (New York: New Press, 2009).

But here we are back with hope for a future different than the present. The question is whether hope is crucial to commitment in the present or whether hope itself presents a series of illusionary possibilities than might prevent giving all to the present.

Israel is now defined by some as a colonial and imperial state that needs to be dismantled. Recent conferences in the United Kingdom, Norway, Canada and the United States illustrate this shift in tone. If recent discourse on the Jewish and Palestinian Left is heard and affirmed, there is also a return of the question of one-state for Israel/Palestine in which Jews and Palestinians would be citizens of the state without reference to ethnic or religious background. This one-state understanding would eliminate the discriminatory and 'racist' laws of Israel and would allow Palestinian refugees to return to their home in what today has become the state of Israel. This, then, would mean the end of a 'Jewish' state.[12]

What do Jews of Conscience say to this prospect? Can they make this argument after the Holocaust and after Israel – meaning after what Israel has done and is doing to the Palestinian people – that in the long run Jews would be safe in a democratic secular state in the Middle East? At the same time, the disappearance of a Jewish state would have a deep impact on Jewish identity. Since most of contemporary Jewish identity revolves around the Holocaust and the state of Israel, the dissolution of the state of Israel as a Jewish state would mean as well the end of the significance of the Holocaust for Jewish identity.

Here we move beyond the contemporary political and religious constructs of identity into the future of Jewishness itself. Without the Holocaust and Israel, is there any future for Jewish identity? Rabbinic Judaism, which was defining of Jewish identity for almost two thousand years, was found wanting after the Holocaust. The Holocaust and then Israel were replacements for a failing Rabbinic Judaism; in the remembrance of the Holocaust and support for Israel, was born a new definition of Jewishness.

---

12   For a book length treatments of this subject from a Palestinian perspective see Ali Abunimah, *One Country: A Bold Proposal to End the Israeli/Palestinian Impasse* (New York: Henry Holt, 2007).

Some even believe that the Holocaust and Israel have become a new religion for Jews, in essence a Holocaust/Israel Judaism. If Israel ceases to be a Jewish state and the Holocaust becomes less and less defining of Jewish commitment, what would take their place?

It is in the crucible of this possibility that revolutionary forgiveness takes on variegated meanings and layerings, making such a movement more difficult and more important. For if a just reconciliation means so much, it carries with it what may have prompted the conflict in the first place. Jews of Conscience may have to jettison these multiple layers to see clearly and do what needs to be done. Jews of Conscience might then be a catalyst for creating a future that, though difficult for them to accept, might force others to a deeper realization of alternatives to the physical and verbal violence that permeates the Israeli/Palestinian crisis today.

Are Jews of Conscience therefore condemned to agents of change, forcing a future compromise that they themselves would refuse? If this is the case, is it worth the harsh exile Jews of Conscience are forced to endure? And does this compromise ensure the ultimate triumph of Constantinian Judaism? This prospect forces Jews of Conscience to think more deeply about the principles they uphold and the values that come within the creation of a matrix, however insufficient and unjust, for ordinary people to live ordinary lives and be free at last of extraordinary violence and insecurity. Is this what the exile of Jews of Conscience is ultimately all about?

Here, then, we reach the beginning of the end, balancing justice and reconciliation, in almost every situation having to abandon parts of both, but never more so than in the reality of Israel and the Palestinians. The question is rendered more complex by the fact that as time passes, there may be so little left of justice or reconciliation that Jews of Conscience may be in an exile without end, never reaching that bittersweet taste of the end of the cycle of violence and atrocity.

So it is, if history continues as it has, at least in our lifetime. Perhaps here we are reduced to a witness for a just reconciliation, seemingly infinitely postponed.

RON ROBERTS, EDINA BEĆIREVIĆ AND STEPHEN PAUL

Truth and Denial: Psychological Perspectives on Reconciliation in Bosnia

Psychology and Reconciliation

In this chapter we shall explore the contribution psychology can make to peace and reconciliation. We shall give an overview of the changing face of psychology, its contribution to our understanding of human conflict and the importance of human relationships. We shall then focus on reconciliation in Bosnia.

Less than one hundred years ago Freud[1] viewed the world as a dangerous place. Groups of people could act mindlessly together in the humiliation and death of others. Leaders could emerge who, people would follow with little consideration seemingly of their own values. In fact, the most 'disturbed' or 'evil' people rose into positions in which their abuse of others was accepted. This was the scenario in Europe in the 1930s, was the scenario in Yugoslavia in the 1990s and has been the scenario in many hotspots around the world throughout the last one hundred years. Terrible atrocities continue to be committed with seeming justification.

There is no doubt that there exists the potential for terrible destructiveness within the human psyche and that given certain conditions, for example a threat to territory and resources, people may commit atrocities at will. The human reaction to perceived hurt, real or otherwise, provokes a similar potential response. However, these responses cannot be resolved by the forceful suppression or repression of the individuals who act in this manner. Attempts must be made to understand why they act as they do. Consequently we have to try to understand human nature.

---

1 Sigmund Freud, *Civilization and Its Discontents* (London: Penguin, 2002).

Freudian psychology was preoccupied with 'neurosis' and was arguably able to provide insights into what is considered abnormal behaviour.
In Freud's eyes, human nature was essentially destructive. Well-being could
only be achieved by understanding and controlling this, something which
Freud believed was possible. However, more recent work in humanistic
psychology, represented by the work of Abraham Maslow, Carl Rogers
and others has challenged this and argued that the development of a community with shared purpose and common pleasures can be positive and
transformational. Rogers considered this the core of person-centred psychology.[2] His approach to understanding personality and human relationships, was applied to counselling, education, both small groups and larger
communities. Later this was extended to address issues of peace and conflict
resolution. He was nominated for the Nobel Peace Prize for his work on
intergroup conflict in South Africa and Northern Ireland.[3]

Unlike Freud then, Rogers did not see humans as essentially destructive. It is only when 'man [sic] is less than fully man not functioning freely,
that he is to be feared'.[4] Undistorted awareness can lead to healthy living,
while threats to awareness lead to maladjustment and destructive behaviour.
Rogers applied his principles to conflicted groups and communities with
some success, most notably in the peace negotiations with Sadat and Begin
at Camp David chaired by President Carter. There, Rogers worked with
the two leaders, employing his ideas to teach them the values of empathy,
warmth and genuineness in communication, work which contributed to
the subsequent peace accord.[5] Further examples of this work occurred with
black and white leaders in South Africa, both of whom saw the country as
belonging to them. Similar work underpinned the peacemaking in Northern
Ireland. In instances like these political leaders have learnt to understand
their enemies and, as they did so, allowed new ways of working together
to emerge. Understanding human nature is this way is therefore *central* to
understanding political and social change in a way that leads to peace.

2   C. Rogers, *A Way of Being* (Boston: Houghton Mifflin, 1980).
3   C. Rogers, 'Steps Toward World Peace, 1948–1986: Tension Reduction in Theory
      and Practice', *Counseling and Values* 32 (1987), pp. 12–16.
4   C. Rogers, *On Becoming a Person* (Boston: Houghton Mifflin, 1961), p. 105.
5   F. Ibrahim, 'Peace for Kashmir: A Worldview, Psychological Intervention', *International
      Journal for the Advancement of Counselling* 27/2 (2005), pp. 289–97.

More recent developments in psychology, particularly in theoretical transpersonal psychology[6] support the view that humanity and human communities are inextricably bound together and that, for this reason, they can only co-exist through mutual co-operation. The world community is becoming increasingly interdependent with accompanying realization of our common destiny. These bonds are manifests through trade, education, communication, the media, etc. This has to bring benefits to all for it to work.

Clearly, the discipline of psychology has much to offer in areas of human conflict. It does this most explicitly when it helps to explore the ways in which human beings depend on each other for their flourishing.

Truth and Denial in Bosnia

In April 1992, under the influence of the Serbian parliament, the Yugoslav People's Army, began a three year campaign of mass violence and genocide, with intent to destroy the new state of Bosnia and Herzegovina and rid the land of its Bosniak (Bosnian Muslim) and Croat inhabitants. In this project they were aided by the Serbian Ministry of the interior, the army and ministry of the interior of the self – declared Republika Srpska and a host of Serbian paramilitary units[7]. Psychiatrist, Radovan Karadžić, President of the Bosnian Serb parliament and supreme commander leader of the armed forces, had earlier warned that the Muslim people in Bosnia 'would disappear from the face of the earth'.[8] Karadžić provided varying estimates

---

6   R. Metzner, *The Expansion of Consciousness* (Berkeley, CA: Green Earth Foundation & Regent Press, 2008).

7   International Court of Justice (ICJ), Application of the Convention on the Prevention and Punishment of the Crime of Genocide (Bosnia and Herzegovina *v.* Serbia and Montenegro) (2007). Judgement 26 February 2007. http://www.icj-cij.org/docket/files/91/13685.pdf, accessed 3 November 2009.

8   United Nations/ICTY, ICTY Court Records (2009a), Public Transcript of Hearing 27 October 2009. Prosecution Opening statement. http://icr.icty.org/frmResult-Set.aspx?e=o2mj5h453pxv4y45kjsngpiu&StartPage=1&EndPage=10, accessed 15 November 2009.

of what the carnage would entail. In October of 1991 he remarked; 'In just a couple of days, Sarajevo will be gone and there will be five hundred thousand dead, in one month Muslims will be annihilated in Bosnia and Herzegovina.'⁹ He predicted '300,000 alone would perish in Sarajevo.'¹⁰ Should any doubt about intentions have remained, one month into the war, during the sixteenth session of the Bosnian Serb Assembly, Karadžić removed them in declaring 'This conflict was incited so that the Muslims would not exist.'¹¹

In the ensuing war, a systematic genocidal pattern of violence spread across Bosnia, engulfing Prijedor, Brcko, Sanski Most, Zvornik, Bratunac and later Srebrenica.¹² When The Dayton Agreement brought the war to an official close, the overwhelming majority (83 per cent) of civilian casualties had been Bosniak.¹³ The 'justice and reconciliation' process designed by decision makers in the international community during and after the Dayton peace agreement, in reality legitimized the Serbian territorial conquest. By giving the name Republika Srpska, to a separate Serbian entity within the state of Bosnia and Herzegovina, and at the same time depriving the Bosnian state of the prefix of Republic (before the war the full name of Bosnia and Herzegovina was Republika Bosna i Hercegovina – the name under which it is recognized by the EU and admitted to the UN in 1992) Serbian national plans were rewarded. Thus were the aggressors rewarded and victims punished.

The realization the hopes the people of Bosnia have for peace now rests on how its people can reconcile themselves with their own dark memories.

9   United Nations/ICTY, ICTY Court Records (2004), Intercepted conversation between Radovan Karadžić and Mandić Momo on 13 October 1991. http://icr.icty.org/frmResultSet.aspx?e=o2mj5h453pxv4y45kjsngpiu&StartPage=1&EndPage=10, accessed 15 November 2009.
10 (UN/ICTY, 2009a).
11 'The Assembly of *Republika Srpska*, 1992–95: Highlights and Excerpts'. Statement of Expert Witness Robert J. Donia submitted 29 July 2003, ICTY.
12 S. Power, *A Problem from Hell: America and the Age of Genocide* (London: Flamingo, 2003).
13 Research and Documentation Centre Sarajevo http://www.idc.org.ba/.

They also have to learn to understand and live (again) with those who participated in the criminal enterprise against them, many of whom might well be in a state of continued denial about their misdeeds.

Radovan Karadžić and Ratko Mladić (and a number of other political leaders) were indicted for genocide and war crimes and banned from public office after the Dayton agreement. However a number of other political and military leaders on whom war crime dossiers were maintained remained in power. Momcilo Krajišnik and Biljana Plavšić are just two examples of those who continued in high office, both were principal allies of Karadžić during the war. Considered by the international community post 1995 as leaders who have the potential to reform the country, they were subsequently indicted by the Hague Tribunal.[14] Facing the past and acknowledging any personal responsibility for its errors is an essential pre-condition of bringing about effective reconciliation between people in conflict. Appeals for reconciliation, as Cohen[15] notes, explicitly assume that perpetrators, victims and bystanders have already acknowledged what happened.

> It is impossible to expect reconciliation if part of the population refuses to accept that anything was ever wrong, and the other part has never received an acknowledgement of the suffering it has undergone or of the ultimate responsibility for that suffering.[16]

Desmond Tutu expressed this forcefully when he remarked that 'reconciliation based on falsehood, on not facing up to reality, is not reconciliation at all'[17]. In comparison with Bosnia, in both Northern Ireland and South Africa past injustices have been more readily acknowledged by all. What has

---

14   United Nations/ICTY Case information sheet (IT-00–39) (2009b), Momčilo Krajišnik. http://www.icty.org/x/cases/krajisnik/cis/en/cis_krajisnik_en.pdf, accessed 6 January 2010. See also http://www.icty.org/case/plavsic/4#ind.

15   S. Cohen, *States of Denial* (Cambridge: Polity Press, 2001).

16   Letter from Human Rights Watch to President F.W. de Klerk; cited in Cohen, 2001, p. 239.

17   E. Garver, *For the Sake of Argument: Chicago: Practical Reasoning, Character, and the Ethics of Belief* (Chicago: University of Chicago Press, 2004), p. 16.

been disputed, however, is the meaning of those events and the justifications for them. Cessation of violence brought about the creation of a common public space for story-telling. This created effective dialogue and the sharing of narratives across communities. Cultural change emerged from this as did the reconstruction of the institutions of state. This has been further aided by outside international economic and political pressure. The situation in Bosnia, though better than it was, is still very different from that in South Africa and Northern Ireland. The war led to considerable ethnic segregation. Also, very little shared narrative exists between the victims and aggressors. Transitional justice arrangements, where they do exist (e.g. extradition of war crimes suspects and domestic criminal trials), have played no active role in the reconstruction or reconstitution of the aggressor state, Serbia or its allied entity within the Bosnian State, Republika Srpska.

In fact, as Subotić[18] argues, reforms to the Serbian educational system, media and the culture of human rights have escaped attention. Serbia has meanwhile complied with the requirements of international justice in ways which favour its own domestic political agenda. This includes movement toward EU membership, and protection of the very nationalistic culture and mythology which was responsible for the instigation of mass violence.[19] Serbia was judged by the International Court of Justice to be in breach of the genocide convention[20], and must, therefore, be considered a failed state which continues to pose grave threats to any realistic prospects of reconciliation in the region. Consequently, there are no signs of a viable common space being created in which a shared version of the past can facilitate public discourse and reconciliation. Serbian public opinion still lacks any willingness to reappraise either the events of the war or the exploits of its wartime 'heroes'. For example, of those surveyed in 2006 only a minority

---

18   J. Subotić, *Hijacked Justice: Dealing with the Past in the Balkans* (London: Cornell University Press, 2009).

19   An illustrative example of the success this strategy has yielded in the Western media can be found in D. Korski, Serbia deserves to feel proud (2008), *The Guardian* Tuesday 22 July http://www.guardian.co.uk/commentisfree/2008/jul/22/radovankaradzic. warcrimes, accessed 15 November 2009.

20   See ICJ (2007).

believed that Sarajevo had been besieged for three years or considered the mass killings of Muslim civilians in Srebrenica to be a crime.[21] Recent opinion polls show that a majority are opposed to the capture and extradition of General Mladić to The International Criminal Tribunal for the former Yugoslavia. The number supporting his capture, at 26 per cent was barely half the figure of the previous year.[22] Whilst The Hague Tribunal as well as domestic war crimes trials at the State Court in Bosnia have documented the overall war events, Serbian political elites have persistently ignored the ICTY judgements, and have continued to deny genocide. The general population has therefore been under no pressure to change its attitudes or learn from its past mistakes. This has been questionably tolerated by the international community in the interests of *realpolitik*.

Sadly, social scientists and psychologists in particular, have made their own contribution to this culture of denial. They have recycled the myth that all ethnic groups (Croat, Serb and Muslim) were equally responsible for the wars accompanying the break-up of the former Yugoslavia. Agger[23] for example rehashes the tired rhetoric that the Bosnian war can be satisfactorily summarized by reference to 'three ethnic groups who fought each other', whilst Biruski et al.[24] assert with misplaced confidence that 'as is well-known, ethnic minorities fled as atrocities were committed by

21   OCSE, Public opinion in Serbia. Views on domestic war crimes judicial authorities and the Hague Tribunal (2006), http://www.osce.org/documents/srb/2007/03/23518_ en.pdf, accessed 16 November 2009.

22   BBC news online, Bosnia, a 'world of parallel truths' (2009a), 17 October. http:// news.bbc.co.uk/1/hi/programmes/from_our_own_correspondent/8311452.stm. Accessed 17 October. BBC news online, War Tribunal Head in Serbia visit (2009b), 4 November. http://news.bbc.co.uk/1/hi/world/europe/8342035.stm, accessed 5 November 2009.

23   I. Agger, 'Reducing Trauma During Ethno-Political Conflict: A Personal Account of Psycho-Social Work Under War Conditions in Bosnia' (p. 242), in D.J. Christie, R.V. Wagner and D.D. Winter (eds), *Peace, Conflict, and Violence: Peace Psychology for the 21st Century* (Upper Saddle River, NJ: Prentice Hall, 2001).

24   D.C. Biruski, I. Jerkovic, M. Zotovic, and I. Krnetic, 'Psychology in Bosnia and Herzegovina, Croatia and Serbia', *The Psychologist* 20/4 (2007), pp. 220–2.

all sides'. Marchak[25] adds to the common refrain with 'war crimes were committed by all participants'. 'Well known' though these claims may be they serve only to confuse and leave in their wake a portrayal of events that is far from the truth. In a strictly factual sense, of course, it may be correct to say that in Bosnia or for that matter Rwanda, Cambodia, Vietnam, Iraq or German-occupied Europe in World War II, that 'atrocities' were 'committed by all sides'. But would such a description accurately describe the broad sweep and scale of events, to say nothing of the motivations behind the instigation of violence? The 'all sides were to blame' representation reinforces the line taken by the 'pro-Belgrade'[26] British government at the time of the Bosnian war (and again in Iraq) and repeated *ad nauseam* in the British press.[27] This evasion of moral responsibility obscured the misreading of events on the ground. It also turned a blind eye to genocide, ethnic cleansing, mass rape and murder. This enabled Milošević and his allies to perpetuate the slaughter in Bosnia – a slaughter in which the predominant victims were Muslim. Biruski et al.,[28] emphasize the 'considerable challenges (that) remain from the 1990s war violence', but amongst these challenges they make no mention of denial. Their own denial, the denial of the Serbian community, the denial of the intellectual community, the denial of the negotiators, diplomats and policy makers of the international community – do not appear in the landscape of necessary change. Yet as described by Power[29] these can all be said to have succumbed to the mantra that 'all sides' were 'equally responsible'.

25   P. Marchak, Why do states kill citizens? Or, why racism is an insufficient explanation (2008,p. 185), in V. Esses and R. Vernon (eds), *Explaining the Breakdown of Ethnic Relations: Why Neighbors Kill* (Montreal: McGill University Press).

26   M. Klemenčič, The international community and the FRY/Belligerents, 1989–1997 (2009, p. 178). In C. Ingrao and T.A. Emmert (eds), *Confronting the Yugoslav Controversies* (West Lafayette, IN: Purdue University Press).

27   B. Simms, *Unfinest Hour: Britain and the Destruction of Bosnia* (London: Penguin, 2002).

28   Biruski et al., 'Psychology in Bosnia and Herzegovina, Croatia and Serbia', p. 222.

29   Power, pp. 307–9.

The recent publication of presidential confidant Taylor Branch's record of Bill Clinton's time in the White House[30] confirms this and adds to the mounting evidence of anti-Islamic sentiment in the corridors of European power determining policy on the ground:

> Clinton said US allies in Europe blocked proposals to adjust or remove the embargo. They justified their opposition on plausible humanitarian grounds, arguing that more arms would only fuel the bloodshed, but privately, said the President, key allies objected that an independent Bosnia would be 'unnatural' as the only Muslim nation in Europe. He said they favored the embargo precisely because it locked in Bosnia's disadvantage. Worse, he added, they parried numerous alternatives as a danger to the some eight thousand European peacekeepers deployed in Bosnia to safeguard emergency shipments of food and medical supplies [...] While upholding their peacekeepers as a badge of commitment, they turned these troops effectively into a shield for the steady dismemberment of Bosnia by Serb forces...President Clinton only shrugged. He said President François Mitterrand of France had been especially blunt in saying that Bosnia did not belong, and that British officials also spoke of a painful but realistic restoration of Christian Europe.

Thus, through the Faustian marriage of Western polity and Serbian artillery is the 'phantom Europe'[31] demystified. It would be reassuring if in the face of this rather disgusting reality the academic community was able to take a step away from its usual 'conformist subservience to those in power'.[32] Sadly in the professional expositions of Agger and Biruski et al. the Muslim voice is conspicuous by its absence. Their accounts of the Balkan conflict, carry disturbing intimations of a Eurocentric anti-Islamic world view, exhibiting a fear of the Muslim voice and what it might have to say, not just about the Bosnian war but about 'us' here in the West. In excising it and window dressing its removal in the language of 'objective'

---

30   T. Branch, Excerpts from The Clinton Tapes: Wrestling history with the President (2009), *New York Times*, 24 September http://www.nytimes.com/2009/09/25/books/excerpt-clinton-tapes.html?pagewanted=5&_r=2, accessed 7 November 2009.

31   J. Baudrillard, *The Perfect Crime* (London: Verso, 2008), p. 135.

32   Noam Chomsky, *Hegemony or Survival: America's Quest for Global Dominance* (London: Penguin, 2004), p. 48.

psychological science, what we are actually left with is 'a disintegration of rationality'[33], leaving in its wake a strand of psychological discourse, which like the actions of the policy makers, makes common cause not just with the fantasy that Serb forces were protecting 'Christian Europe'[34] but with the Serbian genocidal project itself, an act of intellectual elimination to parallel and accompany the prior existential elimination.

For all these reasons, reconciliation between the parties involved, cannot be a matter solely confined to relations between Muslim and Serb peoples in the Balkans. It must involve the wider international community. Denial of mass crimes is as much an issue now in Bosnia as it was in Germany after World War II. The intellectual community has an obligation to point this out. It must also show exactly why the acknowledgement of such denial is a precondition of bringing about effective reconciliation between the peoples of the region. However, Anglo-American social psychology has been complicit in the Western 'all sides to blame' analysis. By following an essentialist anti-historical discourse is it has been able to direct blame onto a warring 'Balkan mentality'. Such a portrayal of violence as being intrinsic to human nature has been a mainstay of psychological argument running through Milgram's[35] explanations of obedience to malevolent authority and Tajfel's[36] explanation of in-group favouritism/out-group hostility. Tajfel's social identity theory has been particularly influential in psychological reasoning about human conflict and while such 'primordialist' perspectives

33   Cohen p. 148.
34   For example Dobrica Ćosić, so called 'spiritual father of the Serbian nation' writes 'Serbs, the cast-out Serbs, are bound to fight for the historical truth about the Bosnian war and prove to the world and to their own offspring that when fighting in Bosnia for their freedom they were once again defending Christian Europe from jihadist Islam' (cited in S. Biserko and E. Bećirević, Denial of genocide – on the possibility of normalizing relations in the region (2009). *Bosnian Institute*. 23 October. http://www.bosnia.org.uk/news/news_body.cfm?newsid=2638, accessed 30 November 2009).
35   S. Milgram, Obedience to Authority (London: Pinter and Martin, 1974).
36   H. Tajfel, *Differentiation between social groups: Studies in the social psychology of intergroup relations*. European Monographs in Social Psychology, no.14 (London: Academic Press, 1978).

have not gone unchallenged.[37] It is only in the outer limits of psychology and in the broader social sciences where one is more likely to find a reasoned account of the role of the (Serbian) state in creating violence and conflict in the former Yugoslavia.[38] The key question for us is whether, despite these flaws, psychology has anything to offer in addressing the problems of reconciliation in Bosnia. To consider this we must first pause and consider what we mean by reconciliation and who is to be reconciled to what and to who and where. Only then will we be in a position to comment on the feasibility of reconciliation and the potential contribution psychological knowledge and practice might make to it.

Reconciliation

Reconciliation between parties can be understood in two basic ways; rapprochement – re-establishing cordial relations or resolving differences between former adversaries – and balancing; harmonising relationships between groups and accommodating and accepting the past. What both these aspects have in common is the idea of arriving at a stable, peaceful and dignified state – with former adversaries and/or with oneself. But what allows this to be achieved in practice?

37   M. Hewstone, N. Tausch, A. Voci, J. Hughes, J. Kenworthy, and E. Cairns, Prior intergroup contact and killing of ethnic out-group neighbours (2008). In V. Esses and R. Vernon (eds), *Explaining the Breakdown of Ethnic Relations: Why Neighbors Kill* (Montreal: McGill University Press). See also J.D. Fearon and D.D. Laitin, Violence and the social construction of ethnic identity. *International Organization* (2000), 54, 845–77.

38   D.B. Macdonald, *Balkan Holocausts? Serbian and Croatian Victim-Centred Propaganda and the War in Yugoslavia* (Manchester: Manchester University Press, 2002). See also F. Wilmer, *The social construction of man, the state, and war: Identity, Conflict and violence in the former Yugoslavia* (London: Routledge, 2002).

Lederach[39] has argued that the necessary ingredients of reconciliation comprise truth, forgiveness, justice and peace; components which implicitly traverse both private and public spaces, and embrace both rational and emotive practices. There is a real problem however in supposing that these components can be considered as objectively measurable or achievable truths. If we take justice as one example – does it make sense to believe that a truly just outcome (an objectively true just outcome) could be attained irrespective of what the contesting parties actually make of matters? Hafer, Olson and Peterson[40] point to the numerous difficulties that such a stance engenders, noting that almost everything about justice – its meaning, utility, relevance and scope may all vary or be contested outright. The perspective[41] adopted by these authors, suggests that it is the actual circumstances on the ground (historical, political, cultural, psychological realities) that in each instance will determine how effectively ideas of justice contribute to either the commission or prevention of harm.

Even within the realist/positivist investigative tradition however[42] scepticism has been expressed as to whether, given the current state of knowledge, the components of effective reconciliation, can be clearly set out. Methodological and empirical arguments have been adduced to challenge the view that truth and justice necessarily have a causal relationship to reconciliation. Mendelhoff[43], for example, maintains that truth and justice are concepts to clarify. For example, are they matters of process

39   J.P. Lederach, *Building Peace: Sustainable reconciliation in divided societies* (Washington DC: US Institute of Peace Press, 1997).

40   C.L. Hafer, J.M. Olson, and A.A. Peterson, Extreme harmdoing: A view from the social psychology of justice (2008). In V. Esses and R. Vernon (eds), *Explaining the Breakdown of Ethnic Relations: Why Neighbors Kill* (Montreal: McGill University Press).

41   This view can be described as 'constructionist' – as the reality which people perceive and participate in is one of their own making.

42   Such a view upholds the primacy of objective measurement in a world which is independent of what we take it to be. Its assumptions are therefore directly opposite to the constructionist perspective.

43   D. Mendelhoff, Truth-seeking, truth-telling, and postconflict peacebuilding (2004), *International Studies Review*, 6, 355–80.

or outcome? He adds that there is, in fact, little evidence to support the claim that they bear as directly on effective reconciliation as many claim. Notwithstanding, Long and Brecke[44] believe that these ideas are critical to understanding reconciliation, and that they are well supported by case studies. Their view is that positive (reconciliatory) outcomes are more likely to result from the public acceptance of past wrongs. Allport's contact hypothesis[45] has also provided an empirical basis for work attesting to the possibilities of reconciliation. Drawing on this in the South African context, Gibson[46] reported increasing levels of inter-ethnic contact were related to increased understanding and rejection of stereotypes which were perpetuated by misunderstanding of the past.

So how do the above ideas relate to Bosnia? Unlike Rwanda where local reconciliation initiatives (the Gacaca Courts) have been pursued, or South Africa where the Truth and Reconciliation Commission operated, the reconciliation process in Bosnia has since 1995 largely rested on war crimes trials (both in The Hague and in domestic courts). Bosnia certainly bears witness to the difficulties of establishing an agreed truth or justice as externally verifiable entities. It also shows an antipathy toward any signalling of reconciliatory intent by the perpetrators of war and their political masters. To the contrary, the spoilers have achieved the territory they sought and now enjoy it under little or no political pressure to concede anything, let alone volunteer it.[47] There is little effective inter-ethnic contact with neighbouring states or among the relationships of the various parties living within it.

44   W.J. Long, and P. Brecke, *War and reconciliation: reasons and emotion in conflict resolution* (Cambridge, MA: MIT Press, 2003).

45   G. Allport, *The Nature of Prejudice* (Reading, MA: Addison-Wesley, 1954).

46   J.L. Gibson, Does truth lead to reconciliation? Testing the causal assumptions of the South African truth and reconciliation process (2004), *American Journal of Political Science*, 48(2), 201–17.

47   S. Pecanin, The disgraceful US and EU game in Bosnia-Herzegovina (2009), *Bosnian Institute*. 5 November. http://www.bosnia.org.uk/news/news_body.cfm?newsid=2643, accessed 30 November 2009.

Further complications arise from the consequences of ethnic homogenization and the *de facto* partition of the state. Following the genocide, the political leadership of Republika Srpska has maintained the ethnic homogeneity of the entity by preventing the return of Bosnian Muslim and Bosnian Croat refugees. At the same time, in the second half of the country, in the Federation of Bosnia and Herzegovina, due to the demographic breakdown caused by the war, ethnic pockets of majority Bosnian Muslim and Bosnian Croat areas are formed. Some larger urban settlements sought to resist ethnic homogenization but with little result. Of the small percentage of refugees who did return to Republika Srpska many are exposed to apartheid-like treatment. So not only do the levels of possible inter group contact vary considerably across the country, but where there is contact there is also the uncomfortable truth that victims may be living cheek by jowl with perpetrators.

Any process of reconciliation consequently must address the desire for Muslims, Serbs and Croats to arrive at an understanding of each other and their common past. It must also address the very specific problems of people who happen to live in neighbourhoods where war criminals, both in and outside the forces of law and order, can be found 'every day in the streets'[48]. As many as one thousand direct perpetrators of the Srebenica massacre for example are estimated to be in the police forces of Republika Srpska (ibid). In such a fractal environment reconciliation cannot be fashioned from the general and universal, but must instead be wrought from the specific and local.

One outstanding example of this is to be found in a remarkable achievement. *Pontanima* (a bridge to the soul or bridge between souls) was established in 1996, as an interreligious choir based in Sarajevo, and has since been widely acclaimed for its unusual and innovative approach to peace making. It offers instructive lessons about the promises and prospects of reconciliation. Pontanima in its practice bypasses the logic of verbal reason and expresses its hopes in the power of spiritual music to heal and reconcile the people of Sarajevo and Bosnia-Herzegovina. To date the choir has managed to gather some two hundred people from different layers and segments

48   Subotić, p. 157.

of Bosnia-Herzegovinian society, held several hundred concerts and made numerous public appearances throughout the country and abroad, receiving in its wake a variety of accolades. Its distinctiveness and its strength lies in the fact that its members belong to different religions, and at their concerts perform spiritual songs from all the four mainstream religions: Judaism, Orthodox, Catholic and Islam. It also boasts in its repertoire a number of Hare Krishna and African-American songs. For the people of Bosnia and Herzegovina, accustomed to the mutual intolerance of official religions this is an exceptional experience. Unique though it now is, its roots lie deep in the cultural soil of Bosnia, a seat of multiculturalism where for centuries people of different religions lived and worked together; a tradition of tolerance disturbed in the second world war and thrown to the wind in the Serbian aggression of the 1990s, a period when the Serbian Orthodox Church allegedly made its own contribution to the dissemination of hatred toward Bosnian Muslims, and endorsed the Milošević regime. For this no apology has been forthcoming and its intolerant stance has abated little.

Fra Ivo Marković, Bosnian Franciscan, professor of practical theology at the Franciscan School of Theology in Sarajevo, is founder of the chorus and also the director and founder of the interreligious service 'Eye to Eye'. The role of the Bosnian Franciscans he believes may be of great significance. They are no interlopers to the scene. The presence of the religious order in the region can be traced back to fifteenth-century Ottoman times. During the Bosnian war, the Franciscans remained loyal to the Bosnian State, unlike the mainstream Catholic Church which aligned its interests with the aggressive Croatian president Franjo Tudjman. The model of change which Marković's work speaks to falls under the umbrella of social diffusion[49] and centres on the key roles which influential individuals can play in specific communities. In the Bosnian context such individuals are likely to be those who, despite extensive propaganda and the threat of force, continued and continue to provide help and assistance to members of the targeted group even though they lie across community lines.

49 S.R. Friedman, D.C. Des Jarlais and T.C. Ward, 'Social models for changing risk behaviour', in J. Peterson and R. DiClemente (eds), *Preventing AIDS: Theory and Practice of Behavioural Interventions* (London: Plenum, 1994).

Such people might be able to provide valuable information not just on the possible characteristics/personal histories of resilient individuals but also, and more importantly for the present context, the opportunities, means and prospects for such people to promulgate changed norms and narratives of the past within their own community. The extent to which such people can play a unifying role is as yet unknown.

Interviewed by one of the authors (EB) Marković was clear about the limits of his own initiative:

> In Bosnia-Herzegovina, reconciliation is first the healing of people, and healing starts from politics, meaning that first the disease called nationalism must be removed.

In matters of reconciliation, says Marković:

> The key lies in communication and cooperation, in the opening of people toward one another by crossing over the differences (to make them) too small to be able to ever create a gap between people again. In my view, reconciliation is a process of removing fear from our Bosnia. We must begin making an environment of reconciliation where every person represents an opportunity in their own right, regardless of their faith, nationality or other orientation.

Where many see religious affiliation as a problem in Bosnian society, Marković sees it differently, explaining why the Pontanima choir was formed he articulated the connection of religions through music, through a mighty symphonic statement which fills the hearts and souls of people with pleasure and joy:

> Religion is the basis of peace in every society, it is what produces perceptions and understandings of the 'different other'. If we see religion as a concept of togetherness, not of separateness, we will understand how alike we are between ourselves. All of us are witnesses: Muslims, Serbs, Orthodox, Gnostic, non-believers, believers, all functioning together, all accepting of each other, all friends to each other, and all singing a symphony of religions.

Music can bring people together and yet in this milieu politics cannot be ignored. Elaborating his understanding of the political situation as an obstacle to effective reconciliation, Fra Marković stated that reconciliation in Bosnia-Herzegovina would remain an impossible goal for as long as the society refuses to accept what has happened. He stressed the importance of a decisive attitude being taken toward those who have committed crimes, and who must be condemned. Accompanying this there must be absolute clarity about who the victims have been. Only then, he opined, can projects leading to reconciliation be truly effective. While the basis for these processes is to be found in politics, contemporary Bosnian society proffers a political world built on the ashes of hatred and intolerance, around identities, rather than a politics of general interests and compassions. Accordingly, political obstacles must be addressed and to do so Marković makes an impassioned plea for outside assistance:

> Only once we remove people such as Milorad Dodik, prime minister of Republika Srpska, the one person who is a motor for evil in our society, a person who uses the same recipe for his actions like Karadžić and Milošević, only then will our society be able to begin healing and reconciliation leading to prosperity and progress. There are good people in politics in this country, too, people who wish to help and achieve something good, who support projects like our own as they know it is an honest initiative worth supporting. There are good people we work with and if we didn't have such good friends our society couldn't possibly survive. Unfortunately, a good many politicians in this country are corrupt. They therefore need ways to hide their criminality, they don't need compassion. They are pursuing a policy of personal interest and abusing identity as a political means, identity in the sense of religion and nation. We were not able to stop the war ourselves and we cannot get through this reconciliation process on our own either.

But Marković also holds the international community responsible for the current condition of Bosnian society and considers the war in Bosnia is still going on, though by different means through political repression and corruption:

> [...] they've been sending only incompetent people to get the job done in Bosnia-Herzegovina, where their actions only produce the opposite effect (to that intended). That's why I'm cross with Europe [...] they've been sending us incompetent administrators, not people who'd do the right thing. Had the international community removed some two-three hundred politicians or rather political criminals, we would have a different society by now.

While Marković puts forward one brand of hope there are stark warnings here for those who think the issue of denial can be pushed aside and that peace and reconciliation in Bosnia is a done deal, awaiting only the smooth passage of time.

Conclusion: Recovery and Reconciliation

Our deliberations have pointed to international and domestic structural, cultural and psychological obstacles to public truth telling, justice and reconciliation. While these difficulties certainly do not contribute positively to creating an environment conducive to people dealing with their losses, either individually or collectively, it would be a mistake to pin all hope of psychological recovery on political process alone. Recovery and reconciliation are not the same. One of the obstacles to establishing peaceful relations in any society which has been riven with conflict is the propensity to consider one's fate as being solely dependent on others. If everyone construes themselves as victims, movement cannot occur.[50] Sometimes the real victims in a conflict have to abandon the apparent security of that position in order to advance – a move that does not mean denying the truth. Over and above the possibilities and prospects of establishing cordial relations between members of Bosnia's different ethnic groups it is important to reflect on the extent to which psychological recovery from the war and its consequences can be considered independently of public truth telling, justice or forgiveness. At present this is an unknown and warrants further investigation. Fra Marković believes that initiatives to rebuild the bridges between communities can proceed, prior to any political initiative, and can contribute to the reconstruction of public space, a necessary part of any healing process. At the same time, he contends, the successful fulfilment of the goals which such initiatives strive for will ultimately depend upon coordinated political action in the domestic and international spheres – this itself will be responsive to a melding of interpersonal social processes with institutional action.

50   Macdonald, op. cit.

LAKSHMAN DISSANAYAKE

Social Reconciliation in Sri Lanka

Introduction

This chapter examines reconciliation activities in post-conflict Sri Lankan society. The consequences of the thirty-year 'civil war' in Sri Lanka have been disastrous, creating development and humanitarian challenges. The majority of Sinhalese, as well as other communities, including most of the Tamils, have welcomed the cessation of armed conflict. However, those involved remain in what is called *conflict trap*.[1] Countries that resolve conflicts peacefully are disposed to continue living in peace. This is more difficult to achieve for other countries, particularly in situations involving diverse ethnic groups, but this does not mean that Sri Lanka cannot work towards peace successfully. One issue is that reconciliation activities are frequently top-down. This overlooks the importance played in them by traditional social structures; I will examine this issue in detail in the chapter. Youth unrest has been central to the conflict. Although some assert that the rights of the Tamils have been denied by the successive governments since independence in 1948,[2] it is important to remember that the majority of Sinhalese have been similarly affected. Sinhalese youth unrest notably erupted in 1971 and was militarily suppressed. This unrest recurred

1   P. Collier and N. Sambanis, 'Understanding Civil War: A New Agenda', *Journal of Conflict Resolution* 46/1 (2002), pp. 3–12. M. Duponchel, 'Can Aid Break the Conflict Trap?' (2008), available online at http://www.csae.ox.ac.uk/conferences/2008-EDiA/papers/316-Duponchel.pdf, accessed 26 August 2010.

2   Chelvadurai Manogaran, 'A Political Solution to the Ethnic Conflict in Sri Lanka', *Refuge* 13/3 (1993), pp. 23–5. A. Balasingham, *War and Peace: Armed Struggle and Peace Efforts of Liberation Tigers* (London: Fairmax Publishing, 2004).

throughout the conflict, noticeably in 1986–9.[3] Reconciliation activity needs to be brought to bear on this central issue.

The Sources of Conflict and its Emergence

The conflict eroded respect for many everyday social values which had previously allowed multi-ethnic communities to live together. These included mutual respect and toleration. The conflict also reduced economic growth, discouraged investment, destroyed human and physical capital, redirected natural resources to non-productive uses, and caused a dramatic deterioration in the quality of life in the entire island.

It is important to acquire an understanding of the issues that contributed to the emergence of the war and its persistence in Sri Lanka in order to achieve effective reconciliation between all the parties involved. It occurred because of a demand for the establishment of a separate ethnic homeland by a militant group among ethnic minority Tamils in the North and East and because of the refusal of successive governments to grant this.[4] Previous contact between the two ethnic groups had not always been hostile. It was, however, occasionally exacerbated whenever external threats from South India transpired. Another factor was the determination of the Sinhalese kings to protect Buddhism and the Sinhalese nation. This can be seen in Sinhala school text books. Children influenced by them grew up with the view that Sri Lanka belonged only to Sinhalese Buddhists.

---

3   J. Uyangoda, 'Social Conflict, Radical Resistance and Projects of State Power in Southern Sri Lanka: The Case of the JVP', in M. Mayer, D. Rajasingham-Senanayake, and Y. Thangarajah (eds), *Building Local Capacities for Peace: Rethinking Conflict and Development in Sri Lanka* (New Delhi: Macmillan, 2003). K. Ratnayake, 'Sri Lanka Elections: JVP in Sordid Alliance to Back Fonseka', World Socialist Website, http://www.wsws.org/articles/2010/jan2010/jvp-jo5.shtml, accessed 26 August 2010.

4   J. Spencer (ed.), *Sri Lanka: History and the Roots of Conflict* (London: Routledge, 1990), p. 247.

The root-cause for the war also goes back to the beginning of about 152 years of British colonial administration. (Africa also has been similarly affected.[5]) Since colonial rule began, a national political movement has existed with the intention of obtaining political independence from the British. This was finally granted in 1948. When the first post-independence constitution was drawn up, extensive disagreements immediately occurred between the majority Sinhalese and minority Tamil communities.

It is also important to note that because English was previously the common official language, all the communities were able to communicate with each other. The first break with this tradition took place in 1936 when a leftist party called the Lanka Sama Samaja party demanded the official replacement of English by the local Sinhala and Tamil language groups. In 1956, the enactment of the Sinhala Only Act significantly paved the way to the ethnic war. At the same time, the emerging Sinhalese national- ist forces perceived that Sri Lankan Tamils had access to an unequal share of power because of favourable educational opportunities they had ben- efited from in the colonial period. As a consequence, the Sinhalese were disproportionately represented in the civil administration of the country. A further consequence was that considerable trade interests were guarded by non-Sinhalese groups in their own interest. These issues were the source of the emergence of a 'politics of language'. It thrust the language issue into the forefront of Sri Lankan politics. The Sinhalese language, along with the Buddhist religion, sought supremacy in Sri Lankan society. In 1987, Tamil was decreed an official language along with Sinhalese under the 13th Amendment to the Constitution. The conflict this caused meant that issues behind the politics of language remain unaddressed.[6]

5   K. Obiekwe, 'In Search of Appropriate Peacemaking/Peacebuilding Paradigm in Dealing with Africa's Intrastate Violent Conflicts: Considering Lederach's Faith- based Conflict Transformation and Peacebuilding Approach', *Journal of Peace, Conflict and Development* 13 (February 2009), pp. 1–27.

6   R. Edirisigha, 'Trying Times: Constitutional Attempts to Resolve Armed Conflict in Sri Lanka', *Conciliation Resources*, http://www.c-r.org/our-work/accord/sri-lanka/ trying-times.php, accessed 26 August 2010.

The formation of the Tamil United Liberation Front (TULF) with its Vaddukaodai Resolution in 1976, which expressed the view 'that minority Sri Lankan Tamils needed separation from the rest of Sri Lanka to resolve their political problems', actually lit the flames for potential conflicts between the two ethnic groups.[7] (The civil war emerged in 1983.) The resolution also claimed that factors such as access to higher education, employment and issues about land ownership had jointly contributed to worsen the distrust between majority Sinhalese and minority Tamils. During British rule, as mentioned above, Tamils were in a more privileged position than the Sinhalese and therefore eligible to attend English language schools. This disproportionately increased their access to higher education and, thereby, they acquired better employment. This was all supported and even encouraged by American missionary activities in the Tamil-dominated Northern Province. Consequently, this resulted in the relative over-representation of Tamils in higher education, the professions and the administration in relation to their numerical presence in the general population. It can, therefore, be argued that post-independence Sinhalese nationalism erupted in order to secure Sinhalese status which was progressively lost during the British Colonial era. For all these reasons, the new constitution in 1972 favoured: Sinhalese language, Buddhist religion, and educational policies which benefitted the majority Sinhalese. Many Tamils were then led to believe that that they were now being treated as an underprivileged community.

Tamil politicians also felt that post-independent land colonization schemes, which were meant to re-settle poor farmers from the highly-populated South-West wet-zone of the country to less populated dry-zone areas in the North-Central province and Eastern Province, were a deliberate attempt to marginalize their communities. This was also regarded as an significant obstacle to the achievement of the 'traditional Tamil homeland'. The Muslim community, which is in the majority in most parts of the Eastern Province and who speak the Tamil language, also completely rejected the claim for the establishment of a traditional homeland.

---

7   TamilNet, 'Vaddukkoaddai Resolution' (Sunday 8 June 1997).

In the face of all this, Tamil politicians modified their earlier claim and proposed a Federal system of governance. Two pacts, the Bandaranayake–Chelvanayagam Pact (1957) and the Dudley–Chelvanayagam Pact (1965), were formulated but never implemented because of contrary political pressures. However, in 1980, the District Development Council Act was passed in Parliament and elections to the councils were held in July 1981. However, the persistent lack of government commitment to the decentralization of power frustrated its purpose. As a result, there were increasing signs that the politics of the Tamil people were changing from a loyalty to parliamentary democracy to a commitment to armed struggle. The latter, for reasons already explained, was favoured by considerable sections of the Tamil youth. Their numbers were the product of a post-war population explosion. They were more educated yet remained unemployed and, of frustration, searched for violent solutions to their problems. By contrast, the Sinhalese youth who took arms only twice in 1971 and during the 1987–9 in the South of Sri Lanka.

The failure to implement these federal measures led to enhanced Tamil demands for separation. A disintegration of confidence in parliamentary politics then became increasingly apparent. The 1977 general election could be regarded as turning point in Tamil politics. The Tamil United Liberation Front (TULF) won an overwhelming electoral success on a stimulating political platform of separatism. They were then the leading opposition party in the parliament.

Although ethnic riots emerged in 1958, 1977 and 1981, the most violent and destructive occurrence of them was in July 1983. Many believe this was a turning point in the conflict. The Tamils were, by then, totally devoted to and united in their pursuit of independence from Sinhalese authority. The major Tamil armed group was the Liberation Tigers of Tamil Elam, popularly known as LTTE. Following 1978, they carried out a series of bank robberies, and subsequently massacres of Sinhalese and Muslim civilians in the border villages. In the 1980s, all this evolved into haphazard bomb attacks in the Sinhalese-dominated South. Consequently, the conflict escalated into a civil war and Indian peacekeeping forces were sent to Sri Lanka in 1987. Tamil majority areas were then placed under direct government supervision, while the Sinhalese majority areas in the North and East of Sri Lanka remained mostly under the control of Sri Lankan forces. The Indian forces were withdrawn in 1990 and the civil conflict between the Government and LTTE resumed in only three months time. The conflict escalated further in the late-1990s into conventional battles being fought to capture territory.

The conflict reached a deadlock by 2001 by when it became clear that neither side were able to advance their political aims merely through military means. The United National Front Government (UNF) and LTTE peace discussions agreed a phased approach to ending the violence, creating a peace dividend, and dealing with the core political issues.[8] International participation in this approach was essential in setting up the peace negotiations. Although they achieved some success, they could not deliver the expected long-lasting peace. This was principally because the Cease Fire Agreement (CFA) allowed both sides to rearm and strengthen their military capabilities. As a result, there were incredibly over 3,000 cease-fire violations. Insecurity then grew in the East due to the emergence of the Karuna break-away faction of the LTTE. It was widely held that that macro economic reforms introduced by the UNF destabilized the economy and led to the perception that the government was unconcerned with the plight of the poor among the Sinhalese. It was however, still hoped that the benefit of a limited peace enjoyed during the CFA would eventually pave the way to a lasting and transformative peace. The absence of a clear long-term plan for peace talks created apprehension among internal and international participants. This was also experienced by the re-emergence of Eastern regionalism and the ever growing radicalization of some Muslims. Although one might expect that, as in Banda-Ache, the tsunami response would provide a space to re-energize peace negotiations, here it proved otherwise. Lingering negotiations about the institutional arrangements for delivering tsunami support were expected to work through the P-TOMS (Post-Tsunami Operational Management Structure) agreement, but it never materialized due to the lack of trust between the two sides. P-TOMS received sharp disparagement from the leftist party Janatha Vimukthi

8   J. Goodhan and B. Klem, *Aid, Conflict and Peacebuilding in Sri Lanka 2000–2005* (Colombo: Asia Foundation, 2005), p. 117.

Peramuna (JVP) which led several protests against the government. This was also challenged in the courts and ultimately P-TOMS was scrapped. The time covered by the CFA came to be seen as a pause in the conflict rather than as significant post-conflict development.[9]

In 2005, the Sri Lankan Foreign Minister, who was a Tamil and greatly esteemed by the local and international community, was assassinated by the LTTE. The international community became increasingly critical of the LTTE following this event. Notwithstanding, following the election in 2006, the LTTE leader warned the government that they would renew their armed struggle if the government did not make clear moves towards peace. This prompted the government to take military action against the LTTE in 2006 when the LTTE provocatively closed the *Mavil Aru* sluice.

From early 2008, the focal point of the war turned towards civilian targets mainly in and around Colombo. These killed a substantial number of innocent people. During this period, the co-chairs of the Tokyo Donor Conference called both parties to the negotiating table. The US was particularly critical of the numerous LTTE breaches of the CFA. As a result, Norway initiated a series of talks in Geneva. These gave rise to a high expectation for peace. Both parties agreed to restrain from violence and hold more discussions. In spite of all this the LTTE resumed its attacks on the Sri Lankan military and further peace talks were cancelled. Nevertheless, in the midst of the continuing war, new talks were scheduled in Oslo, but the LTTE refused to meet with the government delegation over a supposed 'travel issue'. The Norwegian mediator then stated that the LTTE should take the direct accountability for the failure of the talks. The violence which followed raised the question about whether the ceasefire agreement was effective at all. However, most political analysts continued to think that it was and that a return to full-scale conflict was unlikely. As expected, the LTTE continued to carry out attacks against civilians in government held territory. However, in 2007, the whole of the Eastern province was liberated by the government forces. By 19 May 2009, the LTTE was entirely defeated. The UN Secretary General said on that day:

9   Ibid.

I am relieved by the conclusion of the military operation, but I am deeply troubled by the loss of so many civilian lives. The task now facing the people of Sri Lanka is immense and requires all hands. It is most important that every effort be undertaken to begin a process of healing and national reconciliation. I listened very carefully to what President Rajapaksa said in his address to Parliament today. The legitimate concerns and aspirations of the Tamil people and other minorities must be fully addressed.[10]

The final stage of the war created about 300,000 internally displaced persons who were transferred to camps in the Vavuniya district. Over 2,000 LTTE militants were identified by the military. Those who surrendered, including child soldiers, were provided with facilities and were sent to rehabilitation camps. In the meantime, Tamil Diaspora communities around the world have been actively protesting about the Tamil civilian causalities in order to persuade world national leaders that the Sri Lankan government committed war crimes.[11] The thirty years of war tragically killed over 90,000 people. These comprised of 27,639 LTTE, 23,790 Sri Lankan forces, and many more civilians. The Sri Lankan government now states that it is attempting to resettle all displaced persons in their native lands. So far it has resettled over 180,000 displaced civilians in the former battlefields after the areas were cleared of buried mines and explosives. Another 100,000 IDPs still remain in the welfare villages. Meanwhile, the government planned to provide schooling to all children in the war-torn North by the end of April 2010.[12]

10   United Nations, 'Joint Press Conference held by UN Secretary-General and World Health Organization Director-General, Margaret Chan' (19 May 2009), http://www.un.org/apps/sg/offthecuff.asp?nid=1291, accessed 26 August 2010.

11   TamilNet, 'Tamil Diaspora Agitates As Civilian Death Toll Rises' (Monday 11 May 2009).

12   'Sri Lanka Resettles Over 1,000 IDPs in North', Colombo Page (24 February 2010), http://www.colombopage.com/archive_10/Feb1267030305CH.html, accessed 26 August 2010.

What Next?

Identifying Dimensions of Conflict

It is quite apparent that the war which cost so many lives during the last thirty years is completely over and will not immediately recur. However, aspects of the conflict still need to be resolved. Unless this happens reconciliation between the parties will not be totally effective, As they were described in the preceding section, the root-causes of the war were generally clear. However, the foregoing interpretation of the conflict failed to identify the role played in it by the failure of indigenous social structures. The restoration of these will be essential if reconciliation is to be effective and a lasting peace created.

Bandarage rightly claims that it is necessary to look beyond the previously dominant bipolar ethnic approach and take a multi-polar one which recognizes the multifaceted interplay of local, regional and international issues.[13] Although India, the United States, Canada, the United Kingdom and the European Union banned the LTTE as a terrorist organization, they still interpret the Sri Lankan conflict in the majority–minority ethnic framework. At present, this is being further endorsed by the Tamil Diaspora and many NGOs.

It is fairly obvious that the government enfranchisement of the Sinhalese majority has threatened the political and economic rights that the Tamil elite, but not the Tamil majority. The Jaffna *Vellala* caste had enjoyed more political and economic privileges than any other group in the country during the British colonial period. This elite maintained the illusion of there being a majority of Sinhalese against a minority of Tamils in order to safeguard their own interests. They did not do it to further the interests of the majority of ordinary Tamil citizens. This prevented the recognition of

13   Asoka Bandarage, 'The Sri Lankan Conflict: A Multi-Polar Approach', *Harvard International Review* 15 (June 2008), available from http:www.harvardir.org/articles/1725/1/, accessed 10 October 2008.

and action being taken about the common social and economic problems faced by various other Tamil groups. The elite also ignored the important dissimilarities and variations within overall Tamil ethnicity. This was clearly demonstrated when the LTTE were even prepared to use their own Tamil civilians as a human shield in order to protect themselves. Effective reconciliation must redress such sectional self-interest by respecting rights of all Tamil peoples.

More widely, one can argue whether or not the Sri Lankan conflict is a domestic one, or one which reflects a wider regional South Asian conflict.[14] The bipolar model perceives it as a domestic conflict which then ignores its regional relevance. When Dravidian-speaking Dravidasthan lost its fight against Hindi imperialism in the mid-1960s, the hunt for a Tamil homeland moved from India to Sri Lanka. The Sri Lankan Tamil homeland concept under separate Tamil Eelam was then sought by Tamil Nadu politicians who pressurized the Indian central government, through their influence in its coalition, to safeguard the Tamil separatist cause in Sri Lanka.

Lipschutz argues that the settlement of civil conflicts has generally come about not because societies have become 'exhausted' by war, or because people have mobilized in peace movements to demand an end to fighting.[15] They are, rather, the result of the decisions and actions of specific individuals, elites, and groups in who are in positions of power and authority. These act when they realize that there are greater benefits to be had from achieving peace than from the continuation war. This seems particularly appropriate in the case of Sri Lanka. The Tamil Diaspora has reflected this by consistently gaining support from wider interests in the international human rights of their people in the island. Although the battle for a separate homeland was there lost, the Tamil Diaspora has not given up on the establishment of a 'Tamil homeland'. They are currently attempting to set up a 'transnational Eelam government'. In all this, they use their

14   Rohan Gunaratna, *Indian Intervention in Sri Lanka* (South Asian Network on Conflict Research, 1993), p. 55. Bandarage, 'The Sri Lankan Conflict'.

15   D. Lipschutz, 'Beyond the Neoliberal Peace: From Conflict Resolution to Social Reconciliation', *Social Justice* 25 (1998).

international networking to the maximum potential. Their long-established expertise in English-language skills, as well as their access to the internet, are both vital in this endeavour. This does not necessarily mean, however, that the ordinary Tamil poor, who are denied access to such resources, are well served by such aspirations.

The shadows of the prolonged conflict will linger unless the government looks beyond the framework of the ethnic conflict and pays more adequate attention to the fact that the grievances of the impoverished need to be acted upon. The latter are not only peculiar to one ethnic group or race. Tamils whose rights have been denied are similar to ordinary Sinhalese who are in the same situation.

The Need for Social Reconciliation

The word *reconciliation* derives from the Latin word *conciliatus*, which means 'coming together'. Reconciliation entails a process of restoring traumatized relationships between individuals. Prefixing the word with 'social' indicates that the emphasis needs to be on group, and not only individual, reconciliation.[16] John Paul Lederach recognized this when he played a vital consultative role in the conflict resolution process between the Sandinista government and the Miskito Indians on the east coast of Nicaragua in 1988. Outstandingly, his approach is based on actual practice rather than simply grounded in theories. It focuses on what can realistically be achieved in local cultures. Lederach's definition of conflict transformation 'is to envision and respond to the ebb and flow of social conflict as life-giving opportunities for creating constructive change processes that reduce violence, increase justice in direct interaction and social structures, and respond to real-life

16   J.P. Lederach, *Preparing for Peace: Conflict Transformation across Cultures* (Syracuse, NY: Syracuse University Press, 1995), p. 129; J.P. Lederach, *Building Peace: Sustainable Reconciliation in Divided Societies* (Washington, DC: United States Institute of Peace Press, 1997), p. 191; J.P. Lederach, *Little Book of Conflict Transformation* (Intercourse, PA: Good Books, 2003), p. 64; J.P. Lederach, *Journey Toward Reconciliation* (Scottdale and Waterloo: Herald Press, 1999), p. 176.

problems in human relationships'.[17] This further suggests that we need to understand more about the social dynamics of conflict as they were described in the previous section.

According to Lederach, there are three distinguishable hierarchies that are recognizable in any conflict. Namely, those found at its top level, its middle range and the grassroots. The top-level is comprised of an elite group of military, political and religious leaders. This will be small in number but have immense influence because of its high profile. In the middle range, those are found who are not directly controlled by government authority. These include ethnic and religious leaders, academicians and humanitarian leaders of non-governmental organizations. In the Sri Lankan context, many in this group were, in fact, controlled by the government during the war, although they had more freedom than others to express their views. Their status and influence arises from their established relationships relating to familial, professional, institutional and formal friendships and acquaintance. Their peace-building activities and roles draw on these. They include problem-solving workshops, training in conflict resolution and peace commissions.[18] The third level is the grassroots, where the majority of the population is burdened with the needs of daily survival. Leaders in Sri Lanka at this level include those close to everyday society such as government officers, village and other local leaders, teachers and priests. The participation of the grassroots population in social reconciliation processes is vital. They are the always the majority and therefore carry the most widespread and lasting influence.

The brutal aspects of war are still a vivid memory in Sri Lanka. This makes it imperative that strategies are found that will enable the restoration of trust between the two overall communities and the diversity of interests they embrace. This trust largely existed before the conflict, so it is not an impossible ideal. Tamils often once lived with Sinhalese without any conflict. As conceptualized by Krishna Kumar, reconciliation 'is a process that begins with the adversaries' acceptance of each other's right to coexist in war-torn societies. Social reconciliation does not presuppose tolerance;

17   Lederach, *Little Book of Conflict Transformation*, p. 64.
18   Lederach, *Building Peace*, p. 191.

it seeks to promote it'.[19] Social reconciliation interventions are therefore specifically designed to foster inter-group understanding, strengthen non-violent conflict resolution mechanisms and heal the wounds of war.

It is essential to remember the importance of placing social reconciliation in the wider context of overall economic, social and political development. To this end, it has been claimed that a social reconciliation intervention is supposed to realize one or more of the following objectives:[20]

- To prevent or resolve the occurrence of violent conflict by facilitating communication and by developing peace structures
- To reduce deep-seated anger, prejudices, and misunderstandings among the conflicting groups through reciprocal dialogue, cooperative action, and acknowledgment of the past
- To establish or re-establish positive relationships among conflicting parties through communication and cooperative activities.

In all these objectives, clear communication has to be created among the participating groups. To achieve this, the following strategies have been proposed:[21]

1. Uncovering the past
    a. Truth commissions
    b. Indigenous mechanisms of acknowledging the past
2. Promoting dialogue
    a. Problem-solving workshops
    b. High-profile conferences
    c. Conflict management training
    d. Sustained dialogue

---

19   Krishna Kumar, *Promoting Social Reconciliation in Post Conflict Societies: Selected Lessons from USAID's Experience*, USAID Program and Operations Assessment Report No. 24 (Center for Development Information and Evaluation, US Agency for International Development, January 1999), pp. 10–12.
20   Ibid.
21   Ibid.

3. Promoting understanding through media
    a. Documentaries and films promoting mutual understanding
    b. Peace radio and television
    c. Professionalization of media, both print and electronic
    d. Institutional infrastructure for independent media
4. Developing grass-roots structures for peace
    a. Peace committees and commissions
    b. Peace research and training organizations
5. Collaborative activities
    a. Scientific and technical collaboration
    b. Collaborative development interventions
    c. Collaboration in sports, music, and arts

The first strategy, uncovering the past, will not necessarily work in Sri Lanka because the armed conflict was settled with the defeat of the LTTE by the Sri Lankan Army. It could be argued that neither the government nor the captured LTTE members would like to uncover too much of the past, lest painful memories thwart peace initiatives in the future. The Tamil Diaspora, with the help of international participants, attempted to uncover the past through the Tamil Global Forum. A danger here was that they were simply perpetuating their separatist agenda simply by calling attention to past grievances.

Promoting dialogue through problem-solving workshops, high-profile conferences, conflict management training and sustained dialogue are strategies which do not necessarily reach the general public. In Sri Lanka, these are being conducted by non-governmental organizations, professional institutions and private foundations. One doubts whether their effects have trickled down to the bottom structures of the society, to the people who have suffered the most. The media plays a key role in promoting dialogue. It helps to disseminate accurate information and dispel rumours and false propaganda. This beneficially promotes constructive dialogue among large numbers of people. Without this effective reconciliation is impossible.

Sri Lanka realized peace by defeating what some people saw as one of the world's most vicious terrorist organization (LTTE). This organization wanted to divide the country in its own interests. That has been avoided.

However, the Tamil grievances still have to be addressed. This is why a just reconciliation process is needed because it can help both the Sinhalese and Tamil communities to recognize the importance of sustaining peace in both of their interests. Primarily this means providing for their everyday needs. When this is seen to happen, the possibility of recourse to arms is diminished. These needs are experienced by and can only be articulated by local communities. Once this happens the foundations can be laid for national reconciliation. Recognizing this, Lederach claims that peace *building* involves a long-term commitment to a *process* that includes investment, gathering of resources and materials, architecture and planning, coordination of resources and labour, laying solid foundations, construction of walls and roofs, finishing work and ongoing maintenance. He also emphasizes that peace building centrally engages the transformation of basic relationships.[22]

Local societies contain the indigenous means for managing conflict without violence. Respecting these is very important.[23] Local leaders are central to this. In Sri Lanka, every Sinhalese and Tamil village community has its own leaders. They are respected by their communities and no outsiders can influence their communities without their involvement. They hold sway in every community at village level. In addition to this, it is always important to remember that villagers are usually clustered around caste and or other socio-economic groupings. No effective reconciliation can take place unless all this is understood. For example, fishery co-operatives in the North of the island play a very important role in structuring their own communities. Labourers will not do anything without letting *thaleivars* (leaders) know. Similarly, each socio-economic and cultural grouping has its own leader and accepted way of interacting with other interests. Understanding the details of such cultural specificity is an important key to creating lasting reconciliation between not only the main ethnic groups, but also their sub-divisions in Sri Lankan society.

22   Lederach, *Building Peace*, p. 191.
23   L.N. Kubasu, 'Grassroots Approaches to Conflict', presentation transcript (16 October 2008), p. 80.

It is vitally important to remember all this when aid is distributed. Sadly, this is not always the case. So often aid workers work at grassroots level without understanding the cultural structures they encounter. This is why effective aid distribution is of often thwarted at the point of most need. The agencies seem to believe that because they have the funds and logistical apparatus, they can override the local community structures. Even though, they nominally stress the significance of a bottom-up approach by involving local communities, their approach is frequently top-down. This is an all too common reason for their failure. Amid all this, as we have previously noted, it is also important to understand that people at grassroots level are in a continuous struggle to acquire the means of their daily survival. It is, therefore, vital that external aid workers have a proper understanding of the huge worries that conflict has brought to these communities. Most basically, they need to treat people with admiration for their human dignity and with compassion for the seriousness of their needs. If they do not do this, people soon feel that the attitudes aid workers have towards them are humiliating and disrespectful. These feelings can be so strong that they, in turn, lead to the non-acceptance of subsequent reconciliation activities. This is an all too common reason why they fail. This cannot be rectified at the point of failure. For the reasons we have explained, it has to be prevented by a proper understanding of how aid agencies should relate to indigenous social structures in the first instance.

Collaborative activities between members of conflicting groups help to foster positive attitudes among them. This, in turn, paves the way for the development of effective reconciliation activities. This is now happening in Sri Lanka. Various social, cultural and sports programmes have been created in order to construct a bridge of trust between the North and the South. It is intended that such programmes will provide a real opportunity for the conflicting groups to work together in other shared activities. Through such efforts, they eventually come to perceive each other as human beings who can share endeavours and pleasures and not as opponents who distrust everything about each other. These are the basic reasons why even seemingly simple collaborative activities so frequently lay the foundations for lasting reconciliation. One of the ways they often do this in the first instance is in the collaborative provision of basic social services such as child care, recreation, and educationally related activities. Such simple achievements have a huge potential for making possible wider programmes of political, economic and community reconciliation.

The Importance of Strengthening Local Governance Structures

In the preceding we have seen, in some detail, why even basic local customs and practices have to be respected before social stability can be established as a precursor to developing effective reconciliation between previously warring parties. This is now becoming more widely recognized that it was. Morris, for example, claims that peace building

> involves a full range of approaches, processes, and stages needed for transformation toward more sustainable, peaceful relationships and governance modes and structures. [...] To be effective, peace building activities require careful and participatory planning, coordination among various efforts, and sustained commitments by both local and donor partners.[24]

However, it is sadly apparent that local governance structures in Sri Lanka are not being utilized as fully as they should be. This needs to be redressed if deep seated social stability is to be achieved.

In Sri Lanka, the formulation and implementation of policies, strategies and interventions have been exclusively confined to the political bureaucracy. The active participation of the local people for whom public policies, strategies and interventions are formulated and implemented, has been minimal. This has contributed to several negative outcomes. For example, one such has been the failure of poverty-reduction related polices and strategies. The absence of a sense of ownership of them on the part of the poor whom they are intended to benefit has been a common reason for their failure. The prevalent governance culture in Sri Lanka has meant that their cadres consider their accountability to be to their superiors within the politico-administrative system and not to the poor themselves.

---

24 Catherine Morris, 'What is Peacebuilding? One Definition', available at http://www.peacemakers.ca/publications/peacebuildingdefinition.html, accessed 26 August 2010.

A provincial council system of governance was created to help prevent this, but it is not effective.[25] It is however important to recognize that this is not a weakness of the devolution of power in principle but the consequence of only its partial implementation. The two public local governance institutions, namely the Divisional Secretariat and the *Pradeshiya Sabha*, which operate at local level, do not have an effective relationship with each other. The former is headed by a civil servant while the latter is led by an elected member. The Divisional Secretariat largely remains within the central government while the *Pradeshiya Sabha* functions solely under the provincial council system. This is an anomaly in local government that requires the urgent attention of policy makers. Again, it leads to the neglect of local people in decision-making and is, for this reason, a serious problem.

I have previous claimed that the administrative district set-up in Sri Lanka creates weak civil societies.[26] One of the main reasons for this is the lack of understanding among the local people about their rights, duties and responsibilities. Local people are completely unaware of the rights that they have in relation to the functions of *Pradeshiya Sabhas*. Although these people are acutely aware of their needs, they are usually not in a position to express them properly to the local government officers. They are also not aware that some of their needs are universally recognized as basic rights which are included in the country's constitution.

It is more than apparent in all this that there is a need to provide local governance structures not only with more effective powers, but also with the increasing participation of local communities. Only in this way will the peace accords were which signed by the top level politicians/administrators and LTTE top-level authorities, reach into the communities they were designed to benefit in the first place. This is why the accords so often fail in their intention to prevent the recurrence of violence at local level. In addition, frequent party conferences organized by various governments during

25 See Lakshman Dissanayake, 'Participatory Rural Development and Local Governance in Sri Lanka', in Lakshman Dissanayake and Edward Halpin (eds), *Regional Development Perspectives* (Colombo and Chennai: Kumaran Book House, 2010), pp. 145–88.
26 Ibid.

the past thirty years also seem to have not encouraged the vast majority of Tamils to reject the LTTE's separatist agenda. The agendas of these conferences have to percolate to village level before they will ever become effective. This, again, will need to involve the 'village headman' and associated representatives of religious leadership. These leaders are capable of steering their communities through effective consultation processes. There are examples of this happening. The government's development programmes directed to the East and the North, namely *Negenahira Navodaya* (Eastern Awakening) and *Uthuru Wasanathaya* (North Spring) work at village level and address most of the grievances of the people such as food and shelter. For this reason, they proffer better chances of success.

The *Uthuru Wasanthaya* programme was initiated to develop the province according to a well designed community based strategy. Infrastructure development, electricity, water supply and sanitation, agriculture, irrigation, livestock development, inland fisheries, health, solid waste disposal, education, sports, cultural affairs and transportation are some of the important areas that will be covered in this programme. Projects worth Rs. 1010 million have been already allocated. The total cost of developing the A-9 Highway with ADB assistance was estimated to be Rs. 710 million. A total of Rs. 380 million will be spent on the Vavuniya–Horowpathana road and Rs. 360 million on the Medawachchiya–Mannar road. Road construction in relief villages currently housing IDPs is nearing completion at a cost of Rs. 150 million. Electricity will be provided to all houses in the Vavuniya District within the stipulated 180-day period. At present, sixty two percent of the households in the district have access to electricity. It was stated that the process of providing electricity to the remaining areas should commence immediately after they are cleared of landmines. It appears that the Northern Spring Programme is being implemented by officers who come from the area itself and that they are, therefore, fully aware of the needs, aspirations and sensibilities of the people it exists to serve. For all these reasons. it has been claimed that *Uthuru Wasanthaya* programme is a gateway to development, recovery, revival, reconciliation and resuscitation.[27] All this is a shining example of what can be achieved once all local people have a proper say in the provisions for their welfare. As they become effective, reconciliation become a reality through the real benefits people experience from the peace process.

The Role of (I)NGOs at Grassroots Level

Both local and international non-governmental organizations were widely criticized during the war for damaging the image of Sri Lanka by directly or indirectly helping the LTTE and their supporters overseas to achieve their separatist agenda. It was held to be proven that some of the International Non-Governmental Organizations – (I)NGOs – had helped LTTE in various ways to carry on the war rather than helping both parties to terminate it by camouflaging peace building mechanisms.[28] This has now led the government to monitor all the (I)NGOs which operate in Sri Lankan. It now checks carefully, for example, that the (I)NGOs genuinely help Sri Lankan people irrespective their ethnic background.

I have observed[29] that one of the significant causes underlying the failure of adequate and need-based relief and rehabilitation by the (I)NGOs was because relief was considered as 'charity' and the survivors as 'victims'. If the right to humanitarian relief is not recognized as a basic human right it will fail to reach those who most need it. It is, of course, widely accepted that humanitarian aid agencies must respect and protect the dignity of those in need. What it has to do to achieve this is to ensure that the right to get

---

27   T.C. Rajaratnam, 'Uthuru Wasanthaya: A Gateway to Development, Recovery, Revival, Reconciliation and Resuscitation', *Lanka Web* (posted 19 June 2009), http://www. lankaweb.com/news/items/2009/06/19/uthuru-wasanthaya-a-gateway-to-development-recovery-revival-reconciliation-and-resuscitation/, accessed 26 August 2010.

28   Walter Jayawardhana, 'LTTE Used Notorious Norwegian NGO's Vehicles for Military Activities', *Asian Tribune*, http://www.asiantribune.com/?q=node/12428.

29   Colombo University Community Extension Centre, Disaster Relief Monitoring Unit, United Nations Development Program, *The Report on the People's Consultations on the Post-tsunami Relief, Reconstruction and Rehabilitation in Sri Lanka* (Colombo: United Nations Development Programme, 2005).

assistance from both the government and other institutions is recognized without any discrimination based on ethnicity, geographic location, caste, religion and gender.

During the post-tsunami period, it was observed that there were many NGOs and voluntary organizations with little previous knowledge or experience at local level.[30] Although these organizations were supposed to work through the divisional secretaries, they often operated on their own with minimal government interference. almost all the divisional secretaries said that it is very difficult to make these organizations accountable for what they do at grass-root level, ironically, because of the welcome given to them by the desperately affected communities in need. Some case studies carried out by the author in Trincomalee district in 2008 provide an opportunity to understand the impact of humanitarian aid delivery on conflict, particularly in the context of war-affected, tsunami-affected and poverty stricken areas. Other case studies carried out in Vavuniya district, another war-torn district in the North, showed that conflict was actually prolonged because of political interference and discriminatory treatment by authorities in the process of humanitarian aid delivery.[31] However, it is very important to mention here that, in contrast, some people in the district were, at the same time, aware that some (I)NGOs did employ more proper methods in aid distribution. However, the fact remains that some distribution of humanitarian aid had led to prolonged conflict in war-torn districts.[32]

It is evident in all this that humanitarian aid providers must adhere to principles of good governance, transparency and consultation in what they do. They should not leave any room for even the slightest suspicion that some people are treated favourably whilst others are denied what is due to them. This applies particularly to the provision of financial assistance for self-help economic activities. Without proper training and learning from careful viability studies, granting loans or subsidies will not achieve the desired results. To the contrary, it might make the victimized even more dependent on others and thereby prolong their vulnerability.

30   Ibid.
31   Ibid.
32   Amarasiri De Silva, 'Ethnicity, Politics and Inequality: Post-Tsunami Humanitarian Aid Delivery in Ampara District, Sri Lanka', *Disasters* 33/2 (2008), pp. 253–73.

Avoiding Subjective Judgements in Humanitarian Interventions

As reconciliation activities are interwoven with humanitarian interventions during the post-war period, subjective judgements by aid providers are capable of creating more conflicts between and among communities. These are inevitably expressions of opinion which will favour some interests over others. One good example of such a subjective judgement is the dispute over post-tsunami humanitarian aid delivery. The Tamil Diaspora and associated (I)NGOs were of the opinion that the government favoured the South over the North in delivering such humanitarian aid. This is quite possible because the East and North are associated with different caste-based systems. To prevent this, reconciliation and associated humanitarian activities need to be based on careful empirical findings. Examples of these were developed by the author during the post-tsunami period after researching with people in both tsunami and war affected areas.

Natural disasters invariably intensify the pre-existing vulnerabilities of communities already at risk. Poverty stricken groups living in substandard housing, on unstable ground or in flood plains are usually the victims of these disasters. Often these groups have already experienced ongoing discrimination because of their ethnicity, religion, class or gender. It has been pointed out that a number of people, in particular women and members of certain ethnic or religious groups, do not receive equal assistance.[33] Many organizations were engaged in tsunami Relief, Rehabilitation and Reconstruction (RRR) work in Sri Lanka. These often replicated conflicts, discrepancies, malpractices and discriminations in aid distribution. One reason for this was because they used uniform, previously conceived, programmes of delivery. These did not fit many of those victims who had racial, ethnic, language, religious, cultural, geographical, literary and various other differences. Some (I)NGOs often failed to consult survivors and their communities about decisions they made about aid distribution, resettlement and reconstruction. They prioritized their own targets over those which should

---

33   *After the Tsunami: Human Rights of Vulnerable Populations* (Berkeley: Human Rights
      Centre, University of California, 2005), p. 113.

have been drawn up in consultation with those in need. This top-bottom approach adopted by both governmental and non-governmental institutions has, in fact, caused most of the problems encountered in the field.

The conceptual framework developed by in this chapter[34] suggests that districts or affected locations need to be looked at separately when humanitarian aid is delivered. If this does not happen and if the same humanitarian aid effort is carried out everywhere, significant differences in the level of progress made in different districts or locations may be observed.

Southern Polity and Social Reconciliation

It is important to understand that post-civil war societies are significantly more likely to experience civil war again than societies with no prior experience of war. Walter argues that two factors can cause this vicious circle to recur: 1) people feel that continuing life in the current condition is worse than the possibility of death in war; 2) there is a closed political system that does not permit change (except by use of violence).[35] Walter's study also suggests that, conversely, improvement in economic well-being, together with increased political transparency, significantly decreases the risk of experiencing war anew. Therefore, political and economic issues in Sri Lanka need to be addressed in the awareness that that the war affected not only minority Tamil people but also the entire population of the country. The total reconciliation of the country needs to embrace the interests of all. If this is not done, the majority of the Sinhalese and minority groups who live in the South will not accept reconciliation efforts.

As we have seen throughout, the feature in contemporary Sri Lankan society which affects everyone is the legacy of war. This was a civil war which divided people on ethnic lines for more than three decades. It created

---

34   *The Impact of Humanitarian Aid on Conflict in Sri Lanka* (Colombo: Colombo University Community Extension Center, 2008).

35   Barbara Walter, 'Does Conflict Beget Conflict? Explaining Recurring Civil War', *Journal of Peace Research* 41/3 (2004).

many incidents of terrorism, counter-terrorism and human rights violations. However, the victory over the LTTE terrorism would never have
been possible if the government had not promoted Sinhalese nationalism
in the South. This was necessary because the government had put aside a
large budget for the war at the expense of social and economic development
throughout the country. Therefore, people in the South were expected to
bear the high cost of living because they had to make such a sacrifice in
the short term in order to secure a long-term future. For this reason, it
is now argued by the Sinhalese nationalists that a hasty decision should
not be taken to grant further devolution of power to the Tamil minority
areas. The government is now in a strong position to respond to this. Due
to the support of the South, the president won the recent election with a
majority of 1.8 million votes over his major opponent. Therefore, there is
no pressure on the government to take a hasty decision. It needs, rather,
to consult all the parties concerned about creating a sustainable future in
the interests of all. There is an enormous pressure building for this from
the international community, particularly from the West where Sri Lanka
has strong economic, trade and tourism links. The West is also raising a
number of issues in the area of human rights violations. Possible reduction
in Western aid may, however, be compensated by China, India, Russia and
some Middle Eastern countries such as Iran and Libya.

The West has perhaps not fully recognized the Sri Lankan need for
total national security. Its support for the views of the Tamil Diaspora has
influenced this. Therefore, there is an obligation on the part of the wider
international community to help Sri Lanka in its programme of socio-
economic development. The Bosnia-Herzegovina and Croatia experiences
provide good examples of how his can be achieved. In its efforts to restore
peace and rehabilitate the shattered economy of that region, the international community has supported a vast array of projects that concentrate on
micro-enterprises and small businesses, business organizations, and physical
infrastructure. These have the power to generate interethnic cooperation,
thus promoting mutual tolerance and understanding. Activities such as
funding for the improvement of welfare camps, resettling of displace persons, supporting the provincial councils for their development, economic
reactivation projects both in the North and South would be immensely
worthwhile in this respect.

Conclusion

This chapter has shown that the Sri Lankan conflict eradicated many pre-existing social values which are essential in uniting multi-ethnic communities and promoting internal community cohesion. The conflict also reduced the socio-economic development of the country and thus the quality of life of not only of the communities in the North and East but also of all the communities in the entire island. This inquiry into the issues that contributed to the emergence of the war and its persistence in Sri Lanka then explored the factors which are crucial in implementing an effective and strategic social reconciliation process. It has also noted that the rights of both the Sinhalese and the Tamil communities have been compromised. For this reason, effective social reconciliation needs to adopt a rights-based approach across all the communities irrespective their ethnic background. The United Nations Agency for International Development's social reconciliation approach was reviewed and broadly approved.[36] The chapter recognizes the significance of reinforcing local governance structures, and the need for (I)NGOs to work through them at grassroots level. It also cautioned against making subjective judgements about humanitarian intervention which militate against local interests and needs. It also stressed the importance of recognizing Southern needs as the key to effecting effective social reconciliation throughout Sri Lanka. It was claimed that local governance is the proper place where conflicting and diverse interests need to be reconciled and that the participation of local people in this is essential to its success.

I have asserted in this chapter that humanitarian aid providers in Sri Lanka must hold to the principles of good governance, transparency and consultation in the planning and the execution of their work. They should not leave any room for suspicion that some sectors of society are treated by them more favourably while others are denied what is rightly due to them. It is essential to accommodate Southern interests into any social reconciliation effort initiated in Sri Lanka. This is important because the

---

1   Kumar, *Promoting Social Reconciliation*, pp. 10–12.

majority Sinhalese and other minority groups who live in the South will not endorse any reconciliation effort that is only directed towards Tamils in the North. Just as all suffered in the conflict, so all must benefit from the ongoing process of reconciliation.

It has been stressed throughout this chapter that the process of reconciliation between the previously warring communities must be interwoven with the creation of effective programmes of political and economic reform. It has also been shown why none of this will succeed unless it involves consultation with local people. Above all, it has been emphasized that these people must be allowed to speak through the local tribal and village structures which they trust and which serve their interests in ways they understand. The way that disaster aid is distributed must work with rather than against the aims of the reconciliation process.

For all these reasons, I have argued that effective social reconciliation is central, rather than peripheral, to everything that is sought in the peace process. The various national and international agencies that work for peace need to respect this by embracing programmes for its development. This needs to apply to local small-scale initiatives as well as countrywide ones. The development of trust and shared endeavour, which these can create, is an important part of a mosaic which creates support for larger-scale undertakings. Those who labour for reconciliation between the various communities and interests in Sri Lanka need to be involved in all these undertakings. They also need to ensure that people of influence nationally and internationally are constantly aware of them.

DONALD REEVES

Peace Building Is Not for Wimps: Reflections on Progress towards Reconciliation in the Balkans

Monasteries

As my colleague Peter Pelz and I approached the monastery an armed soldier emerged from a camouflaged bunker. He introduced himself as a captain in the Italian army, his soldiers from NATO guarding the monastery 24/7. 'Are you carrying weapons?' he asked. 'No,' I replied, acknowledging the possibility I might be concealing a gun under my cassock. He waved us on to the next check point, and as we stopped again an armoured personnel carrier roared up to the bunker. After more questions and waiting as they checked our passports we were allowed to drive to the monastery, along another wall, to another bunker and eventually we entered a gate into a spacious courtyard and at last saw the great church itself.

We had arrived at Pec, the ancient seat of the Serbian Orthodox Patriarchate in Kosovo. The thirteenth-century monastery with three adjacent churches sumptuously decorated with frescoes stands at the entrance to the Rugova valley. Mountains rear up beyond, their tops capped with snow even in high summer. Pec, the second largest city in Kosovo, after the capital Pristina, is now mostly Kosovo Albanian: the Serb population a greatly diminished minority after the conflict in 1999.

We saw the elderly abbess in a black wimple covering a crown leaving the church after morning service, following the twenty nuns who make up the community of Pec. She made her way towards the convent along a path edged with roses, and noticed our arrival, inclining her kindly and sorrowful face in welcome, fingers counting long strings of prayer beads hanging from her black robes. A timeless image: in dress and manner she might have been walking along this path several times each day for centuries, a scene from a pre-Raphaelite painting, a solemn presence surrounded by meticulously painted roses against the background of an ancient wall.

After she and the nuns had told us about the stress of living under constant threat of violent attack, the importance of the high walls, the necessity of barbed wire and for many more soldiers to protect them we were invited to a generous lunch of soup, curd cheese pie and salad. Several nuns peered at us with curiosity through the kitchen hatch, their faces lined with anxiety. 'We are in a prison here,' the Abbess said, raising her eyes and hands. 'Only as we look to the sky, there is freedom.'

We left the nuns to their daily rituals of prayer in a haven of ancient buildings, walking through un-weeded gardens, un-mown lawns and surrounded by walls beyond which lurked menace. This small group of mostly elderly women lived isolated from the locals, in perpetual fear of them.

From Pec we travelled a few miles to the monastery at Decani which stands in a valley surrounded by thickly forested hills, the air invigorating. A source bubbles from a fountain in the monastery courtyard and runs in a stream by orchards and cultivated fields.

As at Pec we had to run the gauntlet of checkpoints, interrogations and passport examinations. Italian soldiers encased in chunky camouflage jackets packed with ammunition and wielding heavy rifles confronted us at the entrance where bunkers, netting and signs with instructions on the use of fire-arms made the monastery look under siege.

'How do you feel about being here?' we asked the soldiers. 'We are not allowed to talk to you!' they responded with grins, most of them teenagers, but quickly relaxed and chatted in broken English, telling us they came from poor suburbs of Italian cities, that being soldiers was a good option for them because otherwise they would be unemployed.

The monastery is separated from the world by a thick wall which had protected the community living inside from centuries of invasion. A massive heavy door opened onto a cobbled courtyard leading to the church, the best preserved medieval monastery in the region. Living quarters for the monks, the bishop, guests, and workshops surround the courtyard. The monks keep a herd of cows, run a dairy, make cheese, and cultivate large orchards. There are also studios where they paint icons in the traditional style, using gold-leaf.

There are thirty monks in Decani, mostly young and well-educated, and apart from working long hours they rise early for worship, which continues at regular intervals throughout the day. It is a life of rigorous discipline, and, as with the nuns of Pec, following a tradition going back centuries. They also look after guests, listening to them, attending to their needs, unhurriedly, giving their whole attention. This is an important part of what the monastery does, how it relates to the outside world, and we were impressed by the calm manner with which they met the demands of their calling.

Bishop Theodosius, the Abbot of Decani, spent a morning telling us of his determination to preserve 'the holiness' of the monastery, and its traditions and not to allow the municipality of Decani to develop the area for business and tourism. He spoke of the criminal element in the Kosovo Albanian community and how another wall being constructed around the monastery would protect the monks from 'murderers and terrorists'. The Kosovo Liberation Army had been established in this municipality. Veterans of the KLA had made it clear they wanted the monks to leave Decani, and extreme factions wanted to destroy all the Orthodox churches and monasteries in Kosovo. 'The municipality sees the monastery as a problem', the bishop told us. 'It wants the church to be a museum. We have to resist this. Ten years ago they tried to destroy us, but these same people now regard this place as a national treasure, even saying it was built by Albanians.'

The bishop insisted, along with the monks, that the place needed even more protection. They preferred the Italians, because after the war these soldiers had come to the defence of the monasteries telling the KLA, 'if you attack these monasteries we will shoot you.'

We had come to Pec and Decani to see if we could be of help to both sides, bringing the monks, the nuns and the municipalities, Kosovo Albanian and Muslim, together to improve dialogue, build trust and create space for conversations that were not just a list of demands and accusations, but openings for future cooperation and living with mutual respect – in short, to normalize relations. Since the year 2000 the Soul of Europe had gained experience in creating processes of mediation in Bosnia.[1] Per-

---

1   Peter Pelz and Donald Reeves, *The White House: From Fear to a Handshake* (O Books, 2008), describes one such process. See also: Peter Pelz and Donald Reeves,

haps this experience could be useful in Kosovo, a situation complicated both by the ambivalence to our process by the international community (about which more later) and also by the difference of language and culture between the two main communities, the majority of Kosovo Albanians and the minority Serbs, who, before the independence of Kosovo had seen themselves as part of Serbia's majority.

Kosovo Albanians find the monks intimidating in their black cassocks, long hair and beards, and the intensity of their religious devotion, seeing them as some kind of elite, an outpost of Serb authority in their newly independent country. As Muslims the Kosovo Albanians are puzzled by the Eastern Orthodox tradition of monasticism. Few Serbs bothered to learn and speak Albanian, because when Kosovo was part of Serbia they never felt the need. Kosovo Albanians for political reasons, mainly a reaction to the atrocities and ethnic cleansing which Milosevic and Serbia had committed before NATO's intervention, did not care to communicate in Serbo-Croat, although we discovered that many could speak it fluently.

Before visiting the monasteries we had called at the offices of the mayors of Pec and Decani. The mayor of Pec, a medical doctor, offered to give us a few minutes of his time but listened for an hour, along with members of his cabinet who looked more like a friendly posse of bodyguards than an elected group of councillors, all with growing interest and some amazement to our proposal for normalizing relations between the municipality and the monasteries. No one had come to them before with such a proposal. The mayor expressed enthusiasm, pleased to be involved and sensing the tourist potential of the Pec Patriarchate. 'What can we do to help?' he asked. We explained the process of preparing carefully for productive meetings and suggested that to start breaking the ice between the communities he should invite the nuns to his office for coffee. 'Of course, no problem,' he declared. The nuns too were delighted to hear of this invitation, all they wanted was to be able to sit down and talk with the mayor. First we would have to overcome many problems and obstacles.

A Tender Bridge: A Journey to Another Europe (Sheffield: Cairns, 2001); Donald Reeves, *The Memoirs of a Very Dangerous Man* (London: Continuum, 2009).

Given that the nuns had been 'walled-up' for ten years, how would they reach the mayor's office? Would it be safe for them to walk there? Should they be accompanied by a military escort, or would this be regarded as a provocation by the Kosovo Albanian community? Perhaps the mayor should fetch and accompany them. These problems needed to be solved, and we could help.

The mayor of Decani was less independent of his political masters than the mayor of Pec, so despite also being enthusiastic about our proposals, outlined a number of issues that were preventing normalizing of relations between the monks and the municipality. He saw his priority as finding a solution to the unemployment in the region, thirteen thousand out of forty thousand. He wanted to open the land around the monastery to tourism and industry, and resented the monk's resistance to his plans, they did not understand the seriousness of his situation, and were blocking plans to build roads and factories. When we explained our process of preparing for meetings where both sides could discuss productively, rather than making declarations and demands, he realized, as did Bishop Theodosius, the possibilities of reaching agreements through mutually beneficial compromises.

Both sides were eager for us to get started. 'Can we set up a meeting as soon as possible?' Bishop Theodosius wanted to know. We then had to explain in more detail the process whereby such a meeting could only take place after careful and thorough preparation, in which we helped both sides to work in small groups on the nature of the event, its shape, questions and aims. Both sides would have to agree an agenda, decide on the number and status of the participants. We pointed out the significance of these details, also the location and length of the meeting, the lay out of the room. We hoped both parties would agree on a media black-out until after the plenary. Then the Soul of Europe including our Kosovo Albanian and Serb project managers would shuttle between the parties to agree on necessary compromises concerning these 'talks about talks'.[2]

---

2   The Soul of Europe is a small NGO. In the UK it has two full-time members of staff, Donald Reeves and Peter Pelz. In Bosnia and Kosovo we worked with local partners.

After the meeting there would certainly be difficult matters still to be resolved, issues raised there which would not find immediate or easy solutions or agreements, such as property rights and security. A number of working groups would then be set up made up of Kosovo Albanians and Kosovo Serbs who would meet separately and then bring their reports to the next plenary.

Given the regional and international significance of the monasteries, not only for the Serbian Orthodox Church, but for Kosovo's cultural heritage, the Soul of Europe would meanwhile search out influential opinion formers and leaders in Kosovo, Serbia and beyond who would publicly support this initiative; some we had already identified and met. These would become allies of the process. We would also identify the spoilers, some of whom the bishop had mentioned. Spoilers left out of the process could create mischief. If they were approached to find out how they could be involved, at least what they were doing would be known. It would not be for us to confront the spoilers on both sides: not only extreme members of the KLA, but some might come from within the monasteries themselves, people who could not accept the independence of Kosovo and whose aim was eventual reunification with Serbia. These negotiations would have to be undertaken by moderate Kosovo Albanians and Kosovo Serbs.

We reminded the mayors, the bishop and the monks and the nuns that the Soul of Europe took inspiration from the words of Nelson Mandela to the Northern Ireland political leaders: 'If you want to make peace, do not speak to your friends. You must speak with your enemies.'[3]

The mayors had guaranteed support. The bishop, moved by these words, remained silent for a while before announcing: 'This is a holy idea. I respect your efforts, your maturity and energy. Feelings are important, what is in your heart. We need this process you are offering.'

In Kosovo we work with the Pro Peace Initiative and in Serbia with TransConflict. See www.soulofeurope.org.

3   Nelson Mandela's words express the aims of the Soul of Europe, working in post conflict situations in the Balkans.

Also the Abbess of Pec was silent for a long time before responding, looking directly at me: 'Yes. Please come.'

We had achieved our first objective: to be invited to create a process of peace building between the monasteries and the municipalities. Without this invitation we could not and would not have returned.

There are no short cuts in the preparations of a peace-building process. Before our first visit to Kosovo we had to obtain the support of the highest authority in the Serbian Orthodox Church, as well as the government of Kosovo. Therefore I visited the headquarters of the Church, the Patriarchate in Belgrade and received the blessing of the 'acting' patriarch, Archbishop Amfilohje. I also had a useful meeting with Dr Mohamed Hamiti, the Kosovo ambassador to the UK. Both the archbishop and ambassador used identical words: 'It will not be easy, but it is certainly worth doing. Good luck.'

Following these meetings we wrote to the monasteries and municipalities:

> The Soul of Europe is encouraged to produce a plan for implementing a process of peace building. We are very grateful to all those who gave their time to meet us. We are conscious that all whom we met had significant obligations, so their time and attention was most appreciated. We are also aware that many of the issues raised, particularly those issues about land and property at Decan/Decani and Peja/Pec are already being addressed elsewhere. But as far as we can tell there is no process in which these issues and particularly underlying attitudes are being addressed. A successful outcome to the peace building process will be when the monastic communities at Peja/Pec and Decan/Decani and the municipalities recognize they are truly neighbours, thus contributing to the flourishing and well being of the region.[4]

For our part we had to remember the huge significance of Pec and Decani not just for their manifestation of Serbian orthodox culture but also a culture which informs what it means to be Serb. 'Destroy these monasteries and we will be nothing,' we have often been told.

---

4   In correspondence with both Kosovo Serbs and Kosovo Albanians we use the Albanian and Serb spelling of places.

When Patriarch Irenje was enthroned on 23 January 2010 he said: 'Our first duty is to safeguard our Kosovo, a holy and martyred land, to help our state to defend it from those who wish to seize it. Kosovo is our Holy Land, our Jerusalem. We must go to Pec to complete this ceremony, but can we visit our relics? Without them Serbia is not Serbia; without Kosovo it is deprived of heart and soul.'

As we began to establish foundations for the project the question arose: 'how was it to be funded?' Given the invitation from Kosovo Albanians and Kosovo Serbs it seemed natural to approach the many international organizations working in Kosovo, particularly the European Union. By February 2008 the EU had donated almost €2 billion to Kosovo and from 2007 to 2010 more resources had been earmarked than for any other region in the world: around €330 million.[5]

The Republic of Kosovo was established in February 2008 and declared its intention of being a modern democratic state in which all ethnic groups and religions were welcome. We assumed the EU and other international organizations would be interested to support our process. We were mistaken. Our approach was not welcomed. No international organization expressed interest in the Soul of Europe's initiative. It was greeted with indifference. Here is a sketch I wrote which describes the reaction typical of the meetings we had with people whose interest we hoped to engage:

5   From a press statement from the EU Press Office, February 2008.

AN OFFICE IN SOME ORGANIZATION

DR, PP, our partners in Belgrade/Pristina and a Spokesperson: third secretary/ researcher/assistant at embassy/major foundation/European Commission

Spokesperson: Thank you for coming in (*indicating we should sit opposite at a spacious empty table. Sometimes someone in the corner is poised to take notes*).

DR: (*Looking around disappointed to see if the director/ambassador or first or even second secretary is available.*) Thank you for seeing us.

DR gives a by now well-honed, persuasive and lucid presentation of the Monasteries Project, explaining how we intend to normalize relations between the Serb Orthodox monastic communities, now protected in their enclaves by heavily armed Italian soldiers, and the surrounding mainly Kosovo Albanian municipalities; and concludes by asking if the spokesperson has ever visited Decani or Pec.

S: (*Only slightly embarrassed*) No unfortunately I have not. But thank you for your presentation. This is a most necessary and important project. Something should happen. (*Pause*) Your valiant work of peace is admirable. I am very sorry our Director/Ambassador is not here. He/She is travelling (*even though we fixed a date some time ago and we were promised a meeting*). Unfortunately we are not able to offer funding since our funds are already allocated for the next twelve months.

DR: Could I ask why you cannot help us, if this work is, in your words, so important and necessary, and no one has ever tried to do this before?

S: (*defensively*) We must tell you that we are already supporting many
       people who work in this field.

DR: Really? Please tell us about them! We would love to meet and learn
       from them.

Embarrassed pause

S: Your project is very difficult, and....

DR: (*interrupting*) Isn't that just why this work is necessary?

S: (*looking uncomfortable and defensive*) Well, we don't fund religious
       projects, much as we would like to...

DR: Of course there is an inter-faith aspect to our work. I am an Anglican
       and we will be bringing together Muslims and Orthodox Serbs. But
       there is more to it than this. This is a project about:

       Democratization – people taking charge of their situation
       Security – ensuring the protection of minorities
       Human Rights – freedom of movement (*the Spokesperson shows
       more attention, we are on more familiar ground*)
       Public Relations – good for Albanians and Serbs, and the chance of
       long-term Economic Development for pilgrims and tourists

S: Yes, that is very interesting. (*The secretary writes something*)

DR: And of course we shall look out for allies and spoilers.

*Donald then explains the mapping exercise in which allies and spoilers will be
identified and brought into the project. The spokesperson looks nonplussed.*

Pause

S: I have to go now. Do keep in touch. We have much to learn from
       you.

The secretary stops writing and stares at us blankly.

*The spokesperson stands up from behind the table. We shake hands and
leave.*

S: Good luck.

Throughout our work in Bosnia we learned about the reasons for this
indifference: the work of conflict transformation which I have been describing is regarded as too risky and unpredictable, too long-term, too emotional,
too complex to squeeze into planning boxes with measurable concrete
outcomes. In a word the process is too 'difficult'.

Kosovo 1999

To understand this anomaly further (after all, don't we all want peace?) I
will describe in more detail the situation in Kosovo. Kosovo belongs to that
part of our memory which is the day before yesterday. It has slipped into
the black hole of our consciousness. The events leading to the intervention
of NATO in 1999 seem distant; the circumstances of the intervention are
unlikely to be repeated. The invasions of Iraq and Afghanistan have made
future interventions considerably more questionable. There are many arguments for and against the right to intervene. In the case of Kosovo was it
an example of 'Western Imperialism' or a matter of 'taking responsibility
to protect innocent victims of oppression'? NATO's intervention has since
been judged a success. Milosevic's attempt at ethnically cleansing Kosovo
of its non-Serb majority failed.

The four-month conflict ended in June 1999. By then Kosovo had ceased to function on any social, economic or political level. Towns were deserted, shops shuttered. Smoking ruins lined the streets; there was no water, no work. Revenge attacks continued the destruction and murder. Dead bodies lay around along with garbage. For a while people starved, they could not lay their hands even on a loaf of bread. Children did not attend school. Most of the livestock in the countryside had perished. Mines made the fields unsafe to plough. Kosovo lacked any institution of governance, the rule of law, public service structures and a functioning economy.

To make this bad situation even worse hundreds of thousands of Kosovo Albanians, the majority, who had been forced to flee returned to their homes, only a minority being welcomed in Europe. At the same time one hundred thousand Serbs (half of the Kosovo Serb population) were also forced out of their homes. This mass movement of peoples was accompanied by inter-ethnic violence, rapes, tortures and revenge killing.

Kosovo is not a large region – roughly the size of Devon and Cornwall together. The UN was authorized to reconstruct a new Kosovo. Fifty thousand troops were deployed to keep the peace, one NATO soldier for every forty Kosovars. Other organizations were authorized to oversee the reconstruction of the economy, the development of democratic structures and the creation of police and an independent judiciary.

With impressive speed an infrastructure was created so within months of the end of the conflict and before the onset of a long hard winter, schools reopened, many roads were repaired, homes re-roofed, postal services and telecommunications began to function. Along with the UN and other major institutions like the Organisation for Security and Co-operation in Europe a vast army of bureaucrats, experts and around five hundred NGOs appeared.

Over ten years later (at the time of writing) the energy and determination of the 'internationals' has evaporated. The North of Kosovo, mostly Serb, looks to Belgrade for support and refuses to cooperate with Pristina. Serbia has consistently declared that it will never recognize Kosovo as an independent state, and the legitimacy of the declaration of Kosovo as a republic has been questioned. Sixty-six countries have recognized Kosovo, but the refusal of several super-powers, Russia foremost, backing Serbia, means that Kosovo's independence remains in question.

These matters occupy the attention of analysts, commentators and Balkan watchers, while the lives of the people of Kosovo show few signs of improvement. The country is the poorest in Europe. Unemployment is officially 40 per cent but most figures show that up to 70 per cent of young people have no work and no prospects of work. Many would leave if they could. There is virtually no market economy. Families survive on money sent from abroad by those lucky relatives who managed to find asylum, or who were already working there.

It is therefore no surprise that increasing numbers of Kosovo Albanians want to see the back of 'internationals'. The unemployed resent the considerable international presence visibly privileged and protected, driving around in gleaming white four by fours.

These international organizations have the task of advising, monitoring, supporting and mentoring initiatives to create with the Kosovo authorities what Peter Feith, the equivalent of the High Representative in Bosnia, calls 'the promise of a homeland for all'. A parliament was established in 2008 after the Declaration of Independence but Kosovo MPs are limited in their powers. Ultimately that is rested in the International Civilian Office and the European Union special representative: Peter Feith. After ten years what is there to show for the huge resources poured in Kosovo?

It is beyond the scope of these reflections to chart the ineffectiveness of these international organizations. But a report by the Institute of Democracy and Cooperation: *Ten Years of International Administration, One Year of Independence: An Appraisal* makes a trenchant comment:

> The various international and national institutions each claim their own share of legitimacy. Tensions are numerous between the international institutions, and the Kosovo authorities know how to exploit this... so the goal of the internationals is to prolong the status quo as long as possible without Kosovo undergoing any real change.

This 'do nothing' approach is particularly pertinent where the situation of minorities is concerned.

A highly critical report by Minority Rights Group International (November 2009) maintains that minority communities are beginning to leave due to persistent exclusion and discrimination. The report: 'Filling the Vacuum: Ensuring Protection and Legal Remedies for Minorities in Kosovo' demonstrates the emptiness of statements by members of the international community asserting the multi-ethnic character of Kosovo. So, for example, a meeting of the EUs general affairs and community relations council 'noted with satisfaction the initial results achieved by the European Union Rule of Law Mission in assisting the Kosovo authorities in consolidating the rule of law, and in contributing to a safe and secure environment for all inhabitants regardless of their ethnic origins.'[6]

The report describes how 'a lack of political will among majority Albanians and poor investment in protection mechanisms have resulted in minority rights being eroded or compromised in the post-independence period' – and not just for the Serb minority; also for the smaller minorities: the Bosniaks, Egyptians, Ashkali and Roma communities.

What has happened since 1999 is that the international community has allowed and tacitly encouraged a segregated society to develop and become entrenched. The Ahtissari Plan[7] which prepared the way for the eventual declaration of independence further legitimized this segregation, so that the Serbian Orthodox monastic communities were to be independent from their municipalities, guarded and protected as though they were Serb territory within a sovereign Kosovo state. The international community has ignored the difficulties faced by minorities, but proclaims success with respect to their protection. There is little political will to reconnect segregated minorities which now exist in enclaves where poverty is endemic to the mainstream of Kosovo's public life.

Thus when a small but experienced NGO like the Soul of Europe is invited by the people themselves to help 'normalize' the relations between the minority Kosovo Serbs and majority Kosovo Albanians our analysis appears to contradict the 'all's well' picture and therefore our activities call into question the validity of the 'do little, do nothing' approach.

6   Ian Bancroft's 'The Flight of Kosovo's Minorities' (on *The Guardian*'s website section Comment is Free, 3 June 2009) is the source for the quote from the EU General Affairs and Community Relations Council.

7   Martti Ahtissari, a former president of Finland, was the UN special envoy to Kosovo. His team produced the blueprint for the Kosovo constitution.

Representatives of the international community, from the Council of Europe to embassies and philanthropic organizations, all met with us unwillingly and were unhelpful, not even proposing possible contacts.

Our experience in Bosnia and now in Kosovo has revealed to us another reason for the international community's reluctance to support this work: peace building, as opposed to peace keeping, is a countercultural phenomenon. It goes against the grain.

Against the Grain

Over ten years we have discovered six requirements for those committed to peace building:

A positive orientation is essential. This is nothing to do with being a cheerful optimist. There is often very little to be cheerful or optimistic about. It is about having a conviction to search out and nurture hope that lies buried even in the bleakest of situations. I have met too many internationals who are disengaged and cynical: 'done it all; seen it all.' We were told several times by different people, including a British diplomat: 'At least the Kosovars are not killing each other.'

An accurate perception of human nature is necessary. This requirement may seem too abstract, but such perception affects the way the work is undertaken. This perception recognizes the potential for nobility, goodness and selflessness, but also the potential for greed, selfishness and appalling acts of brutality. Acknowledging these contradictory notions of human nature recognizes life as it is and creates a pragmatic approach to solutions. This kind of understanding bears no relationship to the reductionist, mechanistic and materialistic interpretation of human nature expressed in 'management speak' by international organizations.

The peace builder is required to work with everyone, fairly and equally, even where there is no justice and where war has left a society shattered. It is exactly in these difficult circumstances where peace building is needed most, and there will always be 'spoilers' from both sides, who try to disrupt the process. I referred to these above in my presentation to Bishop Theodosius, how they must become part of the process and how the participants themselves deal with them. No one must be left out. For example: in 2001, when we were painstakingly bringing the religious leaders in Bosnia to cooperate with each other, a member of the EU parliament expressed disgust that we were being too fair to the Serbian Orthodox bishop. As far as she was concerned he had been directly responsible for the ethnic cleansing; he had influence and could have stopped it. She refused to speak or have anything to do with him. There is of course the issue of bringing the bishop to justice, and this is what she as a politician and the EU needed to do. That was her task. However she could do little to influence the political circumstances in Bosnia, agreed and signed in the Dayton Accord, so she preferred to stand apart from our process, pontificate and take a 'moral stand'.[8]

Attention to process. The process affects the quality of the outcome so the way the work is planned, and at each stage reflected on, is crucial. There are dilemmas about the relationship between justice and peace. Certainly there can be no peace, no reconciliation without justice being done. On the other hand, peace builders have to work in particular situations doing what they can to normalize relations as fast possible in the knowledge that sooner of later the wheels of justice will have to start turning. The stability which peace builders help to create may be limited, but it is certainly better than nothing and may create the conditions where something like a Truth and Reconciliation Commission could be established. Moreover, as Archbishop Tutu has remarked: 'Never underestimate the importance of a handshake.'

Time has to be taken for careful listening on all sides. In Bosnia we discovered three 'movements' in conversations round the table. The first is 'blaming the other'; the second is more reflective where each party considers its own situation and the third happens when the parties begin 'to stand

8   Nigel Biggar (ed.), *Burying the Past: Making Peace and Doing Justice After Civil Conflict* (Washington, DC: Georgetown University Press, 2007), explores this dilemma.

in the shoes of the other'. For disagreements to be solved a step taken away from the adversarial is essential. In practice the process is messy and not so clear cut. The 'movements do not progress as easily as I have described. And before these conversations get under way, those who have been invited to be bridge builders need to be trusted; we had to assure our Bosnia friends (as they became) that we were not researching for a PhD on post-conflict trauma etc, proselytizers, or even spies for the CIA.

Time is needed: plenty of time. Bringing former adversaries round the table, particularly after a bloody war, and creating webs of former enemies so they become partners takes time and infinite patience. As with all human relationships, building trust, even between friends, cannot be hurried. Time is needed to imagine and create webs of relationships within the life of communities, at the grass roots, but also at the middle range, among professionals, teachers, lawyers and business people, those responsible for building society.[9] People at the top, religious leaders, politicians and diplomats, find it easier to meet, usually at lavish expensive locations, to have satisfying discussions and sign agreements declaring peace and reconciliation. Such gatherings may have a positive purpose of keeping the issues in the public eye, but disappointment at subsequent failure to carry out what is agreed tends to make the situation worse, leading to resentment and despair. Rarely is there an attempt to link the top to the grass-roots. Hence the concept of the web, reaching out and across every corner of society. That is where the difficult work lies. Time has to be taken to recollect and treasure nostalgia for a past when life was different. In Prijedor in Bosnia, place of some of the worst ethnic cleansing during the Bosnia War, Serbs, Muslims and Croats expressed nostalgia for a time when all communities shared this once beautiful town and surrounding landscape, churches and mosques side by side, without thought of conflict. In Pris-

10   John Paul Lederach is the Professor of International Peace Studies at the Institute of Peace Studies at the University of Notre Dame, Indiana. His writings have been a major inspiration for our work: '[...] the pursuit of social change initiated through spatial strategies and networking. This strategy identifies, reinforces and builds social spaces and intersections that link individuals, groups, networks and organizations formally and informally across the social divide, sectors, levels and geographies that make up the settings of protracted conflict.'

tina we met Skender Boshtraka, a former Minister of Culture, Youth and Sport. He described an idyll of holidays in Decani where children from all over the former Yugoslavia, from all ethnic and religious groups, Muslim, Orthodox and Catholic, came to spend the summer months, helping the monks on the farm, spending evenings round camp fires. These memories are a foundation for working towards a positive future.

These fresh understandings do not just happen. A skilled mediator is needed to help the healing process, particularly where there has developed a culture of demonizing each other, a consequence of war and atrocities. Without a mediator such healing tends to be deferred indefinitely, the perpetrators trying to avoid their culpability by declaring that healing can only take place in future generations. They are wrong: unhealed traumas lie dormant until a generation grows up with no memory of war and its deprivations, only with the burden of revenge and scores to settle and prepare for even worse wars and traumas. In this case time is of the essence. But even so, the mediator has to be given all the time needed to help the adversaries to understand each other. And the process takes time. 'As long as it takes' as George Mitchell said about the peace process in Northern Ireland.

Pay attention to religion. Over ten years we have met just a handful of international people who took the trouble to attend Friday prayers or the Serbian Orthodox Liturgy. Churches and mosques are routinely described as 'cultural heritage' as it its clerics were museum keepers. There is considerable suspicion about religion among internationals: religion may encourage extremism and sanction violence. The EU professes 'neutrality' about religion, because of the unspoken belief in the clear Enlightenment doctrine of universal liberties; so there is much suspicion of religious propaganda and proselytizing, and working with religious organizations which are committed to beliefs not universally held.[10]

11   In a lecture given at the Royal Society of Arts on 12 November 2009, 'New Perspectives on Faith and Development', Rowan Williams, the Archbishop of Canterbury, urged NGOs working in development to acquire 'a better level of religious literacy', adding that there is a need for 'a deepening fluency in the language of religious discourse'.

The Soul of Europe regularly met with religious leaders in Bosnia. On one matter they were agreed: they all felt slighted and ignored by the international community. This is a serious mistake because more than politicians, religions (not so much the mosque worshippers or church goers) identify and strengthen the identities of different ethnic groups. But religious leaders should also reflect critically on their own failure to provide witness to the fundamental values of their respective faiths.

Peace Building: Has It a Future?

Peace building is too important to be left to independent NGOs. Governments are already beginning to renege on their commitments to 'making poverty history' and development projects are finding it difficult to secure funding. Peace building is the poor relation. So any strategy where military intervention is being planned needs to include peace building. This means establishing working relations between the military and civilian peace builders. In other words, the sort of processes that have been described needs to be established as soon as it is safe to do so.[11]

There is now a considerable body of experience and knowledge about conflict prevention, conflict resolution and conflict transformation. Throughout the world there are some four hundred Universities, Colleges and Institutes for Peace Studies offering courses and study in the roots of armed conflict and terrorism and the preparation of war. Peace building initiatives of the sort I have been describing need to draw on this growing body of knowledge and be properly resourced and funded, as they are no longer regarded as an 'add on' but can make a substantial contribution to the rebuilding of communities.

1   These ideas are developed in Scilla Elsworthy and Gabrielle Rifkind, *Making Terrorism History* (London: Rider 2006), pp. 75–6.

Peace Building: More than a Job

Peace building is not glamorous. The outcomes are always uncertain, because the future of the processes I have described lies in the hands of the people. As catalysts and mediators our role is limited. It is not up to us to impose solutions, and in any case peace building is always unfinished: there will always be more to say and to do long after we have left.

Stamina, patience and a willingness to work with those whom we would not normally wish to meet, because of what they have done or thought to have done. These are qualities which need to be fostered alongside the developing of professional skills: analysis, facilitation, process etc. There is always risk in this work, because as the possibility of peace or reconciliation begins to emerge, it feels safer to remain in the familiar world of recrimination, blame and revenge. Beyond these boundaries the landscape is unclear.

So why do this work? Because peace building is more than a job. It is a vocation which is not so much a goal to be pursued as a calling that is heard. It is a prompting. That prompting is born out of the moral imagination, that capacity to bring to birth something new, something unforeseen which suggests a shared future into which those former enemies step towards a horizon on an epic journey striving for connection and community. The developing and nurture of the imagination keeps that prompting fresh and vibrant.[12] And yet for all the newness which the idea of the imagination suggests, whenever a moment of reconciliation is reached it seems as if it had always been like this – the enemies now together round the table. We had just forgotten what it was like.

2   See John Paul Lederach's *The Moral Imagination: The Art and Soul of Building Peace* (Oxford: Oxford University Press, 2005) and a lecture I gave at Lambeth Palace on 18 May 2006 on the Moral Imagination. I draw strength from philosophers and theologians, who particularly treasure the imagination, such as Paul Ricoeur.

So when the nuns of Pec and the monks at Decani sit together with their new Kosovo Albanian friends, then for all the seeming impossibilities of ever reaching such a conclusion, it will in the event be a natural, beautiful and graceful celebration. To have had some part in bringing former enemies together is a privilege. It is certainly worth the struggle, the betrayals, the indifference, the cynicism, the threats of violence, the apathy and the pessimism which we will have encountered on the way.

Peace building is not for wimps.

R. JOHN ELFORD

Concluding Reflections

This book has accepted the fact that some military interventions are a sad necessity of last resort in the modern world. The reason for this is that, though they use force, they are intended to establish peace. The means by which this is achieved are, of course, the classic subject of scrutiny in just war theory. We have referred to them in passing throughout. They broadly focus on last resort, proportion and discrimination. All war is wretched and to be avoided in any but dire circumstances. Just war theory exists to facilitate the identification of those and to control the use of force once it is engaged. It recognizes that there are some circumstances of human conflict that are worse than those of a limited warfare which can be used to bring about their cessation. In this sense, war can never be anything other than a sad necessity of strictly last resort. Of course, establishing the possibility of such justice does not settle all the questions which have to be asked before military intervention can be justified. Disputes about them invariably remain long after interventions have taken place. Many of these focus on the nature of the authority which is required before intervention can take place. Here, the role of the United Nations and the status of its resolutions are, invariably, controversial. Our not discussing any of this in this book does not mean that we overlook its importance. It is a subject that needs constant attention. The legal and other expertise that its discussion requires is not particularly found in this volume. Here, it has simply been accepted that some interventions will be necessary, whatever that might precisely mean in any given instance. We have, therefore, focussed on what then has to be done to bring about their lasting cessation and restore civil-society in their aftermath.

There have been two *foci* in all this. The first is the recognition that there are now numerous instances in which reconciliation activities which bring together warring parties in the search for peace have achieved tangible success. The second is that, because of this, arrangements for reconciliation, peace building and post-conflict reconstruction must become a premeditated part of the conditions that have to be met, as a matter of moral requirement, before military interventions can be considered to be just. As the experience gained in the aftermath of the invasion of Iraq has poignantly shown, it is mistaken to believe that peace building follows the cessation of hostilities automatically. It does not. It has to be planned for, preferably well in advance of military intervention. An emphasis in this book has been to stress that this must now happen as a matter of moral requirement.

Conflict no longer ceases as a consequence of once-and-for-all military victory. This point deserves a little more attention before we return, in conclusion, to our main themes.

The way in which conflict ceases has changed dramatically in the modern world. There are many reasons for this but one stands out. It concerns the nature and role of modern military force. Wars no longer cease when one side wins a decisive victory over the other which it reduces to surrender by dint of might. In a recent influential study of the use of force in the modern world by General Sir Rupert Smith, this is described as 'industrial war' and identified as a thing of the past.[1] The two world wars of the last century ended in this way, at particular times on specific dates. There was no doubt about their having ceased, particularly when Japan surrendered after the last one. Moreover, it was expected all along by both sides that the conflict would end in this way. In, that is, final decisive and indisputable victory. Every effort of the war, was directed to this end by both sides. Incredible levels of armaments were achieved, constantly developed and maintained right up to the end. Everything was sacrificed to this purpose. Materials were requisitioned, labour forces were marshalled and valiant sacrifices endured. Nothing was spared. Everyone understood that there was no alternative to what was required. This was the achievement of

3   Rupert Smith, *The Utility of Force: The Art of War in the Modern World* (London: Allen Lane, 2005), pp. 78–90.

outright victory by one side followed by the formal surrender of the other. Maintaining and building the existence of such force, was also held to be a deterrent to a possible aggressor in the first place. Its might and readiness were of its very essence. Little wonder that when opposing sides subscribed to these practices, conflicts which did occur were bloody, prolonged and all-consuming. *Blitzkrieg* by one side and area-bombing by the other were two terrifying manifestations of this.

This is the classic story of war which culminated in the two Great Wars of that last century and finally in the dropping the bombs on Hiroshima and Nagasaki in 1945. Rupert Smith comments that this paradigm on interstate industrial war was 'literally blown to pieces on August 6th 1945'.[2] The then demonstrated awesome power of mass destruction made it unequivocally clear that war could no longer be waged by dint of industrial might and technical innovation. He adds that it is an irony of history that the future of industrial war was ended because of its very nature. The East/West Cold War that followed was the stand-off recognition of all this. This is, of course, still chillingly the case between nuclear weapons states throughout the world. We cannot, therefore, be at all sure that the horrifying lessons of twentieth-century history have been learned. The consequences of having to learn them again do not bear even thinking about. Ironically, again, as has been often observed, all this has seemingly made the world safe for lesser and innumerable conflicts. These have now established a new paradigm of warfare. It has not eradicated forever the spectre of the old one. This is why the world is now such a dangerous place. It has, however, created the proliferation of wars of a very different kind. These are localized conflicts. They are caused by often long-standing territorial and ethnic differences and grievances, tribal conflicts, or the collapse of civil government as a result of internal unrest. Whatever their cause, however, they are all markedly different from the industrial wars of the last century.

4   Ibid., p. 146.

Rupert Smith has analysed this difference and coined a name for it. He says that they are all different on one respect from industrial war; they are fought intra-state 'amongst the peoples'. He writes that after the blocs of the old Cold War ceased their former confrontation, 'these latent conflicts began to emerge – in many parts of the globe but especially in the Balkans and throughout great swathes of Africa – and in most cases they were intra- rather than interstate: amongst the people'.[3] This new paradigm of war amongst the people (WAP) is characterized by six major trends. He writes:

> The ends for which we fight are changing from the hard absolute objectives of inter-state industrial war to more malleable objectives to do with the individual and socie-ties that are not states.
> We fight amongst the people, a fact amplified literally and figuratively by the central role of the media: we fight in every living room in the world as well as on the streets and fields of a conflict zone.
> Our conflicts tend to be timeless, since we are seeking a condition, which must then be maintained until an agreement on a definitive outcome, which may take years or decades.
> We fight so as not to lose the force, rather than fighting by using the force at any cost to achieve the aim.
> On each occasion new uses are found for old weapons: those constructed specifically for use in a battlefield against soldiers and heavy armaments, now being adapted for our current conflicts since the tools of industrial war are often irrelevant to war amongst the people.
> The sides are mostly non-state since we tend to conduct our conflicts and confronta-tions in some form of multinational grouping, whether it is an alliance or a coalition, and against some party or parties that are not states.[4]

WAP of this kind is marked by the obvious fact that military can no longer be separated from civilian activity. It is fought, as Smith stresses, in the fields and streets where people live.[5] They are caught up in it every day. Their images, particularly when they suffer, are prominent in war reportage. Bat-tles are frequently fought not to gain territory, but to win the hearts and

5   Ibid., p. 267.
6   Ibid., p. 17.
7   Ibid., p. 3.

minds of those involved. This is nothing less than the sheer paradox of it all. People are suffering in their own interest. The only possible justification for military intervention is that it will end such suffering. It is understandable, to say the least, why those who suffer as a consequence are not so well placed to see the point of this than those who fight on their behalf. This is the crucial point in the battle for hearts and minds. It is well understood, for example, by the Taleban in the present stage of the Afghan conflict. They align with tribal and other loyalties and are quick to pay for the support they receive. Those keen to receive this often have no choice in their battle for daily survival. Little wonder that confusion reigns in the lives of those for whose hearts and minds both sides compete.

Understanding the people in this sense is vital to the success of military campaigns.[6] Smith stresses that though they may be seen as an entity, it is one that embraces many differences. These are those of family, tribe, ethnicity, religion and whatever. All the things, in fact, that it is often so difficult for outsiders to understand. They are a mercurial mix of ever changing influences and even sheer pressures which make people behave, hope and despair as they do. War amongst the people is tactile, immediate and a daily experience. It is not something decided elsewhere on their behalf. There are no 'foreign fields'. The heat of battle is in their midst.

Smith sharpens this analysis by making further distinctions. Implicit in the argument in *The Utility of Force* is a distinction, in any war, between the confrontation and the battle. These are separated by what he calls the 'level of the fight'. Below this level battles take place. Above it the confrontation has to be resolved. It is possible to win battles and lose the confrontation, the war. These two occur simultaneously. Some seek to resolve the confrontation as others seek to conduct the battles in support of the aim of resolving the confrontation. All this is a melee (not his word). At times it may be seen to be working together to a common purpose and at other times not. A most poignant and sadly not uncommon example of the latter is when civilians are inadvertently killed in battles. Such deaths are a sadly evident serious impediment to those seeking, above the level of the fight, to resolve the confrontation.

---

6   Ibid., p. 279.

Smith further clarifies these distinctions by pointing out that confrontations no longer move in a linear process of Peace-Crisis-War-Resolution-Peace. That was the paradigm of Industrial war. It is not so of WAP. He writes 'Now we are in a world of continual Confrontations and Conflicts in which the military acts in the Conflict (to) support the achievement of the desired outcome of the Confrontation by other means. A parallel activity.'[7] To this he adds that the paradigm shift is in the form of war not the battle. The battle(s) has (have) only one aim and justification – to win the confrontation, the war. Above the level of the fight, other agencies will be earnestly involved. These are those which seek peace, provide medical care and other relief, economists, civil engineers and politicians and interested parties sometimes seemingly beyond number. Whilst all this is taking place there is one importantly identifiable objective to be secured – that of winning the will of the people. Without achieving this, all is lost. It needs no explanation to remind us of the difficulty of achieving this in negotiation whilst, below the level of the fight, battles are still be waged. Calling this a melee is more than justified.

Smith makes an observation about all this which is central to his ongoing work and a forthcoming further publication. It is a telling and powerful one. He claims that the existing institutions we use in the conduct of wars are now unsuited for their present purpose. They originated from a time when war was industrial in the sense previously described. He writes 'Here I refer to the institutions of governance whether they are those of London or any other capital, whether they parliamentary or administrative, and whether they are national or intergovernmental. I refer also to the executive institutions. The diplomatic, intelligence, armed and development services, and the multinational organizations we form from them. And I refer to the institutional relationships, process and authorities that link them into a whole to conduct war.'[8] All these, he adds, now need to change in ways which enable us to understand war as it now manifestly is, to effect its cessation and to reconstruct peace and stability. This development of Smith's analysis to include criticism of the often hallowed institu-

---

7   Unpublished lecture given at Liverpool Cathedral, 22 February 2010, pp. 2–3.
8   Ibid., p. 2.

tions of war is a new development in his work. It will be interesting, to say the least, to observe reaction to it. Most obviously, it will both challenge vested interests and raise serious questions about the way conflicts are conducted and resolved. More pointedly, it will raise the really big question about how money is spent in the conduct of battles and in the quest for their cessation.

An obvious consequence of this new paradigm of war is that political and military objectives are intermingled. They cannot be separated in the sense that politicians can expect to have solutions to conflict delivered to them once and for all by the military alone. The political objectives legitimate the utility of force but they have to work together to achieve their aims. Force has no utility of its own. Failure to recognize this, Smith observes, is a common reason for the failure of military campaigns. He stresses repeatedly that political and military acts must be closely aligned. Success in any operation depends, crucially, on how this is achieved. The utility of force must be linked to political purpose. The aim of the military must be to facilitate this utility. It can only achieve this by understanding the political purpose it serves and reconciling that with operational and tactical activity in battle. In all this it is crucial to recognize what the military can and cannot do. It is, for example, less equipped for peace building and social reconstruction than it is for war fighting. Its experiences, post conflict, in Iraq have well illustrated this. It can well support builders of peace and repairers of damaged infrastructures, it cannot function without them. Above all, the military must play its part in securing the will of the people. Without this all is lost. We have seen in many modern conflicts that this will is often fickle. At its most crude it is even available to the highest bidder in societies where poverty is a daily experience. The structure of the end-game of the military is also crucial. The hand-over to civilian policing is central to this and the role of the military in intelligence and information gathering is as important as its war fighting capability. Smith also stresses that, whilst the there is need to protect soldiers, as they seek to restore civil society their visual profile must become less militaristic and more civilian. In this way they will be less alienated from the people they seek to assist.

Smith's analysis is based on extensive command responsibility at the highest level in modern theatres of conflict.[9] This is the main reason why his arguments are so compelling. They relate to and have arisen out of the analysis of actual confrontations, wars and battles. More than that, they make plain common sense to any informed and concerned observer of what has been and is still happening in confrontations throughout the world. For our purpose, in this book, they illustrate an important point. Military intervention, war fighting, peace building and social reconstruction are all of a seamless piece. Moreover, they require the integrated labours of all at every point. What individuals and particular organizations have to offer cannot stand alone to win the day, as of old. Nor can each player wait in the proverbial wings for the time to come to make their contribution. Only the whole team working together at the same time can now achieve desired ends. As in all teams every player is important, sometime one more than others as things develop. Never one alone. All this sounds simple and self-evident. Our frequent disarray in theatres of conflict suggests that it is not as understood as it should be.

We have seen that the military has roles to play right through from intervention to withdrawal. We have also seen why Rupert Smith thinks that these roles change as campaigns proceed and why they are of a piece with roles played by others. It is now abundantly clear that these others must include those who have the skills to create relationships between still warring parties. Given the obvious sensitivities at stake, these activities are often covert. Knowledge of them, if gained at all, often comes long after they have taken place. Whilst the UN properly has facilities in place to achieve these ends, their cumbersome nature often makes them unfit for at least initial purpose. This is where delicate reconciliation activity is crucial. As we have seen in the foregoing, it is often most effective when it is carried out by small groups and even by lone individuals. They have the sense and courage to tread where others fear. To achieve this they may, as

9   He commanded the Armoured Division in the 1990–1 Gulf War, commanded the UN forces in Bosnia in 1995, was GOC Northern Ireland 1996–9 and then served as Deputy Supreme Allied Commander in NATO.

in the case of Andrew White in Baghdad, have had to be in the area for a long time during which trusts and contacts have been created. Others, like Donald Reeves and Peter Pelz, will use their independence to create fresh opportunities for reconciliation where others have failed.

Given the importance of these fragile reconciliation activities, we cannot know too much about them. About how they begin, proceed and become effective. Though there is now a growing literature on all this, it is in its infancy. This book has been aware of this and attempted to make some contribution to it.

One feature of successful reconciliation activity is becoming clear. It is the importance of the involvement of religious people. This is hardly surprising given that conflicts so often involve religious differences and leaders. Andrew White's work in Iraq exemplifies this. He is accepted because he is a religious. It is of little matter that his religion is different from that of many of those involved the conflict. They recognize, understand and appreciate his religion for what it is. It is an entrée'. More than that it is also a catalyst. It creates opportunities for meetings, friendship and the creation of trust where it has been lost. Of itself such reconciliation activity may be transitory as it opens opportunities for others to pursue. Chief among these is making arrangements for the cessation of hostilities.

Ceasefires and truces, are tentative arrangements. They are often reluctantly participated in and can collapse without notice. This fragility is caused by the fact that passing from open hostility, war-fighting, to even its temporary cessation requires a total change of perception by both sides. Whereas hitherto they had perceived each other as enemies and, therefore, felt justified in taking military action and, specifically, killing, now that changes, of a sudden. This transition from war to fragile peace is not now marked by previous formalities. In the transition from war to peace, there are now no clear signposts. Everything is in suspense. Initial communication will invariably be through the third party. All this is governed, at best, by international law.[10] The main aim of it all is an immediate one, simply

---

10   Sydney D. Bailey, *How Wars End: The United Nations and the Termination of Armed Conflict 1946–1968* (Oxford: Clarendon Press, 1982), p. 30.

to suspend hostilities for long enough to enable discussion to begin anew under slightly improved conditions. This, in itself, is not peace. The conditions of war still prevail. They are, simply, temporarily suspended.[11] This is the point at which so much of what has been discussed in this book comes into effect. It is where trusts and conversations between warring parties, some of which were previously established, can be brought to bear. This may well require enemies sitting face to face with each other for the first time. At this point even learning how to listen can seem an insurmountable difficulty.

In the meantime, external agencies, including where appropriate the UN, will come into play.[12] Ceasefires will be supervised, demarcation lines established. Medical facilities and other forms of humanitarian aid will be made available. Shelters for protected persons, pregnant women, the elderly, and children, can be created, Previously impossible infrastructure repairs to services might even begin. In all this independent observers will play crucial roles in giving the parties the assurances they require as they begin their discussions. A role for, usually international, peacekeeping forces emerges from all this as cease-fires hold and prospects for negotiation and agreement improve. Where these are provided by the UN it will decide how long they are deployed for.[13]

In the summation of a discussion from which many of these points have been taken Bailey writes:

> These, then, are questions that are likely to arise when the international community tries to stop war fighting. The effort must be pursued with patience and persistence, for the problems are usually more intractable than the above questions and comments have implied. A society at war devotes so much effort to the conduct of military operations that little energy is left for considering how the armed conflict shall be terminated. It cannot be stressed too much that the decision to fight is almost always easier than the decision to stop fighting, and usually third-party assistance is needed. The United Nations has many defects, but the evidence of the many case studies in volume II suggests that UN help is always useful and occasionally decisive.[14]

11   Ibid., p. 31.
12   Ibid., p. 365.
13   Ibid., p. 372.
14   Ibid., p. 384.

These poignant reflections bring us back to two issues we have addressed throughout. The first is the need for the involvement of third parties and the second is the recognition of the difficulties they face. The work of Andrew White in Iraq and Donald Reevesand Peter Pelz in Bosnia illuminates these difficulties beyond measure. They all pioneer approaches to warring people which many others find difficult to understand. They are both realistic about the prospect of ever making meaningful progress. There are no manuals or blueprints to work from. Every situation is unique in its context and unpredictable in its development and outcome. The only thing that can be predicted is that there will be obstacles and disappointments along the way, as Justin Webb pointed out in the introduction to this volume. There are never any guarantees of success. To state the obvious; a particular sort of tenacity is required of those who work in these ways.

Both White and Reeves draw this from their Christian convictions, though with different emphases. As we have noted, this is often respected by those they reach out to of other faiths. They are seen to be and accepted as the religiously motivated people they are. Even more importantly, they are clearly not doing what they are to further their own ends. They seek only the well being of others. White, as we have seen, is emphatic that he is not an evangelist for the Christian gospel. This is an emphasis that causes some perplexity to evangelical Christians who urge him to be explicit in his desire to convert others. He rejects this and labours only for peace and reconciliation between warring peoples. That, he insists, is what God's love requires. He has long since ceased to perceive himself still to be the sort of Anglican evangelical he once was. We have seen, however, how he still draws deeply on that heritage of faith.

Can we get any closer to analysing and understanding what those who seek reconciliation in these ways actually do? Donald Reeves thinks highly of one attempt to do this. It is by John Paul Lederach.[15] This is a good example of a growing and important literature in this area. It draws upon experience in areas of conflict such as Nicaragua, Somalia, Northern Ireland, the Philippines and elsewhere. It recognizes that lasting peace

15   John Paul Lederach, *The Moral Vision: The Art and Soul of Building Peace* (Oxford: Oxford University Press, 2005).

can only come from within conflicts. It cannot be imposed on them. Such imposition as that conducted by the UN may well be important in the initial stages of conflict resolution, particularly in the arranging of cease-fires. All they can do, however, is to create space for other things to happen. Things without which lasting peace cannot be established. Lederach argues that these 'things' are made up of both learned skills and creative art. Drawing on his earlier *Building Peace*, he focuses on the observation that reconciliation is always context-specific. There are no blueprints. It always embraces a tension between destructive violence and constructive social engagement. This tension is not just manifest in externalities it is, as he says, 'present within myself'.[16] He wrote *The Moral Vision* to try to understand just that. Understood in this way, reconciliation activity is all-consuming and demanding of its practitioners. Their own vulnerabilities are part of the raw material with which they work. These vulnerabilities are deeply personal. However, and this is important, their recognition does not drive people apart. To the contrary, they are shared vulnerabilities. Those who experience them recognize them in each other. This seeming paradox of the personal is something which creates opportunities for interactive empathy, communication, mutual understanding and innovation. It is as Lederach observes, 'a mess'.[17] Making progress with it is more of an art than a science. This emphasis is a caution against believing that peace building activity can be reduced to and communicated in tables of skills. Important those these may be in a wider context, Lederach insists that art remains an important element in the process of peace building.

Any who have ever reflected properly at all on the nature of human interaction under duress will recognize the importance of Lederach's opening reflections. So often words and hope fail. Here silences and gestures, a smile even, a tear, a handshake, can come to mean a great deal more than words can express. These elemental human emotions are not reducible to textbooks. They can only be experienced and recognized for what they are. They might touch on ultimate things, but they are strictly penultimate in

16   Ibid., p. viii.
17   Ibid., p. ix.

their manifestation. They are what they are; tactile, humbling and, above all, self-revealing. They are awesomely real. None of this gives place for intervention by the pretentious and the devious. Only those with *bona fide* are welcome. No wonder so few of us can undertake these things! Lederach stresses that making progress with all this requires a 'worldview shift'.[18] It source lies in what he defines as 'the *capacity to imagine something rooted in the challenges of the real world yet capable of giving birth to that which does not yet exist.*'[19]

Although his book does attend to practicalities its main emphasis is to ask why the work is undertaken and what sustains it and how it can remain open to serendipitous insights. These are sought through what he calls the 'moral imagination'. All this might look and sound like an impractical flight of fancy. The reason why it is not is because it is grounded in actual and sustained experiences of peace building. It makes sense against such a background. Time after time, in accounts of peace building, progress is made unexpectedly when participants recognize new opportunities for what they are and seize them. Of course, the conditions have to be created, as far as is possible, for this to happen. Meetings have to be arranged, dialogues opened and sustained in the face of scepticism. None of that is the work of the imagination. It is hard practical work. But it is only prolegomena. That is Lederach's point. It is not enough on its own. Something different also has to happen. Violence has to be transcended by finding shared acts which can become the instruments of peace.[20] Recognizing what these are when they occur and what has to be done about them is more akin to an art than a science. That is Lederach's repeated point.

He makes much of the importance of understanding the centrality of relationships in the peace building process and writes: 'Time and again, where in small or large ways the shackles of violence are broken, we find a singular tap root that gives life to the moral imagination: the capacity of individuals and communities to imagine themselves in a web of relationship

18   Ibid., p. 18.
19   Ibid., p. ix.
20   Ibid., p. 172.

even with their enemies.'[21] What they discover is that, just have they have the capacity to destroy peace, they also have the equal capacity to create it. This is no passing insight. It is the realization of a profound truth. Human societies are collectives of individuals in relation to each other. The unity they create is not just an organic one. That is not a sufficient condition for the creation of a society. John Macmurray has well made this point in his Gifford Lectures for 1954. He writes: 'Any human society is a moral entity. Its basis is the universal and necessary intention to maintain the personal relations which makes the human individual a person, and his life a common life. It is the instantiation of the "I and you" as the unit of the personal. It is constituted and maintained by keeping faith.'[22] Macmurray made this point in the development of his central thesis in the lectures, that individuals are agents and that their agency is a corollary of what they think.

The underlying point here is one often made in Western Philosophy (Marx made it in the Communist Manifesto). It is that what humans beings have made they can change. They are, in other words, the authors of their circumstances and not the victims of them. In other words, human society is created out of the shared endeavours of its individuals. Christians would add here that it is also created by the grace and love of God. This is its essence. Those human endeavours can be for good or evil, peace or war. When warring parties realize this they discover that their capacity for war is also their capacity for peace. (Christians would add here, again, that this requires genuine repentance for wrongs and the resolve to lead a new life by the grace of God.) They *can* change from willing one to willing the other. It is in their shared gift. That is the key. They can only effectively do it together. More than that; they can help each other to do so. The vital ingredient here is something as simple, beautiful even, as the creation of a new shared intention. The intention, that is, to bring into being a different state-of-affairs from war as a replacement for the former intention which brought war about in the first place. Changing intentions in this way is the holy grail sought by wise peace builders. White, Reeves Lederach, Welby and others discussed in the foregoing are exemplars of this. They know the

21   Ibid., p. 34.
22   John Macmurray, *Persons in Relation* (London: Faber and Faber, 1961), p. 128.

simplicity and beauty of these truths. These become visible when those in the conflict begin to share their fundamental desires such as wanting peace and prosperity for their offspring. When, that is, shared human needs are acknowledged. These put everything else into agreed perspectives. This can have dramatic effects.

Again, the work of Andrew White also deserves careful attention at this point. He is noticeably skilled at creating the conditions for such interpersonal creativity to occur. First, he has a knack of getting people together in unlikely combinations. Bringing, that is, enemies face to face with each other often for the first time. In this a bus journey, a meal, a walk, or some such ordinary shared activity can be as creative in the peace process as formal deliberation. White knows this well from long experience and he deliberately creates opportunities for it to happen. They might look ordinary and not pre-planned, but they are far from it. They are an essential part of the wider artifice. He is fully aware of this and writes carefully of them as he analyses the emergence of agreement and progress out of stalemate. They are often carefully recorded as spontaneous moments of joy and happiness, the jewels in the crown.

It is more than significant that two such experienced peace builders as White and Lederach write on all this with such a degree of unanimity. This is more than coincidence. It is highly significant. More than enough reason, in fact, to read the records of other such reflective peace builders to see if they concur. The now emerging literature more than suggests that this is the case. What experienced writers such as White and Lederach achieve, among other things, is providing the encouragement to others to seek and find the keys to success in peace building as they are doing.

Important though these seemingly simple, but in truth profound, insights might be they are not of their own enough to secure peace. They have to be instantiated. Only in this way can they become a shared reality, an instrument for the outworking of peace. They have to exist visibly and effectively if they are to serve their purpose. As we will see below, more than that even, they have to initiate effective and determined action. Treaties and Accords are the obvious way to achieve all this. Wise peace builders know this and give them as much care and attention as they give to creating the relationships and intentions which make them possible. Again, how they go about it deserving of careful attention.

Peacemakers like White and Lederach widely acknowledge the importance of agreeing Treaties and Accords. These can be difficult to achieve,
but they are essential if hostilities are to cease and peace created in their
aftermath. Their first aim is to secure cessation of hostilities. The UN has
a wealth of experience of this and it has, again, been analysed by Sydney
Bailey.[23] He emphasizes the importance of the precision of language. They
need to focus on who the text is produced by, who the appeal is directed
towards and what exactly is being called for. There can be no equivoca-
tion if parties are to be held to their agreed obligations. In describing the
creation of the Baghdad Peace Accord, Andrew White carefully records
that many of the parties were meeting for the first time. They also had to
be encouraged to take the initiatives and, subsequently, responsibility for
what they agreed. There were thirty-nine signatures. At this point, the art
of peacemaking clearly lies as much in knowing when to withdraw as when
to take initiatives. A dinner was arranged in celebration. But this was just a
beginning. The real work of implementing the Accord had to begin in earnest. This was achieved, by setting up working groups with responsibilities
in specific areas. As we now, sadly, know their success has been and still is
punctuated by recurring violence. The work goes on. The marvellous thing
about this about this is the fact that White and others believe not only
that it can do so, but that it will succeed. The stamina required to sustain
all this in the face of setbacks is awesome. It is an example to all who seek
to discover how difficult it is to work in war zones year in year out. Again,
the growing body of literature is a resource for all who want to know about
the success and failure of actual initiatives. Lederach records that there have
been over eighty of them since the end of the Cold War in 1990.[24] Many are
doomed to failure, others to partial and others to more complete success.
In all this, the end game is never just around the corner. Post conflict social
reconstruction is an ongoing business. In the progress of this, all that can
be hoped for is that former belligerents take over responsibility for and
ownership of the peace process from those who initiated it.

23   Ibid., p. 123.
24   Ibid., p. 41.

Another extremely important point has been touched on throughout these discussions. It is about the funding of reconciliation activities. This does not fall into place automatically if at all. Once it is recognized, as it is here throughout, that the reconcilers have an important role to play from day one, in readiness at least, and for them to be on hand throughout it must also be recognized that they require financial support. The reason for this is simply because so many of them are, and need to be, non-governmental agencies. Sometimes they are even lone individuals and at others small groups. The do not usually fit into the existing budgeted categories for conflict resolution. That they achieve so much as they so often do is testimony to their good-will, frugality and lack of desire for self-reward. Little wonder that all this can so easily be taken for granted. Moreover, they do not have an over-arching organization to represent them. No one, that is, to stand up for them as a group. In fact, they are not even a group at all and perhaps never need to be. For all that, however, they are all part of a recognisable and necessary activity. They are never likely to band together to stick up for themselves. They are too busy doing what they are doing to take time out for that. All the more reason, therefore why others should recognize their worth, stand up for them and, crucially, help to secure the funding for them to continue what they are doing.

It is not, of course, possible to say, in general, where this funding should come from. The source will vary from conflict to conflict, but it must come from somewhere in the coffers of conflict. More, it is also possible to say that those responsible for essaying the morality or otherwise of a particular conflict should lay it upon those who hold the purse-strings to make such a provision as a matter of moral obligation. This might be easier said than done. However, if we take the point I made earlier in this volume (see p. 54) that provision for securing the *jus post bello* and *jus in pace* should be put in place before an intervention is even begun as a matter of moral obligation, it means that it simply has to be done. The mechanics of it will not, of course, necessarily be straightforward. The right reconcilers in any confrontation have to be identified and the costs of their engagement properly estimated. But none of that is impossible. It is done, as it should be, for other needs in the theatre of confrontation. Given, as we have seen throughout, that the activity of reconcilers is so crucial in conflict resolution, this provision cannot any longer be left to happenstance. The point being made forcefully here is that proper recognition of and provision for the work of reconcilers must become a pre-condition of establishing the justice of military intervention.

Before we turn to considering the role played in reconciliation activity by individuals, we need to consider another theme which has been recurrent throughout the book. This is the necessity of placing specific theatres of reconciliation in the context of wider analyses. Marc Ellis does this poignantly in his chapter on the conflict in the Middle East. This, sadly, is a conflict which has defied attempts at quick or superficial fixes. Ellis' point is that there are fundamental issues involved about Israeli and Palestinian history which have to be addressed. He focuses on the displacement of over 70,000 Palestinians from their land in the 1948 settlement of the State of Israel. At this point his analysis put him at odds with many of his fellow Jews. Many of them, in fact, are hostile to him. He reflects on personal friendships with Palestinians including those killed in the conflicts. In doing so he essays the pathos at the centre of the conflict. It embraces the lives and deaths of decent honest people on sides of an intractable conflict. All this, of course, is exacerbated by the ancient Jewish belief that the land is theirs to the exclusion of others by God-given decree. Not only does Ellis question this, he accuses modern Israel of being apostate, of not being true to their own deeper history. This, he claims, has caused them to become the sort of persecutors they have suffered from themselves in their often troublesome history. His solution is for Israel to engage in an act of Revolutionary Forgiveness with those it has persecuted and for it to then act appropriately.

The suggestion that specific acts of reconciliation cannot succeed unless they are placed in the context of wider analyses of the problems which make them necessary could scarce come in stronger form than this. It reminds us just how wide the canvass of the work of reconciliation actually is and needs to be. Ellis' voice is not alone in this, but his is distinguished by the persistence with which he presses his case in writing and through ongoing programmes of world-wide public lecturing.

Another example here given of the needs for wider and careful analyses of specific conflicts is in the chapter on Truth and Denial in Bosnia. The point is there made that some Western, Freudian, psychological analyses of conflict, in general, actually accepted it without question. This was not corrected until Carl Rogers and others demonstrated that human beings were not essentially destructive. This view was applied by him and others to conflict groups with notable success. This chapter also pointed out how some Western psychological analyses of the conflict effective excluded the Muslim point of view from consideration. It also widely endorsed the 'all sides to blame' analyses of the conflict. This chapter points out that such partisan analyses are unbecoming of a profession which should seek the truth. This, again, shows how complex and inadequate the involvement of professions such as psychology can be in establishing the truth in ways which allow reconciliation even to become a possibility.

The chapter on the meaning of reconciliation raises, of course, a fundamental question. What exactly is it and is it always the same thing in every instance? Is it, for example, a process or an outcome? Is it coming to terms with past or reconciliation with the present? These basic questions are more than enough caution against taking too much for granted whenever the word is mentioned. The chapter also showed how reconciliation is affected by concurrent human rights abuses and the Treaties and Commissions which are framed to correct them.

It is more than significant that throughout this book one of the things we have been focussing on is the work of specific individuals who are involved in reconciliation activity. They are, of course, only a chosen selection from the many more who are also involved. An obvious conclusion we have to draw from all this is that the work of reconciliation in difficult circumstances is uniquely suited individuals often working alone. This does not mean that they are not supported by others. They invariably are. But what they actually do and do most effectively, is done by them alone or by them in very small groups. We need to pay more attention to why this is the case.

There are five reasons why the work of reconciliation is uniquely suited to individuals: access, trust, credibility, spontaneity and wider authority. I will discuss these briefly in turn.

Often by dint of their personal courage, individuals are able to go where angels fear and governments cannot even contemplate. This is why, as with Justin Welby on a recent visit to Nigeria, they often have to be fitted with flak-jackets for the purpose. They do not wait for belligerents to come to them. To the contrary, they actively seek them out and gain audience often by their sheer audacity. The Yiddish word 'chutzpah' is sometimes used here to express the admixture of sheer gall, audacity and even insolence! In the records of reconciliation activity. incidents of this are frequent and deserve to be studied carefully. One thing that come to attention immediately is that those who achieve this are strong characters, to put it politely. Many of them of them are characters in their own right. The best, such as Andrew White, are sensitively self-aware about this and use to great advantage. He is self-deprecating and humorous, movingly, even about his personal handicap as a result of illness. The effect of this can be quite dramatic on meeting him. It is totally disarming. Even the most hostile and suspicious cannot fail to be at first bemused and then engaged. Donald Reeves has a similarly strong character which has been properly noted for throughout his distinguished Anglican ministry. He has, quite simply, often been able to achieve things against odds which others would have found daunting.[25] People like these do not sit around waiting for invitations. They rise to the challenge by dint of their own efforts. They will be in action before others even realize what they are doing. They do not ask for permission and, in fact, even seem to relish not having it. They are self-sufficient at the point of initiative. Nowhere is this more effective than it is when initial access is being created to individuals in difficult circumstances and against their will.

At this point trust is all. Without it nothing can happen. Moreover, it has to be virtually instant. There is no time for preliminaries and niceties. Minutes count as daringly contrived opportunities are made the most of. This where other things we have already noticed come into play. Often, but not always, these individuals have been around for some time. They are

---

25   Cf. Donald Reeves, *The Memoirs of a Very Dangerous Man* (London: Continuum, 2009).

trusted because they are known. Paradoxically, however, others might use the novelty of their presence also to advantage. Again, it all depends on the character of the individual. Another element of this trust is the credibility of their knowledge of the situation. Justin Welby and Lakshman Dissanayake both make this point forcibly. Both take care to attain detailed analyses of the complexity of the situations they work in. Both stress that these are essential. At the very least, all this shows a proper and credible respect for those at odds with each other. It indicates that a desire exists to find solutions from within situations rather than impose them from without. All this is in addition to the wider analyses we referred to above. When there are seconds to establish trust and credibility all this counts beyond measure. It demonstrates serious good-will as well as a willingness to listen to the intricacies of complex and often long-standing grievances.

All this is daunting and demanding enough, but there is more. Two more crucial things remain. The first of these is spontaneity. This is the ability to respond immediately to opportunities created by unexpected turns of events in the field. The importance of this is stressed by Lederach when he stresses that there is an art to the work of reconciliation. It requires the flair of the artist, the ability that is to make the very most of limited resources to maximum effect. This is the work of the moment, of seeing something others have overlooked, nothing less that is than sheer creativity at its best. Reconcilers, like artists, can train for this but the creativity is theirs alone at the point of delivery. Opportunities have to be made the most of, particularly when they are likely not to recur. They may be created by a passing mood, or gesture, or a smile, but they are crucial.

Little wonder that individuals are best placed to achieve all this. They alone can travel light enough to respond in the ways we have been describing, This requires of them immense stamina and sheer resolve, as well as a conviction against the odds that they can succeed where others have failed. When they do, however, their work is far from over. They have to return from the field to integrate their achievements (and failures) with wider and more cumbersome peace processes. Here they have to work in entirely different ways with the machinery of governments. Here too, they still have to retain the trust and credibility they have worked so hard to achieve with those in the field. There will still be much going and coming before anything is achieved. What they achieve in the field is of no account unless it can be integrated with everything else in the conflict and, above all, with the wider desires for peace.

What is abundantly clear from this discussion, however, is that those wider desires cannot succeed without those who engage in the sort of reconciliation activity we have been discussing. This is reason enough to recognize their achievements and failures and to subject them to careful and ongoing analysis. More than that, even, we have been arguing that the work of reconciliation is now so well established that it must become an integrated part of the considerations that are made whenever military interventions is being morally assessed. Such activity might well be but a small part of the wider complexity of conflict and its resolution. We have been considering why it is such a crucial one; why it deserves the increasing study it receives, why it also deserves proper financial support and, above all, why it deserves its proper recognition in the wider consideration of the morality of conflict.

In all, we have seen that reconciliation is a complex and important concept. It is the overall term for what has to happen if previously warring peoples are to live together in peace. We have paid attention to some of the issues involved and to some of the work of people who pursue its ends. All this is more than deserving of the analysis it is increasingly receiving. Only by this means will we be better able to understand and operate in a sphere of human activity which is increasingly vital to the resolution of conflict and the establishment of peace. The fact that, for all its failures, it manifestly succeeds as it does in so many instances is more than enough reason to persist with its understanding and practice in every way that we can. In this way, we will help to do continuing justice to the vision which arose from the ashes of Coventry Cathedral.

Notes on Contributors

SEIDU ALIDU is a PhD student at Leeds Metropolitan University.

EDINA BEĆIREVIĆ is Assistant Professor of History at Sarajevo University.

LAKSHMAN DISSANAYAKE is Professor of Demography at the University of Colombo and is currently Visiting Professor at Leeds Metropolitan University.

R. JOHN ELFORD was formerly Visiting Professor of Ethics at Leeds Metropolitan University.

MARC H. ELLIS is University Professor of Jewish Studies, Professor of History and Director of the Centre for Jewish Studies at Baylor University.

GAVIN FAIRBAIRN is Professor of Ethics and Language at Leeds Metropolitan University.

AYERAY MEDINA BUSTOS is a PhD student at Leeds Metropolitan University.

STEPHEN PAUL is Director of the Centre for Psychological Therapies at Leeds Metropolitan University.

DONALD REEVES was Rector of St James's Church, Piccadilly, London, and co-founded The Soul of Europe.

RON ROBERTS is Senior Lecturer at Kingston University.

D.C. WEBB is Professor of Engineering and Director of the Praxis Centre at Leeds Metropolitan University.

JUSTIN WELBY is Dean of Liverpool.

Index

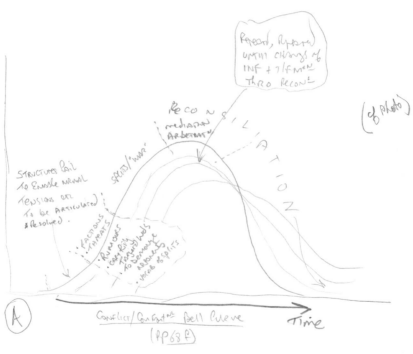

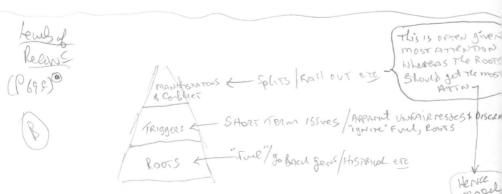

New International Studies in Applied Ethics

SERIES EDITORS
Professor R. John Elford and Professor Simon Robinson,
Leeds Metropolitan University

New International Studies in Applied Ethics is a series based at Leeds Metropolitan University and associated with Virginia Theological Seminary. The series examines the ethical implications of selected areas of public life and concern. Subjects considered include, but are not limited to, medicine, peace studies, international sport and higher education.

The series aims to publish volumes which are clearly written with a general academic readership in mind. Individual volumes may also be useful to those confronted with the issues discussed in their daily lives. A consistent emphasis is on recent developments in the subjects discussed and this is achieved by publishing volumes by writers who are foremost in their fields, as well as those with emerging reputations. Both secular and religious ethical views may be discussed as appropriate. No point of view is considered off-limits and controversy is not avoided.

The series includes both edited volumes and single-authored monographs. Submissions are welcome from all scholars in the field and should be addressed to either the series editors or the publisher.

Vol. 1   R. John Elford and D. Gareth Jones (eds)
          A Tangled Web: Medicine and Theology in Dialogue
          288 pages. 2009.
          ISBN: 978-3-03911-541-9

Vol. 2   D. Gareth Jones and R. John Elford (eds)
          A Glass Darkly: Medicine and Theology in Further Dialogue
          254 pages. 2010.
          ISBN: 978-3-03911-936-3